An Introduction to Political Philosophy

This book provides a comprehensive introduction to political philosophy. Combining discussion of historical and contemporary figures, together with numerous real-life examples, it covers an unusually broad range of topics in the field, including the just distribution of wealth, both within countries and globally; the nature and justification of political authority; the meaning and significance of freedom; arguments for and against democratic rule; the problem of war; and the grounds for toleration in public life. It also offers an accessible, non-technical discussion of perfectionism, utilitarianism, theories of the social contract, and of recently popular forms of critical theory. Throughout, the book challenges readers to think critically about political arguments and institutions that they might otherwise take for granted. It will be a provocative text for any student of philosophy and political science.

COLIN BIRD is Associate Professor at the Woodrow Wilson Department of Politics, University of Virginia. He is author of *The Myth of Liberal Individualism* (1999).

An Introduction to Political Philosophy

COLIN BIRD

University of Virginia

 CAMBRIDGE
UNIVERSITY PRESS

CAMBRIDGE UNIVERSITY PRESS
Cambridge, New York, Melbourne, Madrid, Cape Town, Singapore, São Paulo, Delhi,

Cambridge University Press
The Edinburgh Building, Cambridge CB2 8RU, UK

Published in the United States of America by Cambridge University Press, New York

www.cambridge.org
Information on this title: www.cambridge.org/9780521544825

© Colin Bird 2006

First published 2006
Reprinted 2008

Printed in the United Kingdom at the University Press, Cambridge

A catalogue record for this publication is available from the British Library

ISBN 978-0-521-83625-8   hardback
ISBN 978-0-521-54482-5   paperback

To Adrienne, Nicholas, Teddy, and Tatiana

Contents

Preface

This book has two aims: first, to stimulate critical reflection on political institutions and practices, and on the various arguments that might be offered for and against them; and second, to give readers an appreciation of the most provocative historical and contemporary contributions to political philosophy.

The book could be used as a free-standing text in an introductory course, or in conjunction with assigned readings from some of the major texts discussed (Plato, Hobbes, Rawls, and others). Although I have aimed for wide coverage, the immense scope of the field necessitates some selectivity, and this book does not pretend to be comprehensive or exhaustive. As a general rule, I have tried as far as possible to steer clear of excessive technical jargon, and of those contemporary debates that seem to me to have become boringly scholastic (e.g. "equality of resources" vs. "equality of welfare"; "individualism" vs. "communitarianism," and so on).

Although I have not avoided *all* references to schools of thought, I have also deliberately chosen not to organize the book around ideological worldviews like "liberalism," "libertarianism," "socialism," "feminism," or "conservatism". The most interesting arguments too often flow between these various positions. Moreover, I have found that emphasizing them encourages the false view that these ideological fixtures are natural kinds when in fact they reflect highly parochial political divisions. Focusing on them also implies that political philosophers are servants of ideologies, helping to make them more plausible, systematic, and rhetorically effective. We should discourage this perception. Political philosophers need not be loyal to particular ideological positions or movements and define their activities in these terms. Of course, there are many who today write in this vein – a liberal theory of this, a feminist theory of that, a libertarian defense of such and such – but I think this is clearly the *wrong* way to make philosophy politically relevant. I hope this book helps readers to see a better way.

Thanks are due to Robert Amdur, Steven Wall, George Klosko, Stephen White, Illan Nam, Meghan Sullivan, Ryan Pevnick, Mindy Martin, Chris Zirpoli, Scott Weingaertner, Adrienne Kim Bird, and Graham and Louise Bird, all of whom have been immensely generous, either in taking the time to read and comment on drafts of various chapters, or in providing indispensable support and encouragement as I struggled to complete the manuscript. I am grateful to my current class of Politics Honors students for serving as involuntary guinea pigs, and for providing valuable feedback on readability. I must also thank an anonymous reviewer for Cambridge University Press for helpful suggestions about the final chapter. I am indebted also to Hilary Gaskin, for first floating the idea of this text, and for her patience and encouragement during the writing. Finally, special thanks to the staff of the Alderman Library coffee bar for vital chemical sustenance: I could not have finished, or even begun, this book without it.

Introduction

Like the weather, politics presents two starkly contrasting faces. Often, it comes in the form of calm and seemingly cloudless routine, stability, predictability, and consensus. When we survey the political landscape, for example, we readily observe settled institutions and practices that outlive, by many generations, those who operate and submit to them; widespread acquiescence in particular modes of political organization and acceptance of the values generally thought to underlie them; entrenched rules and principles widely affirmed within particular communities as a legitimate basis on which to criticize the conduct of their members; the regular circulation of bureaucratic forms and instructions, passports issued and honored, wills written and upheld, contracts enforced, wrongdoers peacefully brought to justice in accordance with accepted procedures.

As often, however, politics brings conflict, struggle, disruption, coercion, brutality, uncertainty, disorder, violence, destruction, fear, subversion, and menace: one thinks of bombing raids, pogroms, terrorist attacks, genocides, and "collateral damage"; of coups, revolutions, sweeping legislative change, invasions, electoral reversals, forced evacuations, conscription, hijackings, martial law, and the imposition of violent legal sanctions and penalties; of divided loyalties, naked ambition, sharp moral and religious disagreements, international realignments, and ethnic hatreds; and of intrusive surveillance, invasions of privacy, confiscations of property, arrest, interrogation, and torture.

Some might say that these two faces of politics represent the Jekyll and Hyde of political life. Just as we distinguish between good and bad weather, so we might straightforwardly identify *bad* politics with instability, subversion, and the disconcerting threat of violence, and *good* politics with stability, order, and routine.

But a moment's reflection reveals that this Jekyll-and-Hyde theory of politics is far too simple. When we imagine the menacing hum of bomber formations approaching from the far horizon, our first instinct may indeed be to identify with the potential victims, quietly going about their business without realizing that their homes and communities are in grave danger. But while the raid may be terrible for them, in at least some cases we might reluctantly conclude that it could be justified for the greater good. Rather few, if any, significant political achievements have been entirely bloodless, and it is not obvious that we should never be prepared to use violence for the sake of legitimate political ends. Today, the nuclear bombings of Hiroshima and Nagasaki that ended World War II, or even the "conventional" bombings of Tokyo, Dresden, and Hamburg, are no longer widely defended. But almost no-one says we should not have done *anything* about the Nazis, and there are still many who defend the policy of nuclear deterrence as it was practiced during the Cold War, despite the obvious fact that it involved threatening literally *millions* of innocent civilians with almost instantaneous incineration. Even if we doubt that these very drastic forms of violence can be justified under any circumstances, we might still concede that the more familiar forms of coercion and violence involved in the regular operation of criminal punishment can be more readily defended.

Furthermore, the mere fact that certain patterns of political cooperation are stable, enduring, and routine does not mean that they are therefore desirable or legitimate. Slavery has very often been a routine and widely accepted practice; so have (and are) child labor, the subordination of women, religious intolerance, and racial and ethnic discrimination. On reflection, then, we will often agree that some of these practices, even when hallowed by tradition, deserve to be swept aside in the name of freedom, equality, justice, and other important social ideals.

So political disruption and subversion, even when violent, may sometimes be good, and acquiescence in stable political routines may often be very bad. If there is a distinction between good and bad politics, then, it is not just the same as the difference between order and disorder, or between stability and instability. But when is politics good and when is it bad? Which forms of political action might be justifiable under what circumstances? When ought we to regard the stability of certain public institutions as a good thing and when ought they to be resisted or destabilized? And destabilized by what means and in favor of... what?

Although philosophers are stereotypically regarded as remote from worldly affairs, they have in fact long sought to address these political questions. They have done so in the conviction that thinking philosophically is a precondition for a rational assessment of political life and for constructive political engagement. Is this conviction sound? If so, how exactly can it help? What guidance does it give?

The quest for justification

Humans are not, as Aristotle noted, political animals in the way that ants and bees are, simply programmed by natural instinct to organize themselves in certain iterating structures like nests and hives.[1] Rather, our political communities and institutional practices take many incompatible forms, and people have differed sharply on their relative merits. For example, almost everybody now claims to be for democracy. But until the last couple of centuries "democracy" was more often a term of abuse, rather as the word "fascist" is today. (And we tend to forget, of course, that not *all* Fascists were the power-crazed crackpots we find in old war movies — at least some of them were serious, well-intentioned intellectuals who quite sincerely thought that Fascism was rather a good idea.) More generally, there have been theocracies, aristocracies, oligarchies, and monarchies, and each has had its defenders and detractors. The variability of human political forms and of our judgments about them is one of the most striking facts about us. It means that we cannot avoid thinking of our political practices as alterable, and even (if only in retrospect) as possible objects of choice. We can always ask: Why should we continue to organize ourselves *this* way when we could have done it *that* way instead?

To ask such questions is to seek a justification for the current way of organizing things. This demand for justification seems misplaced when behavior is determined by instinct or reflex. Swarming bees and herds of terrified wildebeest fleeing a predator do not have doubts about or demand justifications for what they are doing. Humans have instincts

---

[1] Aristotle (1981), p. 60.

and reflexes, too, and doubtless much of our political activity is habitual and unreflective. But we strongly resist the idea that our political practices are wholly mindless. "Well, I just *do*," may be a perfectly reasonable reply to the question: "Why do you like strawberry ice-cream?" But "We just *do*" doesn't seem a satisfactory answer to such questions as: Why do we enslave people? Why do we allow enormous disparities of wealth between citizens of the prosperous Western nations and the poor around the world? Why are we sometimes prepared to sacrifice innocent life in war? Such questions demand well-reasoned answers. If we are not convinced by any of the proposed justifications, we may conclude that the relevant practices should be changed or eliminated. This assumes that, at some level, our political arrangements are subject to rational assessment and choice. This assumption lies behind the effort to distinguish political practices and forms of political action that can be justified and those that cannot. That effort, more than anything else, defines the general project of political philosophy.

Ideas and concepts in political life

Aristotle put his finger on another, closely related, reason why our political interaction is not like that of bees, ants, and herds of wildebeest. Wildebeest do not talk and they do not use concepts. They do not recognize "*authority*," they have no notion of what it is to be "*represented*" by other wildebeest, and they do not fuss about "*Wildebeest rights*." Nor do they urge allegiance or resistance to various practices within their herds for the sake of "*freedom and equality*," or on the grounds that they are "*required*" as a matter of "*justice*," that they possess or lack "*legitimacy*," that they are part of or inimical to the "*common good*," and so forth. However, such concepts seem central to human politics and to our efforts to justify our political arrangements to each other.

Broadly, these concepts are of two kinds. Some of them, like the concepts of "justice" or "the common good," refer to certain ethical *ideals* routinely cited in justifications for (or objections to) political practices and actions. Thus we are often urged to reject slavery as unjust, to embrace democracy for the sake of equality and justice, or to topple dictatorships abroad in the name of freedom. Other concepts, like those of "authority," "representation," "rights," "property," "coercion," or "sovereignty," pick out aspects of political practice that themselves stand in need of justification.

Obviously, concepts of the first sort are most directly relevant to the search for justification in politics. We mainly want to know what justice requires, what is ruled out as subversive of the "common good," and so on. And clearly this requires that we reflect on exactly what appeals to "justice" or the "common good" involve, how such concepts have the capacity to justify anything (if indeed they do), how we certify *what* they justify, and so forth.

But concepts of the second kind raise philosophical questions as well. If we are asking (say) whether political authority can be justified, and if so when, we had better be clear on what exactly political authority *is*. Are we? Do we immediately understand, for example, how authority differs from power (does it?), or what exactly it means to say that a judge, rather than my next-door neighbour, has authority over me? Is political authority similar to, or different from, the kind of authority that expert archeologists claim? These questions do not have obvious answers. Facing them often leaves us unexpectedly puzzled about things we at first thought we understood.

Questions about how we should understand political concepts of this kind (coercion, the state, rights, sovereignty, etc.) are not in themselves demands for the justification of political practices. But in order to understand *what* they are trying to justify, political philosophers must address these questions as well.

"Theory and practice"

We have seen how, in the course of investigating the possible justifications that might be offered for different modes of political organization, we are led to reflect on the nature of political concepts like justice, freedom, authority, the state, and so forth. But some become quickly impatient with the resulting focus on concepts and ideas, and complain that it makes political philosophy an unduly "theoretical" as opposed to "practical" endeavor. Such critics charge that political philosophy is an academic diversion from active political engagement, from going out and "making a difference." Instead of wasting our time with philosophy, we should go out and join the Labour Party, become a Young Republican, or sign up for the Peace Corps.

Obviously, getting bogged down in philosophical abstractions is no way to change the world, and I do not want to claim that doing philosophy is exactly like working for Oxfam or formulating public policy. Still, this does not make it helpful to understand the relation between political philosophy and political activity in terms of a broad opposition between "theory" and "practice." Presumably those who want to "make a difference" by becoming politically active do not want to make *just any* sort of difference. They want to make *the right sort of difference.* The Nazi Party made a big difference, but we would not have much patience for someone who said: "Who cares about justice, equality, and all that? That's merely theory. Practice is what matters. So I'm off to do my bit for the Third Reich — at least *that* way I'll make a difference."

In other words, we need to think intelligently about *where* to try to make a difference, about *which* political causes merit investments of our time and energy. This obviously requires some reflection on the proper goals and aims of political activity. Mostly, when people are asked why they become politically involved, they will cite beliefs about justice, the common good, freedom, and equality, among others, as justification. As we have seen, these beliefs, and the question of their soundness, form a major part of the subject matter of political philosophy. But rarely can we separate these beliefs about the goals of political action from our actions themselves; usually the two are seamlessly connected. For example, there is no bit of my voting in an election that is "pure activity," neatly separable from my beliefs about why a particular candidate deserves my support, or about why I should bother to vote in the first place. My vote and these beliefs about it are of a piece.

This has an important consequence. If the beliefs on which we act in politics do not make sense, our actions may not make sense either. In principle, then, philosophical reflection on these beliefs has the power to expose certain of our political activities as confused, to make it clear that we ought to behave otherwise than we do. Neat and tidy distinctions between "theory" and "practice" obscure this point. The important contrast is not between some pure realm of moral ideals ("theory") and a disconnected world of political action ("practice"). Rather, it is between political activity informed by relatively sophisticated and defensible beliefs about its goals and political activity guided by beliefs that are indefensible, confused, or simply stupid.

This is not just a point for those who consciously decide to become politically active in various ways. To adapt a famous remark of Leon Trotsky: "You may not be interested in politics, but politics is interested in you." The point here is that, independently of our decisions to become politically active, we nonetheless find ourselves dragooned into concerted political action in a variety of other ways. This is why so much of our political involvement is expressed in the passive voice. In politics, we are constantly being expected, required, ordered, authorized (etc.) to ..., being manipulated, coerced, recruited, bullied, conscripted (etc.) into ..., and being organized, regulated, controlled (etc.) so that ... Very little of this is in any sense voluntary; much of it goes on without our even noticing, like sales taxes.

Consider, for example, our relationship to the modern state. This immensely powerful and ubiquitous political agency makes significant claims on us. In order to reproduce itself, to promote its goals, to perform its functions, to fight its wars, citizens are recruited, usually involuntarily, into organized action. In this sense, the state makes us all politically active despite ourselves – it transforms us into the agents of *its* projects. Most go along with this out of habit and socialization, encouraged from an early age to believe (perhaps) that the state promotes justice and our common good, that we have some sort of obligation to comply with it, that it represents us and our interests, that it is an agent of our collective self-government, and so forth. These familiar beliefs and habits of thought purport to justify the state and the forms of collective action over which it presides. But as before, when political philosophers ask whether those beliefs make sense, they are also asking whether these forms of collective action and organization themselves make sense. Insofar as these practices and beliefs partly constitute the terms on which we understand and conduct our own lives, the question of whether they make sense is hardly a purely abstract or "theoretical" one.

The plan of the book

There is no closed, ordered list of questions that defines the field of political philosophy. It is better to think of it as an open-ended activity: the effort to reflect in a disciplined, unprejudiced, and critical way on pertinent political issues and on the puzzling features of political phenomena that we might otherwise take for granted. In the body of this book, I discuss a series of largely independent topics in political philosophy, including the justification of authority, the nature and requirements of justice, and the problem of international violence and war.

Disparate as these topics are, the theme of political justification is a thread that nonetheless binds them loosely together. In many ways, the search for justification in political life, the difficulties it raises, and the question of how to proceed with it, are best understood in the context of concrete argument about such specific issues. But the notion of political justification also raises some important general questions: What makes a political justification successful? What does it take to establish that a political arrangement or course of action is justified rather than not? Can disagreements about the justifiability of political practices ever be definitively resolved by philosophical means? How?

The four chapters constituting Part I of the book explore these more general questions. Chapter 1 discusses some of the difficulties raised by the quest for justification in political life. Chapters 2, 3, and 4 discuss two historically influential strategies that political philosophers have developed to deal with them. Chapters 2 and 3 focus on a family of positions that I gather under the general heading of "common-good" arguments. Included in this family are the classical perfectionism of Plato and Aristotle, and the modern utilitarianism of Jeremy Bentham and John Stuart Mill. There are many differences between these views. But, as we shall see, in their understanding of how political justification ought to proceed they are essentially at one.

In chapter 4, I will look at the theory of the social contract, which developed partly in opposition to the common-good approaches just mentioned. The theory of the social contract received its first systematic statements in seventeenth-century English political thought, especially in the writings of Thomas Hobbes and John Locke. The social-contract idea was further developed in the eighteenth century by two continental European philosophers – the Swiss Jean Jacques Rousseau and the Prussian Immanuel Kant – before falling from favor in the nineteenth. However, in the closing decades of the twentieth century, social-contract theory underwent a sudden and dramatic revival, thanks largely to the pioneering work of the American political philosopher John Rawls.

As we shall see, these two approaches are not as starkly opposed as many often assume them to be. Nonetheless, there is an important basic difference between them. As a first approximation, it can be put as follows. The common-good approach understands political justification in terms of claims about our *well-being* and *interests*. On this view, political arrangements are justified insofar as they are collectively beneficial, and impartially promote the welfare and advantage of all. By contrast, theories of the social contract understand political justification in terms of *voluntary agreements* and *choices*. They assert, that is, that political arrangements are justified insofar as agents have, or would have, freely agreed to them.

I discuss these sets of views so extensively in the early part of the book for two reasons. First, they supply a good deal of the conceptual grammar or (less charitably) the *jargon* of contemporary political philosophy. Some understanding of them is therefore essential preparation for decoding recent contributions to the field. Second, and more importantly, they illuminate some of the deepest problems about justification in political life, as well as some of the most ingenious efforts yet devised to solve them.

With this background filled in, Part II considers a series of more specific topics in the field. Chapters 5 and 6 look at the just and equitable distribution of wealth and resources, including the currently fashionable topic of global justice. Chapter 7 discusses the nature and justification of political authority. In chapter 8, I consider the concept of freedom and how it might be understood. Chapter 9 discusses ideals of democratic rule and some of the difficulties they raise. Chapter 10 asks whether and how philosophers might contribute to our understanding of war and violence, unfortunately a topic of particularly urgent concern today. Chapter 11 discusses the basis for toleration and mutual accommodation among groups with opposed ethical views. My final chapter, 12, asks how political philosophers can maintain an appropriate critical distance from the institutions and practices they address; it considers the writings of radical critics like Rousseau, Marx, and Foucault, and the implications of their arguments for the discussions contained in this text.

Part I

Politics and justification

1   The puzzle of justification

To justify something is to give reasons to value it. "Value" is a vague term, but here it means something stronger than the feeble "like" or "prefer." When we question whether political practices like slavery, capital punishment, or redistributive taxation are justified, we do not seem to be simply asking whether they are "to our liking." I might, after all, very much prefer to have a coterie of slaves at my beck and call, but we would not think that personal likes and preferences of this kind (mine or anyone's) decide the question of whether slavery is justified. The question is whether there are general reasons to support or oppose such practices, not whether one might personally prefer them. In other words, then, justifying something seems to require that we demonstrate its value in a rational and impartial way. But how can we establish that we have suitably "impartial" reasons to support or resist some political practice? How can we tell whether arguments purporting to justify it succeed or fail?

One possibility is that they succeed insofar as they actually persuade most people to support (or resist) the practice in question. But we can discount this suggestion immediately. The bare fact that many are led to support something under the influence of purported justifications does not in itself show that the arguments being canvassed are any good. We know that, through skillful propaganda and rhetoric, agents can be manipulated into supporting all kinds of dubious political causes for spurious reasons. Successful persuasion and justification are therefore two different things. What we need to know is not whether people are *in fact* persuaded, but whether they *ought* to be.

But it is one thing to say that we must not confuse justification with effective persuasion, and another to explain how we are supposed to assess and verify claims about which political practices we ought rationally to support or resist. Many skeptics have doubted that such claims can be rationally adjudicated. According to them, our judgments about the value of different political arrangements only provoke endless and irresolvable disagreement. If they are right, the quest for rational justification in politics is ultimately vain, and a central aim of political philosophy misguided. This chapter explores doubts along these lines, and considers some ways one might try to allay them.

Subjective and objective

We can begin by dismissing one currently popular way of expressing such doubts. People often say that claims about something's value, be it a political arrangement or anything (a work of art, an experience, a piece of music), cannot be validated because they are essentially "subjective" rather than "objective." The model of "objectivity" to which this distinction appeals is usually provided by modern empirical science. The thought here is that scientific inquiry involves the "objective" investigation of hard, verifiable, facts. Our value judgments, however, are not objectively verifiable facts, or so many think. Rather, they reflect non-rational preferences and emotional reactions. Like our taste for different flavors of ice-cream, they vary from person to person. Unlike the question of whether the Earth is flat, or revolves around the sun, these claims cannot be "objectively" tested. They are in this sense "subjective."

Those attracted to this line of thinking may think that it undermines the search for rational justification in political life. They could argue: "You have said that the effort to justify a political arrangement requires that we supply general reasons for valuing it. But questions about values are 'subjective.' They cannot be adjudicated in an objective, rational, way. So attempts to assess justifications rationally must be fruitless. Ergo, political philosophy is bunk."

This sort of skepticism is ubiquitous nowadays. It is therefore particularly important to expose its inadequacy. The first thing to say about it is that the distinction between "objective" and "subjective" is far less clear than many suppose. Below are a few of the various meanings that hide behind this distinction:

Subjective	vs.	Objective
	might mean...	
Difficult to prove	vs.	Easy to prove
Biased	vs.	Unbiased
About values	vs.	About facts
Matters of opinion	vs.	Matters of fact
Matters of the "heart"	vs.	Matters of the "mind"
Untestable	vs.	Testable
Doubtful	vs.	Certain
Sentimental	vs.	Dispassionate
Nonrational	vs.	Rational
Expressive	vs.	Informative
Unreflective	vs.	Reflective
Controversial	vs.	Uncontroversial
Prescriptive	vs.	Descriptive
Preferences	vs.	Judgments
Partial	vs.	Impartial
Emotional	vs.	Reasoned
Unscientific	vs.	Scientific
Moral	vs.	Nonmoral
Personal	vs.	Impersonal
Neither true nor false	vs.	True or false

The important point about this list, which could be extended, is that there are clear differences between these various distinctions. Crucially, moreover, it is not obvious that they match up with each other: not all of the items in each column necessarily go together. But the opposition of subjective and objective blends all these various contrasts into a single omnibus distinction. It encourages the assumption that everything on the left must be incompatible with everything on the right. But why assume this? For example, could not some evaluative claims be testable judgments rather than unverifiable preferences (see below)? Are not some moral claims relatively uncontroversial? Is it not possible that some value judgments could be impartial rather than partial? Could not some be based on reasons rather than on emotions? I am not saying here that these possibilities are easy to explain or completely unproblematic. The point, rather, is that the objective/subjective distinction simply discounts these possibilities at the outset, more or less by definition. This prejudges the very questions at issue.

A second problem with this appeal to the "subjectivity" of value judgment is that it implausibly suggests that *all* modes of valuation must be like unreflective tastes and appetites. No doubt my taste for chocolate reflects a predilection that we cannot really describe as rational or irrational. But surely not all evaluations, and rather few *political* evaluations, conform to this model.

Consider my conviction that the practice of slavery is seriously unjust and therefore unjustifiable. Here we have an evaluation – a condemnation of a certain social practice as unjust – that does not look anything like my taste for chocolate. For one thing, we would not describe that taste as a "conviction" about chocolate. Furthermore, there is no immediate reason to doubt that the ground given for this conviction – the claim that racial slavery is unjust – is rationally defensible. My convictions about the injustice of slavery presumably depend on some understanding of justice. At least in principle, by making that conception of justice explicit, we can subject it to critical scrutiny and determine whether, assuming it to be defensible, my judgment that slavery is unjust is indeed among its implications.

A third problem with this line of argument concerns its insinuation that judgments about "matters of fact" are systematically easier to validate than claims about what we have reason to value. Sometimes, of course, they may be. For example, compared to the question of (say) whether justice requires or prohibits affirmative action, it certainly seems easier to determine (say) whether or not the cat really is on the mat. But this is just one example. In other cases, the comparison seems to go the other way.

Consider, for example, starvation, disease, depression, rejection, exclusion, loss, fear, ignorance, delusion, war, violence, insecurity, and pain. Is it complicated or difficult to validate the claim that these are evils that we have reason to avoid? Do we even need to validate it? Consider falling in love, encountering great beauty, laughing so hard that tears come to your eyes, bringing some important and difficult project to completion, experiencing intensely pleasurable sensations, enjoying the trust of a loyal friend, successfully raising healthy children, and achieving knowledge or understanding. Should we hesitate before saying that we know that these things (among others) usually enhance our lives? Can there be any serious doubt about whether we have reason to value them?

Now compare these evaluative claims with the answers one might offer to the following "factual" questions: What caused the French Revolution? Did the universe begin with a "Big Bang"? How does the human brain process visual images? Why did the dinosaurs go extinct? Why is it dark at night when so many stars far more powerful than our sun are still shining?[1] Answers to these "factual" questions look as if they will be much harder to validate than claims about the value of such basic goods as friendship, pleasure, or beauty.

This comparison reinforces our earlier point that not all value judgments are necessarily nonrational preferences, entirely impervious to rational scrutiny. As we have just seen, at the very least there seems to be a category of basic goods, like beauty, friendship, or pleasure, that naturally command our rational approval. Surely one can plausibly maintain that a person who sincerely denies the value of these natural goods exemplifies a form of irrationality. ("Great news: I'm clinically depressed." "Why should I avoid excruciating pain?" "Too bad that my kids are healthy and flourishing!") This certainly looks like a fixed point in any defensible understanding of what it means to be a rational agent.[2]

No doubt such a view about rationality requires further elaboration and defense. But equally, we have no immediate reasons to reject it out of hand. And as long as it is a possible view, it is not clear that judgments about values always compare unfavorably with judgments about facts so far as our ability to assess their rationality is concerned. We shouldn't allow flabby distinctions between "objectivity" and "subjectivity" to bewitch us into thinking otherwise. To the extent that skepticism about political philosophy rests on that distinction, we have no reason to take it seriously.

Essentially contested concepts

Unfortunately, however, this is far from the end of the story. More sophisticated and troubling doubts about the quest for justification

---

[1] This is, of course, the famous "Olbers' Paradox." See Harrison (1987).

[2] Some skeptics have denied even this. I ignore this view here. This would take us too far afield. In any case, I think the most interesting and troubling forms of skepticism about political philosophy arise even after we grant this point.

in political life remain. Consider the following line of argument. We have seen that attempts to justify something involve offering reasons to value it. Notice, however, that it does not follow from this that everything that we have reason to value requires justification. Rather, the need for justification arises only when something's value is not immediately obvious, or seems open to reasonable question. Precisely for this reason, we might claim that we do not need to justify our interest in the sorts of "basic goods" we discussed in the previous section. For, as we saw, it is at least plausible to think that these goods quite naturally command our rational approval. Of course, if we want to be provocative we can always ask, "Do you *really* have a reason to value (care for, support, protect) your children?" or "Do you *really* have reasons to hope that you never lapse into crippling depression?" But there is something absurd about these questions. In these cases we operate with the presumption that people do have such reasons, and we would think it odd if someone demanded a justification for this presumption.

However, skeptics could grant this point but still deny that we can make this presumption so easily when we are evaluating political arrangements, and this for two reasons. First, it seems safe to say that there have been virtually no political practices or actions whose value (or disvalue) has been so obviously uncontestable as to preempt calls for a justification. As I mentioned in the introduction, human political arrangements have displayed an astounding variety, and people have disagreed sharply about their respective value. Indeed, it is quite difficult to think of *any* political practice whose value or disvalue has gone entirely unchallenged. Thus skeptics might point out that even the assumption that the state is an essential human institution, providing such basic goods as security and order, has been questioned by anarchists, often with considerable cogency. Or, they might remind us that several philosophers, including such illustrious figures as Aristotle, Hobbes, and Locke, have defended various forms of slavery even though most people today assume that, if any political practice is clearly objectionable, it is this one. Clearly, this was not as obvious to them as it seems to us.

Second, and more importantly still, the arguments that people use to defend or criticize political practices invariably mobilize concepts that themselves inspire considerable disagreement. The ideal of justice, for example, often figures prominently in arguments for or against political arrangements and actions. But the concept of justice is hardly uncontroversial. Different people interpret it in conflicting ways. How can we demonstrate that any one of these rival interpretations is clearly superior to the others? This is not clear.

Some philosophers conclude from this that ideals like justice are "essentially contested concepts." According to W.B. Gallie, who coined this term, "When we examine the different uses of these [concepts] and the characteristic arguments in which they figure we soon see that there is no one clearly definable general use of any of them which can be set up as the correct or standard use." As a result, we can expect "endless disputes" about the proper uses and implications of these concepts.[3] And what goes for justice, we may fear, also goes for other "essentially contestable" concepts like "the common good," "equality," "democracy," and so on. Faced with such disputes, we may lose confidence in the ability of reasoned reflection to explain definitively which political arrangements justice, or equality, democracy, and the common good, require us to support or resist.

Skepticism along these lines need not rest on any hazy distinctions between "objective" and "subjective." Even if we were confident that many simple value judgments can be criticized as irrational, for example, we might still doubt that we can use reason to resolve disagreements over the "correct" interpretation of a complex ethical ideal like justice. The rest of this chapter explores the dimensions of this problem and the doubts it raises about the possibility of rational justification in political life.

Pacifica and Atlantis

I will focus on the case of justice and the kinds of disagreement it invites. Begin by noting that in many cultures and communities, there already exists a rough consensus on certain basic principles of justice. Imagine, for example, that Atlantis is a democratic regime and that Atlantan political culture revolves around an egalitarian conception of justice according to which humans are each other's equals. Among Atlantans, that is, all human beings are assumed to be independent, free beings, each with an equal right, founded upon justice, to be respected as such by their fellows and the social institutions that regulate their common life. These commitments,

---

[3] Gallie (1956), pp. 168–9.

moreover, are woven into the day-to-day practices of Atlantan public life — judges, citizens and public officials accept the Atlantan political system because they believe that it accords, broadly, with the desiderata of justice as they understand it.

Still, as we know very well from our own societies, which are Atlantan in many ways, there is room for considerable disagreement about what these very broad commitments demand. Do they require the redistribution of wealth, and if so, how much? Do they mandate special forms of assistance (e.g. affirmative action, special rights for cultural minorities) for members of disadvantaged groups? Under what conditions? How far ought the authority of democratic majorities over individuals' lives to extend?

These questions will generate controversy, and the resulting disagreements may be keenly felt and hotly debated. Nevertheless, these disagreements are bounded by a higher-order consensus about the basic desiderata of a just society and are therefore limited in scope. They concern not the validity of a principle of basic equality (that is generally presupposed by parties to the conversation) but rather the application of that general principle to specific cases. And, in principle at least, if I were to make a really convincing argument that fidelity to such a basic principle clearly requires (say) affirmative action, I might be in a strong position to demonstrate that my fellow Atlantans ought to support the policy, given their commitment to an egalitarian conception of justice. This convergence might in practice be quite difficult to obtain, but the presence of an underlying set of shared understandings at least makes it possible.

Indeed, it is tempting to think that just such a convergence has come into being in our own societies, around a similar cluster of values. The arguments made on behalf of women seeking the right to vote, or for extending civil rights to racial minorities in the American South, for example, were forceful precisely because they rested on assumptions about equality that are now very widely accepted within Western societies. If it is difficult to imagine people today opposing these positions and being taken seriously, it is surely because the case for them depends on a commitment to an egalitarian understanding of basic justice that few in our societies question.

But there is another sort of disagreement about justice. Suppose that in nearby Pacifica, an aristocratic regime, political culture and entrenched social practices revolve around a quite different, and strongly inegalitarian, understanding of justice. Pacifica is organized into various castes with different social entitlements and privileges; it practices slavery; women are excluded from positions of public responsibility and status and are expected to remain at home raising children and running households; and it is a requirement of full Pacifican citizenship that one accept a particular religious doctrine, practiced by a majority, but also conscientiously rejected by many others, who are therefore deprived of full legal rights and protections. Let's suppose that these practices are stable and that they are widely accepted as just by members of Pacifican society. Once again, disagreements will arise over how to interpret the conception of justice implicit in these practices. (How should membership in each of the various castes be determined? Are there circumstances under which slaves might justifiably be freed? How exactly should we measure the relative qualities and attributes of different citizens for the purposes of allocating wealth and status?) But, as in the Atlantan case, these disagreements occur against the backdrop of an underlying consensus about the basic outlines of a just society.

Putting these internal debates in Atlantis and Pacifica side by side exposes a deeper form of disagreement about justice. For here we have two apparently contradictory conceptions of justice. From a conventional Atlantan point of view, societies count as just rather than unjust to the extent that they approximate some principle of basic equality; but from a Pacifican perspective societies count as just insofar as they perpetuate and respond to various sorts of inequality. It is hard to believe that both these views can be true at the same time. But it is also difficult to see how we might resolve the disagreement between them. For here there seems to be no consensus in place, no obvious fund of shared assumptions to which Pacificans or Atlantans might appeal to try to vindicate their underlying views about justice against each other.

To be sure, Pacificans and Atlantans both seem to use the same concept — that of justice. And perhaps at a sufficiently general level they might agree on certain elements of that concept: that it involves notions of fairness, of giving people their due, applying the rules impartially, and so forth. But the way in which these two societies interpret this basic concept results in radically opposed *conceptions of justice*. This kind of radical disagreement supports the claim that justice is an "essentially contested concept." It is not clear how, or on what basis, Atlantans and Pacificans could demonstrate to each other that their own understanding of justice is superior.

Does radical disagreement matter?

On the other hand, perhaps this is a disagreement we need not resolve. As long as Pacifica and Atlantis keep out of each other's way, why should it bother citizens of either society? Why not simply encourage Atlantans to get on with organizing their civic life in their own way and Pacificans to do the same? Why not just say, "Diff'rent strokes for diff'rent folks"?

But this effort to sidestep the issue proves ultimately unsatisfying, for both practical and philosophical reasons. As a practical matter, we cannot usually assume that deep disagreements of this kind coincide neatly with the boundaries of different political associations. The more standard case is one in which – to adapt the example – citizens with Pacifican and Atlantan understandings of justice must live side by side within a common civic order. In such circumstances we do not really have the luxury of saying, "Let the Pacificans and Atlantans among us go their separate ways." Unless Pacificans and Atlantans secede from each other, then, the terms of their civic association must somehow coexist with dissensus on the fundamental requirements of justice. Under these conditions, it will surely be difficult for Pacificans and Atlantans (and, for that matter, Mediterraneans, Caspians, and others) to ignore their profound differences over the fundamental requirements of justice.

But there is another, more philosophical, reason why we cannot wholeheartedly ignore deep disagreements between rival conceptions of justice. Even if Pacificans and Atlantans do not live together in close proximity, for example, the mere knowledge that the two societies understand the same concept in conflicting ways should be disturbing to devotees of both views. But to understand exactly why this is the case, it is first necessary to distinguish carefully between two elements of our ordinary thinking about justice.

Recognition and evaluation

When we make judgments about the justness of some social arrangement, that is, there seem to be two elements in play. There is, first, an element of *recognition* or *accreditation*: a person who judges Atlantis to be a just (or unjust) polity recognizes that certain of Atlantis's actual procedures, practices, and characteristics satisfy (or violate) relevant desiderata.

Part of what we seem to do in judging a society as just, then, is to hold that it meets certain standards or expectations. To the extent that a society satisfies these criteria in our eyes we will "see" or "count" it as just rather than unjust, or as more rather than less just.

But second, judgments about justice involve an element of *valuation*: in judging a society to be just, we appraise it in some way – we imply that it is in some rather important sense superior to societies that are unjust. To contend, then, that Atlantis conforms to relevant principles of justice is not only to say that it meets some set of standards. It is also to assert that we have a strong reason to value the Atlantan regime *because* it satisfies those standards. In this sense, justice is a value-conferring property: just societies are good societies and command our approval for that reason.

This seems to be a fixed point in our ordinary understandings of justice. It would be strange to say that there could be an essentially just society that is in no respect better than an unjust one. Indeed, we would normally say that a society we know to be just is in some very fundamental sense a better society than one we know to be unjust. We are likely to believe this even when the adjective "just" is applied to things we otherwise regard as bad. We may think, for example, that war is always regrettable, but would nonetheless accept that a just war is in some important respect better, or at any rate less bad, than an unjust one.

The implications of radical disagreement

This means that the disagreement between Pacificans and Atlantans is not only about how to recognize justice and injustice. It is more fundamentally about which political arrangements we have reason to value. But it is now hard to see how Pacificans or Atlantans could hope to resolve this disagreement by appealing to their own views about justice. For here, it seems that different conceptions of justice are being used to *express* a disagreement about whether we ought to prefer egalitarian over inegalitarian political arrangements. But for just that reason, it is difficult to think that such claims about justice can serve as impartial bases from which to assess the relative merits of egalitarian or inegalitarian political arrangements. The two conceptions of justice take sides on the very issue that needs to be adjudicated.

This line of thought raises doubts about *any* argument that claims to justify political arrangements by appealing to conventional beliefs about how we ought to recognize justice. And this has implications for Pacificans' and Altantans' *own* beliefs about the value of their local political practices. Members of both societies consider their political systems to be justified because broadly they conform to the requirements they recognize as just rather than unjust. But they are entitled to this conclusion only if they are right to assume that arrangements that count as just under their respective conceptions of justice really do command their rational approval. In themselves, however, conventional beliefs about what *counts* or should be *recognized* as just or unjust (whether Atlantan, Pacifican, or otherwise) cannot establish this. They assert, but do not demonstrate, that we have reasons to value the arrangements they mark as just rather than unjust.

The "diff'rent strokes for diff'rent folks" strategy seemed appealing because it implied that Pacificans and Atlantans could simply skip away from their disagreements about justice with their confidence in the value of their domestic political arrangements intact. But the arguments we have considered suggest that they cannot be so complacent. Pacificans and Atlantans cannot validate their belief that their local political arrangements are justified merely by pointing out that they count as just by the lights of a conception of justice they happen to accept. Arguments along these lines are incomplete; they purport to be, but seem not to be, successful justifications.

Faced with this realization, Pacificans and Atlantans may be thrown back into skepticism about political arguments based on claims about justice. They – and we – may come to doubt that such contested concepts as justice have the power to justify anything. If conceptions of justice lack any real justificatory force, then clearly we cannot appeal to them as a basis for rationally evaluating our political institutions. We may instead come to regard them as culturally and historically relative artifacts, merely question-begging "social constructs" that serve to induce compliance with prevailing modes of political organization in different places at different times.

Plato's challenge

Though today they often step forward in trendy black turtlenecks and sleek postmodern spectacles, doubts of this kind are actually very ancient.

In the next three chapters we will consider some of the most influential ways in which political philosophers have tried to overcome them. Among the first to grasp their significance was the classical Greek philosopher Aristocles, better known to us by his nickname, Plato. In his best-known and most important discussion of political philosophy, the *Republic*, Plato attempted to respond to skepticism of this sort. That work is written as a dialogue, in which a number of people discuss the nature of justice with the great Athenian philosopher, Socrates, normally assumed to be Plato's own spokesman in the text. Socrates' interlocutors challenge him to show that "justice benefits its possessor."[4] This challenge is significant for us because Plato believed that, if he could meet it, the kind of skepticism we have just considered could be defused.

To understand this, though, we need first to explain the initially mysterious idea that justice is something that a person can "possess." For Plato, a person who possesses justice is simply one who embraces, and who is disposed to conform to, the requirements of a particular conception of justice. She internalizes that conception of justice, and correctly recognizes which forms of conduct and social organization count as just or unjust by its lights. She also believes she has reasons to value institutions that are in the relevant sense "just." On this basis she is disposed to conform her own actions to its expectations and to praise and support others' efforts to do so as well.

We can assume that in most societies, as in Pacifica and Atlantis, there is some such understanding of justice implicit in the routine patterns of public life. It is reasonable to think that these patterns of social organization persist over time in part because the people who live within them are disposed to accept and comply with these implicit conceptions of justice latent within their public culture. In this sense, members of particular societies typically "possess" the conceptions of justice structuring their public life. For example, if few Atlantan citizens believed that it is just and hence good to treat each other as equals, why would they continue to support and comply with the institutions and practices around which Atlantis' political system is organized?

The cultivation of particular conceptions of justice, then, must have a wide range of effects. They will influence people's system of values, their

---

[4] Plato (1992), p. 42.

ethical beliefs about their proper roles and responsibilities, as well as their views about how others ought to be acting. These beliefs will also tend to guide their actions, and so conceptions of justice will have effects on what agents choose for themselves, how they treat each other, what expectations they make of themselves and others, what they criticize each other for, how they allocate important social and political responsibilities, how wealth and property are divided, and much else. In this way, the "possession" of particular conceptions of justice by members of society will have far-reaching consequences, powerfully affecting the shape and pattern of social relations in particular political communities.

But these consequences might be beneficial or harmful in varying degrees to different people. Once we notice this, Plato's quest in the *Republic* for an explanation of how justice might "benefit its possessors" starts to make more sense. Presumably one way to test whether agents really do have reason to value the arrangements they recognize as just rather than unjust is to ask whether their "possessing" the relevant conception of justice tends to benefit or harm them. It is not controversial that people have reason to value those things that will improve their lives. Investigating the beneficial and harmful consequences of conceptions of justice for those who accept and live by them may therefore allow us to test the claims made by those conceptions from an independent and impartial standpoint. We have seen that agents socialized into "possessing" particular conceptions of justice will believe they have reasons to value arrangements, institutions, and forms of action that those conceptions classify as just. And, on the basis of these beliefs, they will support and comply with the relevant expectations. Plato's hope was that he might falsify or verify such beliefs by asking whether or not the lives of agents who embrace and act on them are enhanced as a result.

In the *Republic*, Plato developed a very ambitious version of this line of argument. He set himself the challenge of developing an ideal conception of justice that would enhance the lives of all those who "possess" it. In a society organized around this conception of justice individuals would recognize justice and injustice in a particular way, and be disposed to conform their own conduct to its expectations. And according to Plato, they would all benefit as a result; their lives would be enhanced for being socialized into this conception of justice and would be harmed if they were not. On this argument, far from being a burden to them, possessing the relevant conception of justice would actually be a precondition of their well-being.

An important advantage of an ideal of justice of which this is true is that it seems immune to the sort of skepticism we encountered in the last section. Unlike Pacificans and Atlantans, members of such an ideal society need not be haunted by the worry that their commitment to the value of political arrangements they recognize as just is founded on nothing more than question-begging conventions or traditional beliefs. For they could deflect such doubts by citing the way in which their acceptance of and compliance with the relevant ideal of justice contributes to their own well-being. They would have an independent reason for embracing the value of just social arrangements.

Plato's anti-skeptical strategy thus involves arguing that acceptance and compliance with justice, properly understood, is in everyone's best interests. Were that strategy to succeed, we could readily explain why we have reasons to value just social arrangements. And this might in turn restore our confidence in ideals of justice as a basis for rational justification in politics. If Plato can show that willing compliance with institutions we ought to recognize as just advances our interests, it would be easier to understand why showing that something is just gives us a reason to value it.

New doubts

But this project raises several new questions. As Socrates' interlocutors in the *Republic* immediately point out, there is something puzzling about the suggestion that adherence to the requirements of justice promotes our own interests. We characteristically encounter conflicts between doing what justice, or morality more generally, requires and doing what we think would promote our own interests. After all, people normally lie, cheat, and steal precisely because they believe they stand to gain from doing so. Conversely, we often assume that those who exemplify ideals of just and moral conduct act on relevant ethical principles regardless of considerations of personal benefit. This suggests that any plausible reconstruction of justice must concede that being disposed to act justly involves a willingness to forgo certain benefits and advantages for the sake of something other than oneself. Properly understood, compliance with justice and morality is selfless, not self-interested.

Interestingly, this assumption seems to hold constant even when the content of particular conceptions of justice changes. Women and slaves in Pacifica may (rightly) suspect that it is in their interest to violate the prevailing norms of justice that keep them in their subordinate social positions. But insofar as they "possess" Pacifican justice, they will be disposed to comply with those norms nonetheless, and to believe that doing so is the right thing to do, for its own sake, on principle, and so forth. Although the Atlantan conception of justice makes very different demands, its "possessors" must sometimes face similar conflicts between their personal interests and compliance with expectations they recognize as just. For example, Atlantis is a democratic regime, and this means that minorities are expected, as a matter of justice, magnanimously to accept defeat when the "democratic process" produces outcomes that run counter to their members' interests. As loyal Atlantans, they embrace and comply with this understanding of what justice requires of them even if this means that their interests are systematically overridden by those of the majority.

These reflections give rise to two related objections to Plato's enterprise. First, the project seems naïvely utopian. The idea that any society could entirely eliminate conflicts between agents' own interests and the prevailing conventions of justice looks like a vain hope. Second, it may seem that Plato indulged this utopian fantasy only because he was fundamentally confused about the kind of value that justice is. A just society is one in which agents fulfill certain duties simply for their own sake, and without regard, not only to their own interests, but also to interests more generally. As one contemporary political philosopher writes: "The idea that considerations of advantage are distinct from those of morality, and that it might be rational to allow the latter to override the former, seems to be at the core of our intuitions about morality."[5] This position is often associated with the great Prussian philosopher Immanuel Kant. He argued that it is a mistake to confuse "moral" values like justice and the duties and obligations they impose with prudential calculations, or considerations of rational advantage. On his view, the defining feature of the rules of justice and morality is that they require me to fulfill my duties and obligations *on principle*, regardless of the ways in which I,

---

[5] Beitz (1999), p. 16.

or others, might benefit. But if this Kantian view is on target, Plato's project seems confused at the outset.

But neither objection is decisive. As to the first, there are several passages in the *Republic* in which Plato seems to concede that his proposed ideal of a just society is utopian, in the sense that it may be impossible ever actually to realize it.[6] But Plato thought that describing such a society is nevertheless informative inasmuch as it provides an ideal criterion for assessing the relative merits of the various possible conceptions of justice that *are* achievable in practice. So, for Plato, the important question was not whether his model could ever actually be achieved, but rather whether it correctly represents the ideal archetype of a just society. If it does (admittedly a rather big "if" in Plato's case), it provides a basis for rationally discriminating among actually realizable conceptions of justice that approximate this ideal to greater or lesser degrees. That is how Plato himself proceeded in the *Republic*. Having first sketched out a frankly utopian ideal of a truly just society, he then developed a typology of non-ideal societies ("timarchy," oligarchy, democracy, and tyranny) and ranked them by their proximity to that ideal.[7] This enabled him to diagnose with some precision the respective merits and deficiencies of the different understandings of justice around which societies might revolve. While we may reject Plato's proposed ideal, and find his list and judgments of regimes anachronistic, the general approach of assessing existing political practices in the light of *some* appropriately validated ideal of justice seems sensible enough.

As for the second objection, the Kantian assumption that moral evaluation and considerations of advantage must be entirely distinct is in some ways even more puzzling than Plato's suggested alternative. If complying with justice and other moral requirements does literally *nothing* to promote anyone's interests, or actually works against them, it surely becomes significantly harder to explain why we have reasons to value doing so nonetheless. Decoupled from claims about their tendency to advance one's interests, justifications that appeal to free-standing requirements of justice may seem no less question-begging than the bare appeals to conventional beliefs we earlier considered. In contrast, the appeal

---

[6] Plato (1992), pp. 147–8.
[7] Plato (1992), pp. 213–40.

of Plato's strategy is that it promises to connect justice with considerations that, if sound, would uncontroversially command our rational approval – claims about our interests, happiness, and well-being. Despite the objections it invites, then, we cannot simply dismiss Plato's effort to explain how justice, properly understood, advances the interests of agents who cooperate in meeting and complying with its various expectations.

In pursuing this line of argument, Plato helped to launch the idea that a society is truly just only when its political arrangements work impartially to the advantage of all. As Plato himself put it, his project in the *Republic* is to "determine which whole way of life would make living most worthwhile for each of us".[8] Plato's attempt to answer this question in the *Republic* became the prototype for a whole tradition of inquiry into the proper requirements of a "common good." Theories of the "common good" raise many questions: How do we determine whether someone's life is enhanced in the relevant sense? Compared to what? How do we ensure that everyone's interests are taken impartially into consideration? What is the relevant standard of impartiality? The history of inquiry into the nature of the common good is the story of various efforts to confront and answer these questions. The next two chapters survey and assess some of the most influential efforts to tackle them.

Conclusions

This chapter considered several different forms of skepticism about rational justification in politics. We began by canvassing and rejecting the still widespread view that judgments about the "value" of different political arrangements are too "subjective" to be rationally assessed. But we then confronted an array of more sophisticated and serious worries about whether appealing to ethical ideals can ever show that we have reason to value political practices and actions. Using the example of justice, we noted that such ideals are characteristically open to radically conflicting interpretations, and that it is not clear how one can vindicate any one interpretation as more "correct" than any other. We also emphasized the way in which conventional understandings about how justice should be recognized tend to beg the crucial question of whether agents really have

---

[8] Plato (1992), p. 21.

reasons to value whatever those understandings mark as just rather than unjust. Since it is precisely this question that successful justifications must answer, we were led to consider the possibility that conventional beliefs about justice lack the capacity to justify anything at all. In the last few sections, we began to reconstruct a line of argument, first developed by Plato, for overcoming this problem.

We will discuss this Platonic argument, and common-good arguments more generally, in more detail in the coming chapters. I end this chapter with a point about the contemporary resonance of the discussion so far. The story I have told about Pacifica and Atlantis is of course fictional and stylized. Still, it is built up from raw materials that we can easily recognize. In particular, it is important to emphasize the similarity between the Western liberal democracies in which we live and the fictional society of Atlantis. What I have called the "Atlantan" conception of justice, committed to the equality of human beings as such, to democratic procedures, and to principles of respect for individuals' freedom and independence, is a close approximation to what we today call "liberalism." And, as at Atlantis, these broadly "liberal" doctrines are not for us mere empty abstractions: they are woven into the routine practices of our public life. In our societies, "equality before the law," "freedom of speech," "respect for the dignity of all," "one person, one vote," are not merely theoretical slogans but actively enforced social practices that many believe they have reasons to value and support.

Many contemporary political philosophers are tempted to view this reservoir of shared understandings as a resource that they can exploit to present justifications for various particular political practices and policies. Thus many political philosophers writing today openly declare their allegiance to "liberalism" and to its organizing assumptions about justice. They then inquire into the question of whether or not endorsing these background assumptions commits one to such specific practices as affirmative action, redistributive taxation, the public provision of healthcare, same-sex marriage, overseas aid, the legal enforcement of moral standards, civil disobedience, and so forth. Understood in this way, the political philosopher's major concern is with a particular kind of coherence — the consistency of specific political arrangements and policies with background principles that are generally professed by participants in a common culture.

As we have seen in this chapter, however, there is a serious question about how much arguments of this general form can establish. They seem open to the objection that, at best, they establish which arrangements *count* as just rather than unjust by the lights of a particular (liberal) conception of justice, but tend to beg the question of whether we have reasons to value (support, defend) such arrangements. Since a successful justification for something must provide us with just such reasons to value it, it is unclear that arguments along these lines are sufficient to justify the things they purport to justify. True, insofar as people in liberal societies believe that justice requires that we treat each other as equals, and so forth, they believe that we have reasons to value social arrangements that are appropriately egalitarian. But as we mentioned at the start, the fact that people believe something does not show that they are correct to believe it. Readers new to recent debates among philosophers about the implications of liberal ideals would be well advised to keep this worry firmly in view.

2   The common good

The last chapter explored some difficulties facing the quest for rational justification in political life. This chapter and the next take up Plato's influential effort to overcome them, and explore some variants of the general justificatory strategy that he pioneered. I will call theories that follow this strategy *common-good arguments*. These arguments form a very broad church and have come in many shapes and sizes. Despite these many differences, however, they share a distinguishing feature. They all assume that the value of political arrangements and forms of collective organization, along with the beliefs about justice and other ethical ideals that hold them in place, must ultimately be explained in terms of their contribution to the well-being and happiness of everyone living within them. Insofar as they meet this condition, these arrangements, practices, and beliefs are part of a common good, or so theorists in this tradition maintain.

This chapter explores Plato's contention that, properly understood, justice is part of the common good in this sense, something that benefits everyone. As we shall see, Plato's seminal proposal launched a distinctively perfectionist conception of political life, one later refined by his pupil Aristotle and still influential today. Having (in this chapter) described the contours of this classical perfectionist account of the common good, in the next we shall consider the most influential modern variant of the common-good approach, utilitarianism. That chapter ends with a critical discussion of some of the problems facing this approach as a whole.

Public and private

To introduce Plato's notion of the common good, it is helpful to begin with a view that he rejected. Consider the following extract from a poem by W. H. Auden:

> There are two atlases: the one
> The public space where acts are done,
> In theory common to us all,
> Where we are needed and feel small,
> The *agora* of work and news
> Where each one has the right to choose
> His trade, his corner and his way,
> And can, again, in theory, say
> For whose protection he will pay,
> And loyalty is help we give
> The place where we prefer to live;
> The other is the inner space
> Of private ownership, the place
> That each of us is forced to own,
> Like his own life from which it's grown,
> The landscape of his will and need
> Where he is sovereign indeed,
> The state created by his acts
> Where he patrols the forest tracts
> Planted in childhood, farms the belt
> Of doings memorized and felt,
> And even if he find it hell
> May neither leave it nor rebel.
> Two worlds describing their rewards,
> That one in tangents, this in chords;
> Each lives in one, all in the other,
> Here all are kings, there each a brother.
>
> W. H. Auden, from *New Year Letter* (January 1, 1940)[1]

Implicit in these lines is a certain vision of justice, familiar in popular discourse today, centered on a distinction between a public and a private realm. To develop Auden's helpful geometrical metaphor, this broadly liberal democratic conception of justice is concerned mainly with the "tangents" that separate our lives from one another. Justice is, on this view, fundamentally a matter of respecting external boundaries, of preventing

---

[1] Auden (1991), pp. 225–6.

collisions and infringements between individuals and their lives. It is a purely interpersonal virtue, concerned with the relations between persons, but not the internal structure of individuals' own lives, the shadowy "chords" that structure our inward life. The private, "inner space" defined by publicly enforced boundaries between the separate lives of different individuals is protected from outside interference. Each of us must make of it what we will. My life thus becomes my responsibility and your life yours, such that *my* life is none of *your* business and vice versa. It would, on this view, be fundamentally unjust for others to meddle in our rights to "pursue our own good in our own way."

Plato agreed that conceptions of justice determine what constitutes improper meddling or interference of something with something else. And as a citizen of democratic Athens, he was familiar with the tendency of democratic political cultures to regard interference by one individual in another's personal freedom as the paradigmatic form of injustice. Plato also granted that this understanding of justice is attractive and invigorating because of the freedom and diversity it promotes.[2] Nevertheless, he regarded the democratic view as a fundamentally inadequate interpretation of justice, for he denied that justice and injustice are concerned solely with patterns of *interpersonal* interference. Plato thought that, properly understood, justice aims not only to map out Auden's public atlas but also to promote a particular pattern of harmonious organization within individual selves.

This led him to draw a famous – some would say infamous – analogy between just societies and just selves. Plato claimed that just as societies are composed of individuals and groups that can get in each other's way, so the individual self is made up of different and potentially conflicting psychological faculties. Each has distinctive functions and generates distinctive desires. Plato distinguished three such elements. As partly *appetitive* beings, we naturally seek food, drink, shelter, sexual gratification, physical pleasure, and relief from pain. As partly "*spirited*" or emotional beings, we rejoice in activity and self-expression and find ourselves inspired to act from such motives as pride, anger, indignation, and love. And as partly *rational* beings, we seek and can achieve knowledge, wisdom, and understanding. According to Plato, our familiar

[2] Plato (1992), p. 232.

struggles to suppress physical temptations, to swallow our pride, to remain resolutely committed to some plan of action, and similar phenomena, all exemplify conflicts that often arise between these faculties of reason, spirit, and appetite.

Since Plato believed that both selves and societies are complex entities in this way, he thought of justice and injustice as possible properties of each. A society is, on this account, just when the individuals and groups that make it up play their proper roles, and unjust when they interfere with each other's functions. And individual selves are justly ordered when the three faculties of reason, spirit, and appetite perform their proper psychological roles and do not get in each other's way.

At first sight, the suggestion that justice is a possible property of an agent's inward psychological organization seems bizarre. But we may be inclined to reject it only because we have been raised to accept the democratic view. Perhaps we should not be so ready to take for granted this democratic understanding of our respective roles and responsibilities, and its account of what counts as unjust mutual interference. Why, then, did Plato reject it? Why did he insist, as against that democratic conception, that an adequate theory of justice be concerned not only with relations between persons, but with internal psychological relations as well? Answering these questions is the key to understanding Plato's influential account of the "common good."

Down with democracy

The excerpt from Auden's poem hints at Plato's basic worry about democratic conceptions of justice. As Auden points out, under the democratic conception each of us is "forced to own" an "inner space of private ownership," one that we cannot escape even if we "find it hell." In these lines, Auden acknowledges that individuals might willingly conform to democratic principles regulating their outward relations (e.g. "respect the rights of others") yet still suffer great distress in their inward lives. And as Auden clearly recognized, the "private hells" in which individuals may find themselves trapped often result from their own decisions: they are "states" created by agents acting as personal "sovereigns" on their own behalf. Plato's major worry about democratic conceptions of justice is that, in "forcing" individuals to "own" responsibility for their own well-being in this way, they leave them too vulnerable to their own mistakes about where their best interests lie. These mistakes will lead them to pursue inappropriate courses of action, and invest in the wrong projects. As a result, their lives may be unhappy and unfulfilled.

Plato thought that if they are to avoid this fate, agents must somehow come to a sound understanding of their real interests. They must learn to discriminate intelligently between desires and choices that would promote their well-being and those that, if indulged, would be toxic to it. They also need self-discipline and resolve. But Plato denied that these character traits come naturally or easily to most people. Unless they are exposed to the right guidance, the chances are that they will fail to develop them and that they will make poor decisions for themselves as a result. Democratic freedom, the freedom to pursue one's own good unimpeded by others, tends to cut too many people off from this needed guidance, or so Plato feared. He doubted whether leaving people to themselves was an adequate way to promote their happiness.

One might be tempted here to excavate a notion we tried to bury in the previous chapter, by retorting that the question of what would make each of us happy is a purely "subjective" one. It is therefore presumptious for Plato to suppose that he or anyone else could know what would make others happy. Insofar as this sort of objection has any real meaning, it alleges that there is no authoritative standpoint outside each individual's own perspective from which we can evaluate judgments about their own good. There is only *my* good understood from *my* perspective, *your* good understood from *your* perspective, *his* good understood from *his* perspective, and so on.

But this view is very implausible. People do make mistakes about their own interests, and there is rarely any difficulty in others' knowing that this is the case. Indeed, it often seems painfully true that outsiders are *more* aware of our own mistakes than we are. We can all think of examples of people who continually "mess up" by pursuing relationships with the wrong people, indulging foolish desires and temptations, lapsing into wasteful and unhealthy addictions, nursing inappropriate ambitions, sabotaging important long-term goals for the sake of trivial short-term gains, and so forth. And, as we know from our own political culture, democratic citizens do not deny that they often make mistakes of this kind.

Faced with criticism or advice from others, for example, they often say things like: "Well, you may be right that X is a mistake, but in a democracy, I have a right to make my own mistakes, and it would be unjust for you, or anyone else, to stop me from making them." Or, invoking Frank Sinatra: "Even if I am making a mistake, at least I will be able to say that *I did it my way*." These claims concede that people sometimes make mistakes about their own interests and that others can know that this is the case. The democratic view is that it would be unjust to interfere in individuals' personal affairs to stop them from making them nonetheless.

One of the enduring merits of Plato's argument in the *Republic* is that it draws our attention to the puzzling quality of such familiar claims. What sort of interest do we have in a system of rights that exposes us to an undue risk of a failed life? To ask this question is to return to the challenge of showing how justice "benefits its possessor." Plato's objection to democratic conceptions of justice is that they cannot meet this challenge and therefore cannot be adequate interpretations of the concept of justice. To "possess" democratic justice, in the Platonic sense, is to be socialized into the belief that each of us is a self-sufficient individual with our own idiosyncratic goals and interests, and to be disposed to respect others' "Sinatra-rights" – their rights to live their lives *their way*. But if Plato is correct, one can possess justice in this sense and lead a miserable, damaged, self-defeated life. In that case, what good is democratic justice to me? If I have wrecked my life, what consolation is it to know that I did it "my way"? Doesn't being implicated in our own failures only make our private hells even more hellish?

Notice that Plato's argument is not just a claim about the specific effects on *me* of *my* enjoying Sinatra-rights. Rather, it is an argument about the overall social effects of encouraging everyone to think of justice in these terms. His worry was that, over time, organizing social life around a "tangents-only" principle of justice cuts individuals loose from the sources of guidance and discipline they need to appreciate and effectively pursue their real interests. Democratic citizens are therefore "forced to own" responsibility for their own lives under social conditions that deny them the means to fulfill that responsibility competently. As a result, democratic justice may inflict real damage on individuals lives, or so Plato concluded.

The politics of the self

The lesson that Plato drew from this line of argument was that it is ultimately impossible to separate Auden's "two atlases" — the mapping of the public world and the inner world of the self. The two are, for him, profoundly interrelated. Thus he thought that some configurations of social roles and responsibilities, of which (on Plato's view) democratic conceptions of justice are examples, will tend to obscure individuals' real interests from them and encourage them to make mistakes about where their good really lies (or at any rate not sufficiently discourage such mistakes). This led him to speculate that other ways of ordering social relations might assist individuals in correctly perceiving and realizing their own good. He hoped to identify an ideal division of social responsibility that would as far as possible promote agents' ability to see their interests correctly and thereby realize their own good. Equipped with an ideal conception of justice of this kind, he thought he might then diagnose the distinctive ways in which other ways of mapping out proper social roles and responsibilities tend to distort agents' understandings of, and ability to pursue, their real interests. This, according to Plato, is the role of the philosopher of justice.

Once we see that Plato's aim was to diagnose the social conditions under which agents are liable to make characteristic mistakes about their best interests, we are on our way to explaining his initially strange thought that justice is a property of the inward organization of the self. For, clearly, in order to make such diagnoses, we need an account of what, exactly, goes awry when people commit such errors. It was in this context that Plato advanced his theory of the tripartite psyche, divided into appetitive, spirited, and rational components.

The tripartite self

Plato thought that each of these three faculties corresponds both to distinctive capacities and forms of action *and* to three distinct sets of basic interests that all individuals share. On the capacity side, Plato associated appetite, spirit, and reason respectively with

1. the capacity to experience physical pleasures and pains, along with natural inclinations to seek the former and avoid the latter;

2. the capacity to throw oneself wholeheartedly, with energy and feeling, into projects and endeavors;

3. the ability to assuage curiosity, solve puzzles, plan, acquire beliefs and convictions, expose error and falsehood, and seek the truth.

But for Plato appetite, spirit, and reason also correspond to three sets of interests. In ascending order of importance, we have

1. interests in satisfying certain physical needs, for food, drink, sex, the removal of discomfort and pain;

2. interests in our character, efforts and activities being appreciated by those around us, i.e., interests in friendship, love, recognition, honor, and respect;

3. interests in achieving knowledge and understanding, and especially in a justified consciousness of our lives as success stories.

So Plato contended that we have a hierarchically ordered set of basic interests, and a linked set of human capacities that we can harness to realize them. For Plato, human well-being involves the realization of these interests, and rational action simply consists in the effective deployment of these capacities in pursuit of this goal. But because he thought they have discrete psychological sources in three disparate parts of our psychological constitution, these goals and the available means for pursuing them are complex. And according to Plato, it is this complexity, and the resulting possibility of internal conflict, that expose human agents to the risk of error and irrationality in their actions and choices. Matching these capacities and interests in a propitious way requires various complicated forms of *coordination*. When this coordination goes wrong, we become liable to mistakes and as a result may fail to realize our interests. The question for him was to explain how agents can avoid mistakes of this kind by mobilizing their capacities to promote their well-being successfully.

Plato's answers to this question in the *Republic* are complex and often remarkably subtle. For our purposes it is necessary to note only that on Plato's view the required form of coordination is at once psychological and social. It is psychological in the following sense. Plato insisted that individuals will be able to realize their deepest interests only if the three components of their psychological make-up (the appetitive, spirited, and rational parts) stand in the proper relation to each other. Specifically, agents must be "ruled by" reason, with their other faculties taking a subordinate role. Being "ruled" by reason in this Platonic sense is not just a matter of possessing knowledge of what is best for us. The rational pursuit of one's real interests will sometimes require that one suppress certain urges and desires in favor of others. This requires a measure of self-discipline. For example, the fact that we know that sugary foods are bad for us will not by itself remove the desire to eat them. To *follow* our reason, we must do more than just listen politely to its recommendations and then disregard them. We must actually submit to its judgments, and cultivate a settled disposition to do so. This, according to Plato, is the proper role for his middle faculty of "spirit": it supplies the determination and resolve to discipline our appetites so that they support, rather than subvert, our best interests.

So, for Plato, our well-being depends crucially on a politics of the self in which reason is in firm and well-informed control. Desires and urges originating elsewhere in our psychological system must not be allowed to usurp its authority or meddle in its affairs. They have no business pushing our reason around as it tries to determine our best interests. This explains the sense in which Plato thought that justice within the self — each faculty performing its proper role and not interfering with the others — was a precondition for correctly perceiving and effectively pursuing our real interests. Our gravest errors about our own interests stem from different psychological faculties improperly meddling with each other; in this way, they are symptoms of internal conflict and therefore of psychological "injustice."

The thesis of social dependence

But Plato simultaneously thought that achieving this sort of psychological coordination is as much a collective as an individual project. For several reasons, Plato thought that individual well-being has deep *social* preconditions. He denied, for example, that agents are self-sufficient when it comes to the cultivation of the traits and dispositions necessary for the sort of well-adjusted character we have just described. He insisted, rather, that the cultivation of these virtues depends crucially on the proper intervention of outside agencies in the formation of individuals' characters.

One reason for this is that, in contrast to our appetitive capacities and needs, those associated with the "spirited" and "rational" elements of our self are not pre-programmed instincts, naturally well adapted to pursue certain self-evident interests like the need for food or shelter. The efficient deployment of these capacities is a potentiality that requires education, training, and practice to perfect. Others must be involved in this educative process; we need them to provide sound guidance and role-models, and sometimes to impose on us various forms of discipline. Obviously we cannot supply these for ourselves, and when others intervene in the wrong way, they can profoundly damage our prospects for well-being.

More controversially, while Plato believed that our three basic interests, and their relative importance, are the same for everyone, he denied that the corresponding three capacities for realizing them are evenly distributed across human populations. When it comes to their skills and natural capacities, individuals are not all appetitive, spirited, and rational in the same proportion. Some individuals are more naturally suited to activities that engage specifically physical, emotional, and intellectual capacities. The most infamous implication Plato drew from this claim was the suggestion that only intellectually gifted individuals should hold positions of political power. Plato's ideal state is governed by a caste of philosopher rulers who must survive a rigorously meritocratic educational curriculum intended to weed out those unqualified to assume public responsibilities. For Plato, only those who prove themselves competent in this academic venue have the expertise to govern society in a way that will benefit everyone.

On Plato's account, then, being ruled by reason and wisdom is not necessarily the same as being ruled by *one's own* rational judgments. Rather, in many cases it requires a settled disposition to defer to the rational judgments of better-qualified others. So, even as it enhances the quality of individuals' lives by inducing the required psychological dispositions, being properly "ruled by" reason is for Plato an inherently social achievement. In this way, Plato held that individuals' chances of realizing their most basic interests are heavily dependent on the particular ways in which social responsibilities are allocated in their society. For Plato, therefore, individuals are socially dependent in a strong sense. The achievement of their well-being depends crucially on the pattern of social forms surrounding them and the terms on which they are encouraged to participate in them. Properly understood, justice describes the conditions under which those terms will tend to promote, rather than hinder, everyone's well-being. It is in this sense a common good.

Perfectionism

Clearly, there is much in this elaborate theory with which one might quarrel. The Platonic objection to democratic conceptions of justice invites several obvious replies. For example, while we may agree with Plato that individuals require guidance and self-discipline to live successfully, we may think that trusting the state, or public officials, to impart these qualities is a terrible idea: these responsibilities are better left to families, churches, and other private institutions. And perhaps, contrary to Plato's claims, we *do* have an important interest in being exposed to the risk of personal failure. As John Stuart Mill suggested, errors and mistakes may be necessary conditions for individual and collective progress: we often learn from them.[3]

Plato's own pupil Aristotle took a similar line. He was concerned that, in his haste to insure individuals against their own mistakes, Plato left so little to individual initiative and discretion as to transform the citizens of his ideal state into programmed automatons, hardly a satisfactory model for human well-being.[4] Plato's disconcerting claim that only a small minority of individuals in any community is intelligent enough to participate in political decision-making obviously also deserves close scrutiny. More broadly, Plato's suggestions about the specific effects on individuals' characters of different configurations of social responsibilities and the governing norms of justice that keep them in place are speculative and often unconvincing.

These all point toward serious difficulties in Plato's view. What is of more immediate interest here, however, is the general idea of the common good that Plato launched in making this argument. This general idea, and the research agenda it defines, has often struck Plato's readers as more promising than his particular recommendations. Indeed, the two critics just mentioned, Aristotle and Mill, took roughly this line. Both embraced

---

[3] Mill (1972), p. 152.
[4] Aristotle (1981), pp. 103–19.

the general research program Plato opened up, but disagreed, often quite strongly, with the particular way in which he developed it.

Two general aspects of this research program deserve stress. First, Plato's argument is *perfectionist*. His position is built around a depiction of a perfectly rational agent directed intelligently and effectively toward the fulfillment of her deepest interests, making the best of her life. Having laid out this perfectionist ideal of human flourishing, Plato sought to describe the social and political circumstances likely to promote its realization in as many lives as possible. The resulting research agenda assumes that Plato's ideal of a well-lived life is the ultimate end for the sake of which social and political arrangements exist and relative to which they ought finally to be evaluated.

In effect, then, Plato's argument takes his perfectionist ideal as the ultimate touchstone of rational justification in politics. Since, on his view, everyone's well-being is (allegedly) equally at stake in the design and effects of our political arrangements, that ideal affords an impartial standpoint from which to evaluate them. If Plato is right, individuals have a reason to support those arrangements necessary for realizing this ideal in their own lives, and to oppose or resist those that would hinder them in this endeavor. On this basis, the skeptical puzzles surrounding the possibility of rational justification in politics that we extensively discussed in chapter 1 can be dissolved. Even if we reject Plato's particular specification of human flourishing and his ideas about how to achieve it, we can still acknowledge that in principle this is a promising way to approach rational justification in politics.[5]

The second general feature of the research program that Plato inaugurated concerns the notion of a "common good" to which it gives rise. As we have seen, Plato insisted that individual well-being is fully attainable only *in concert* with others. When properly interpreted, the flourishing of political society and the flourishing of the individuals who comprise it are not opposed, but merely aspects of each other. This implies that insofar as we see an opposition between them, we lack a proper understanding of both. From this Platonic, and also Aristotelian, perspective, Auden's description of the public and private realms as two separate, disconnected atlases exemplifies a deep misunderstanding, plausible only to people

---

[5] For some contemporary perfectionist theories, see Raz (1986); Hurka (1993); Sher (1997).

unfortunate enough to be socialized into degenerate forms of political community like democracy.

In contrast, Plato and Aristotle thought of the terms on which we cooperate in political community as a potential common good in the following dual sense. On the one hand, each of us stands to gain or lose in very fundamental ways from this political environment being ordered in different ways. When the terms of human association are organized propitiously, each participant can obtain fundamentally important goods that would have eluded him or her otherwise. Conversely, when wrongly configured, the fulfillment of basic individual interests is threatened, and our common good unrealized. Individuals' well-being is in this way *dependent* on their political environment, and its realization as much a collective as an individual responsibility.

On the other hand, this is not to say that for Plato and Aristotle we are dependent on something other than ourselves, for in the end we *are* our political environment. The various different principles for allocating social roles and responsibilities which form the major subject of Plato's research program simply represent different possible forms of collective self-organization. So to say with Plato and Aristotle that individuals depend on their political environment for their well-being is not to say that they depend on some alien agency beyond themselves. Rather, it is to say that they depend on themselves and their own collective resources and assets. The task for the theorist of the common good is to investigate how these internal resources should be disposed so as to promote the flourishing of everyone sharing in political community.

Conclusion

Plato and Aristotle developed this project against the backdrop of a very particular model of political community – the classical Greek city-state. These were largely self-sufficient, culturally homogenous political communities whose territory comprised the immediate environs of individual cities, like Athens, Sparta, Miletus, Corinth, and Argos. By modern standards, these city-states were extremely small. The payroll of some multinational corporations today significantly exceeds the total population of Athens in the time of Plato and Aristotle. Because their speculations about how to realize the common good tend to presuppose this now extinct political form, many modern critics have charged that this Platonic and Aristotelian project, inspiring as it is, is of historical interest only. They argue that the research program they initiated has been rendered irrelevant by the subsequent development of political organization on an incomparably larger scale. The size, cultural diversity, and complexity of modern nation-states make it implausible to suppose that its citizens could ever share in the sort of rich common good Plato and Aristotle hoped to promote by political means.

But the common-good approach did not simply die out with the Greek city-states. One of the most influential paradigms in recent political philosophy – utilitarianism – can be thought of as an attempt to revive that research program and to adapt it to the transformed conditions of modern political life. Before we consider some objections to the common-good approach as a whole, it is therefore important to have before us this modern variant of genus. These tasks form the topic of the next chapter.

3   Utilitarianism

Utilitarianism as a philosophical movement got going towards the end of the eighteenth century in Europe and really took off in Britain in the nineteenth. Its pioneers were Helvetius, David Hume, Jeremy Bentham, John Austin, and James and John Stuart Mill. Later utilitarians include Henry Sidgwick, R. M. Hare, and Peter Singer.[1] For reasons considered below, utilitarianism as a philosophical doctrine is today on the defensive. But utilitarian ideas are fundamental to modern economic theory, and partly for this reason they remain firmly ensconced in contemporary intellectual life.

In its simplest formulation, utilitarianism asserts a basic principle of justification: actions and practices should be considered justified to the extent that they promote the greatest overall happiness. Actions and practices are said to have "utility" to the extent that they bring about overall happiness, and "disutility" to the extent that they produce overall suffering. The overriding utilitarian goal is therefore to seek actions and social practices likely to maximize utility.

Like the Platonic and Aristotelian views discussed earlier, utilitarianism is a *consequentialist* theory. For utilitarians, we decide whether something is justified by considering its consequences for the welfare of those it affects. Influenced by the Enlightenment enthusiasm for science and mathematics, however, the classical utilitarians (especially Bentham) aimed to make consequentialist ethics more scientific and precise. Their hope was that ethical justification might eventually become a matter of scrupulous mathematical calculation, like mechanics and engineering.

---

[1] Sidgwick (1981); Hare (1981); Singer (1993).

The basic idea for this sort of utilitarian calculus is extremely simple. We first assess the likely effects of some action or institution *A* on each of the individuals who stand to be affected by it. On this basis, we determine the costs and benefits (i.e. the utility and disutility) of *A* for each of these individuals. Assigning equal arithmetical weight to each of these individual utility scores, we next add them up and determine the total amount of utility that would result from *A*. We then follow the same procedure for each of the available alternatives (*B*, *C*, *D*) and select the option with the highest aggregate utility.

The utilitarian focus on *aggregate* welfare represents an important departure from the classical conception of the common good, which in contrast favors mutual advantage. On a mutual-advantage view, in order for something to be justified as a common good, each person involved must be shown to derive some benefit from it. On an aggregate-advantage view, what matters is the overall total of welfare, regardless of whether the position of every individual is improved. Utilitarians' embrace of the latter view opens them to the charge that they could allow the imposition of unreasonable sacrifices on the few in order to promote the welfare of the many, a criticism to which we will return. Whatever the merits of this objection, however, utilitarians can still represent themselves as offering an interpretation of the common good. They can argue that, for the purposes of political justification, giving each person's utility scores equal weight in calculations of overall utility is all that is necessary to provide an adequately impartial account of the social good.

Rules and ethical beliefs

Like Plato and Aristotle, utilitarians insist that justifications for political arrangements must ultimately come to rest in judgments about human well-being. Beliefs about ethical ideals like justice are not, for any of these philosophers, the final tribunal before which we assess the merits of different political arrangements. So, according to utilitarians, the question of which particular beliefs about justice we ought to encourage people to accept and abide by in the course of their political interaction is itself to be assessed on the basis of consequentialist judgments. Utilitarians deny that abstract beliefs about justice and other ethical ideals have any value apart from their tendency, once inculcated among members of a population, to have beneficial consequences.

That is not to say that utilitarians generally assume that such beliefs are useless and that agents should simply apply the utilitarian injunction to maximize happiness directly to their own choices and decisions without any reference to independent principles of justice or to other sorts of ethical rules. They have more often argued that this strategy is self-defeating: if everyone is left to apply the utility principle themselves, the effect is likely to be a net loss in overall utility. Utilitarians have therefore usually endorsed forms of "indirect utilitarianism," of which the most common is "rule utilitarianism." According to rule-utilitarians, agents ought to follow rules general compliance with which will tend to promote overall utility more effectively than would be the case if they applied the utility principle to their own choices directly.

By acquiring dispositions to abide by certain ethical rules or principles of justice, agents will tend to act in ways that are on balance more productive of utility than otherwise, or so the claim goes. In the absence of such coordinating beliefs, agents will be collectively worse off. This utilitarian understanding of the function of beliefs about justice and other ethical requirements is essentially the same as that of Plato and Aristotle, despite their many other differences. For both utilitarians and the classical Greek perfectionists, the proper function of such beliefs is to coordinate agents' behavior in rational and collectively advantageous ways. Insofar as all tend to benefit from the general adoption and observance of the relevant rules, those rules and their inculcation among members of society are aspects of their common good.

The problem of incommensurability

As with the classical perfectionist position of Plato and Aristotle, utilitarianism is organized around a conception of welfare that it is rational to promote. But utilitarians understand welfare in a distinctive way. As we have seen, Plato's own understanding of human well-being was quite complex and subtle. The term that Plato and Aristotle used for well-being was the Greek word *eudaimonia*. This is standardly translated into English as "happiness." But, as many have pointed out, this translation is not ideal, since the English word "happiness" tends to connote certain experiential states of enjoyment or pleasure, and this clearly is not exactly what Plato and Aristotle meant when they spoke of *eudaimonia*. Rather, they understood it in terms of the realization of certain basic interests. While they acknowledged that experiencing enjoyment (and being free of suffering) was among our interests, they also recognized other basic interests — for example, in being loved and respected, and in achieving knowledge and understanding — that are not simply reducible to our interest in certain pleasurable, or pain-free, forms of experience. They thought they stood alone as interests in their own right. The sort of human "fulfillment" (a better translation of *eudaimonia)* that Plato and Aristotle equated with well-being is irreducibly complex, something that must be pursued along several tracks at once.

In this respect utilitarianism presents a contrasting picture. Utilitarians are committed to maximizing happiness. But it makes sense to *maximize* something only if it can be treated as a single, measurable, magnitude. For example, we can "maximize" the distance between two objects inside a cube by placing them at diagonally opposed corners. If we were to place them at adjacent corners, they would be closer together by a measurable degree: the length of the sides of a cube can be compared with the lengths of diagonal lines between its corners. Distances are "commensurable" in this way because distance is a simple, measurable quantity.

If the utilitarian injunction to maximize utility is to make sense, human happiness must be measurable in this way. We must be able to measure and compare the different amounts of utility that are produced in different individuals under different circumstances. Unfortunately, it is not clear how, or that, this is possible. This is the problem of incommensurability, arguably the gravest problem facing the utilitarian project.

The early utilitarians tried to deal with this problem by adopting a "hedonistic" conception of happiness, according to which well-being is a simple function of the presence of pleasurable experience and the absence of pain. They thought of the mental states of pleasure and pain as jointly comprising a common denominator by which to determine utilitarian value of anything and to compare it with that of anything else. One proponent of this hedonistic approach, the nineteenth-century utilitarian Francis Edgeworth, even entertained the idea that eventually we might invent a device he called a "hedonimeter." Just as thermometers today determine how high our fevers are, or how cold it is outside, Edgeworth's hedonimeter would be able to measure the amount of pleasure and pain that different experiences (drinking coffee, listening to an opera, orgasm) might arouse in different subjects.[2]

On this sort of view, as Bentham famously put it, pushpin (the eighteenth-century equivalent of an arcade game like pinball) can be as good as, or even better than, poetry: in principle, a game of pushpin may arouse in some subject the same (or more) pleasure as the recitation of a poetic masterpiece. The resulting account of well-being is therefore quite unlike the perfectionist positions developed by Plato and Aristotle. They understood happiness in terms of the realization of intrinsically valuable ideals of human flourishing. Like many perfectionists, for example, they claimed that lives rich in esthetic and intellectual pursuits (like poetry) are better lives intrinsically than those containing only trivial forms of recreation (like pushpin), regardless of the amount of pleasure these activities induce. But on a hedonistic view, well-being does not consist in the realization of any instrinsically valuable ideals of life, but simply in states of arousal that can be experienced to greater or lesser degrees.

Problems with hedonism

Despite its obvious curiosities, one can see why the early utilitarians were attracted to this hedonistic view of well-being. That view holds out the prospect of a universal, empirically based, calculative science of human rationality and welfare. By appealing to hedonism, it seems, utilitarians need not rely on more controversial perfectionist ideals of the kind Plato and Aristotle defended.

The hedonistic view is nevertheless deeply problematic. It is not clear, in the first place, whether it really does solve the problem of incommensurability. For example, some philosophers, including Plato, have doubted whether pleasure and pain are mutually commensurable. It is tempting to think that the relation between degrees of pleasure and degrees of pain is analogous to that between degrees of heat and degrees of cold.

---

[2] Edgeworth (1967).

But while it makes sense to say that heat and cold are on a measurable continuum, it seems odd to say that when I am experiencing the intensely pleasurable aroma of freshly ground coffee I am experiencing much more of the same thing that I (in some measure) lack when I am passing a kidney stone. It seems equally, if not more, plausible to say that the presence or absence of pleasure is *one* thing, and the presence or absence of pain *another*. The same seems true of many pleasures: is the pleasure I derive from a satisfying mathematical proof on a continuum with a sniff of ground coffee?

Moreover, even if the amounts of pleasure or pain that *I* experience in some instance can be compared with those *I* experience in some other instance, it does not necessarily follow that these judgments are comparable *between* persons. This difficulty particularly impressed some of the early neo-classical economists (who integrated utilitarian ideas into economic theory). W. S. Jevons, for example, saw no way to "compare the amount of feeling in one mind with that in another ... the susceptibility of one mind may be, for what we know, a thousand times greater than that of another. But, provided that the susceptibility was different in a like ratio in all directions, we should never be able to discover the difference. Every mind is thus inscrutable to every other mind, and no common denominator of feeling seems possible."[3] This is the problem of interpersonal comparisons of utility. It is a formidable problem facing the hedonistic view, and indeed for any version of utilitarianism.

Even if these problems were solved, however, the hedonistic account would face still other difficulties. Many have doubted, for example, that happiness or well-being can be adequately explained just in terms of quanta of pleasurable experience. Robert Nozick's famous "experience machine" argument provides an elegant formulation of this objection:

> Suppose there were an experience machine that would give you any experience you desired. Superduper neuropsychologists could stimulate your brain so that you would think and feel you were writing a great novel, or making a friend, or reading an interesting book. All the time you would be floating in a tank, with electrodes attached to your brain. Should you plug into this machine for life, preprogramming your life's experiences?[4]

[3] Jevons (1988), p. 14.
[4] Nozick (1974), p. 42.

Nozick thinks that no rational person would choose to plug in on these terms. The example is intended to expose our tacit conviction that there is more to life than experience. We care not only about *feeling* things, but also about *doing* things, and about who we are or what we become in doing them. It also matters to us whether doing those things is genuinely *worthwhile* independently of their pleasure-promoting capacities. People plugged into the experience machine would have no real access to these goods. They might feel good, but they could not know that what they are doing matters, or take pride in a life of successful accomplishment; indeed, there is no sense in which they *do* anything. Nozick suggests that plugging into the machine is therefore tantamount to suicide.

Desire-fulfillment theories

These difficulties have led some utilitarians to move away from mental-state conceptions of welfare. An alternative approach is to understand utility in terms of desire-fulfillment or preference-satisfaction.[5] On this view, I am happy, or well off, to the extent that my preferences or desires are satisfied, so that the utility principle would then say that actions and practices ought to be considered justified to the extent that they satisfy as many of our desires and preferences as possible. The satisfaction of a desire need not be understood as a mental state opaque to outside appreciation, but simply in terms of the actual coincidence between what one wants and what one gets. This seems to mitigate the problem of interpersonal comparisons, at least to some degree. Presumably we can on this basis at least compare the number of my satisfied desires with the number of yours. Moreover, since – as the experience-machine example reminds us – we often desire things other than pleasurable experience, the desire-fulfillment approach seems to meet Nozick's objection. Perhaps a viable utilitarian calculus can still be devised on this model.

A major problem with this alternative is that it equivocates on the question of *which* desires and preferences should matter. It does not seem sufficient to say we can measure individual well-being just in terms of the satisfaction of people's *actual* desires and preferences. For example,

---

[5] Singer (1993), pp. x–xi, 90–101, 127–31.

drug addicts are dominated by overwhelming desires to consume certain narcotic substances. But even if some users had an unlimited supply of the relevant drug, and so could always satisfy their constantly recurring craving for it, we would be hard put to describe them as models of happiness or well-being. Proponents of the actual-desire view might respond by pointing out that the addiction may prevent agents' other actual desires from being satisfied. But then it seems that on the actual-desire view one way in which we could make the drug addict happy is simply to eliminate these other desires. That way, given a guaranteed supply of the drug, the addict could satisfy *all* of her actual desires and would therefore be optimally happy. But, as an account of human welfare, this is crazy.

It seems better to say, then, that what individuals *ought* to desire is more important that what they *actually* desire. This, of course, returns us to the sort of position Plato defended. A significant advantage of Plato's theory of the tripartite self is its acknowledgment that the desires that actually move agents may be a poor guide to their real interests. On his view, well-being is not a simple function of whether one's actual desires are satisfied. Rather, it consists in developing the ability and wisdom to distinguish between one's real interests and one's actual desires and a disposition to ignore or suppress the latter in favor of the former.

Aware of these advantages, some utilitarians have tried to rescue the desire-fulfillment theory by helping themselves to this perfectionist intuition. John Stuart Mill provides the best-known example of such an attempt. He denied that utilitarians are bound to admit that pushpin can be as good as or better than poetry, arguing famously that it is "better to be a human being dissatisfied than a pig satisfied; better to be Socrates dissatisfied than a fool satisfied."[6] Implicit in this formulation is the perfectionist assumption that satisfying Socratic desires is intrinsically better than satisfying more basic desires for food, drink, and sex. Mill suggested that utilitarian calculations ought therefore to attach greater weight to the satisfaction of Socratic desires, what Mill called the "higher pleasures."

---

[6] Mill (1972), p. 10.

It is striking how closely Mill's discussion of these matters tracks Plato's account of the divided self, oriented toward qualitatively different interests in the satisfaction of appetites and in the achievement of understanding and aesthetic sensibility. Mill even borrowed one of Plato's arguments in the *Republic*, claiming that only those who have *both* experienced physical pleasures *and* been acquainted with the "higher" satisfactions of intellectual and esthetic pursuit are in a position to appreciate the latter's greater significance for individual well-being. Similar efforts to integrate perfectionist accounts of human flourishing into utilitarianism were made by G. E. Moore and Hastings Rashdall. The resulting views are sometimes referred to as forms of "ideal utilitarianism."

The problem with all of these maneuvers, however, is that it is difficult to reconcile these more plausible perfectionist accounts of well-being with the essential utilitarian notion of a *calculus* of welfare. The price of admitting, with Mill, Plato, and other perfectionists, that the constituents of well-being are complex and diverse is the reintroduction of the problem of incommensurability in a virulent form. My achieving mastery of some field of study, my becoming a scratch golfer, my commanding the respect of my peers, my dearly loving (and being loved by) my children, my enjoying good food and wine, my having adequate opportunities for sexual fulfillment, my finding a good therapist to overcome my tendency to depression, all seem to be aspects of my good. But does it make sense to assume that they all enhance my life in some *one* measurable way to different degrees? Few perfectionists have thought so. They have usually followed Plato and Aristotle in insisting, rather, that these constituents of human well-being represent incommensurable goods. If they are right, the utilitarian project is fundamentally misguided, because it is fruitless to regard well-being as a measurable quantity that can be optimized.

This is not a point about the *technical difficulty* of such measurements. The objection is rather that it is *conceptually incoherent* to think that levels of human "fulfillment" can be measured and compared along a single dimension in the required way. From this standpoint, Mill's idea that some "higher" pleasures can simply be given a higher numerical score in a computation of a maximizable quantity called "utility" looks confused. The very idea of a measurable common denominator of human well-being may be a chimera.

Utilitarian common goods

Given these difficulties, it is unsurprising that utilitarian political philosophy has worn its commitment to strict calculative maximization rather lightly. In practice, utilitarian assessments of particular political arrangements typically fall back on fairly relaxed and imprecise generalizations about their consequences for individuals' welfare. For example, few would deny (although some have)[7] that, given a choice, we ought to save a larger rather than a smaller number of lives. More often than not, the particular political claims that utilitarians have historically defended appeal to very basic consequentialist judgments of this sort.

Instructive here are the standard utilitarian justifications of the modern liberal state, committed to the rule of law, to the enforcement of prohibitions on force, fraud, and theft. Utilitarians have often maintained, for example, that the value of this institution consists in its ability to provide all individuals with a measure of personal security, which Mill called "the most vital of all interests":

> All other earthly benefits are needed by one person, not needed by another; and many of them can, if necessary, be cheerfully forgone or replaced by something else; but security no human being can possibly do without; on it we depend for all our immunity from evil and for the whole value of all and every good, beyond the passing moment, since we could be deprived of everything the next instant by whoever was momentarily stronger than ourselves ... This most indispensable of all necessaries ... cannot be had, unless the machinery for providing it is kept in unintermittedly active play.[8]

Mill concluded that we all therefore have overriding reasons to "join" with others "in making safe the very groundwork of our existence" by cooperating with and supporting the relevant "machinery," that is, the modern liberal state.

There are two points to note about this argument. First, it is not clear that it is a strictly *maximizing* argument. Plausible as it is, Mill can hardly claim to have established that of all *possible* forms of political organization

---

[7] See Taurek (1977).

[8] Mill (1972), p. 56.

the modern liberal state clearly is the one that produces the *greatest overall utility*. The argument shows merely that each of us would be fundamentally worse off in the absence of institutions that provide us with a measure of personal security. But this is not equivalent to saying that utility is thereby maximized. Indeed, insofar as the argument is portrayed as hinging on the latter claim, it immediately becomes questionable.

Second, once we see that the plausibility of Mill's position does not really derive from strictly maximizing considerations, but rather from a more relaxed claim about mutual advantage, its affinity with classical common-good arguments becomes apparent. As we saw earlier, Plato and Aristotle thought of political association as a potential common good in that any participant will fundamentally gain from his or her being well-ordered. Each individual's prospects improve or diminish as the required forms of social coordination are more or less fully realized. And if those forms of coordination are absent, essential ingredients of well-being will elude individuals. Mill's claim about the value of institutional mechanisms that provide for individuals' security asserts just such a claim. If the forms of legal coordination characteristic of the liberal state are absent, the very "groundwork" of every citizen's welfare is, on his view, threatened. In effect, Mill claims that the modern liberal state is a common good in a sense that Plato and Aristotle could have recognized.

On the other hand, Mill's judgment about the value of the modern liberal state seems significantly less ambitious than those at which Plato and Aristotle aimed. According to them, the state has a responsibility not only to provide such basic public goods as security, the rule of law, and systems of property allocation but also to cultivate quite directly very specific ideals of human flourishing. Mill was famously skeptical of that idea, arguing in *On Liberty* that, even granting a perfectionist ideal of human flourishing, it is a mistake to think of its realization as a direct responsibility of the state and the law.[9] Instead, the state ought as far as possible to leave individuals to "pursue their own good in their own way." Citizens will do better if given the freedom to pursue their own conceptions of the good on their own terms, unimpeded by paternalist legislation and government interference.

---

[9] Mill (1972) pp. 69–185.

But it would be misleading to suggest that this more modest view represents an abandonment of the common-good approach entirely. It is better to think of it as reflecting Mill's pragmatic judgment that, whatever might be said for the more intimate and culturally homogeneous setting of the ancient Greek *polis*, the modes of legal and bureaucratic regulation characteristic of modern states are ill adapted to the direct promotion of perfectionist ideals of human flourishing. Thus Mill's divergent conclusions result from applying common-good considerations to political institutions whose nature and limitations Plato and Aristotle could not have foreseen.

Facts, norms, and "human nature"

I now consider several standard objections to the common-good approach as a whole.

Some have worried that common-good arguments, in both their classical and utilitarian forms, problematically blend factual claims and value judgments. There is a longstanding philosophical view according to which value judgments, if verifiable at all, cannot be verified by appealing to facts. On this view, statements of fact – that is, empirical propositions about what *is* the case – can neither support nor refute "normative" claims – that is, judgments about what is valuable, or about what ought to be the case. This doctrine has a long history but received its canonical statement in Hume's *Treatise of Human Nature*, which accused arguments that move directly from "is" to "ought" of being invalid. According to Hume and his followers, questions about "matters of fact" are logically independent of questions about what we should value, and it is simply a mistake to confuse the two.[10]

Critics have often suspected that common-good arguments commit just this error. Their worry takes the following form. We have seen that a distinguishing feature of common-good arguments is the claim that justifications for political arrangements must ultimately repose upon judgments about the interests and well-being of the individuals who live within them. But, the objection runs, in order to determine what

---

[10] Hume (1969), pp. 520–1.

constitutes human well-being, flourishing, or happiness, common-good theorists must rely on some implicit or explicit "theory of human nature." Such theories are typically constituted by factual claims about people's actual desires, about their natural dispositions or about their social and biological functions, or so the critics charge. If we view common-good arguments in this light, it is easy to portray their (normative) conclusions about how public life ought to be structured as resting problematically on (factual) claims about how human nature is constituted.

Some of the claims historically associated with the common-good tradition undoubtedly lend credence to this charge. For example, Aristotle's conclusion that humans *ought* to participate in political life can be portrayed as depending, questionably, on his famous declaration that "man *is* a political animal." The Thomist insistence that nonreproductive sexual activity is immoral may seem to rest on a similarly unwarranted inference from factual claims about the biological functions of sex organs. More recently, Mill offered a notorious "proof" of utilitarianism that seems to exemplify the same confusion of facts and norms. Mill's argument was an effort to establish, on behalf of utilitarianism, that happiness is "the only thing desirable" as an ultimate end.[11] But his "proof" infers this conclusion from the premise that as a matter of fact people *do* desire happiness. Whether he really intended to make an argument so crude is not actually as clear as Mill's many critics have thought. But if this was his argument, the obvious reply is to say that we cannot show that something is desirable, which requires us to show that we *ought* to desire it, by pointing out that in *fact* we do desire it. Once again, this reply turns on the accusation that Mill is moving illegitimately from facts to evaluations.

But at best these considerations amount to a circumstantial case against the common-good position. While some common-good theorists may, in unguarded moments, have confused factual and evaluative judgments in these ways, there is no reason to think that common-good justifications must depend on "facts" or strictly empirical propositions about "human nature" and our characteristic desires. In the previous chapter, we canvassed the view that there are certain basic goods, like friendship or beauty,

---

[11] Mill (1972), p. 36.

that anyone has reasons to seek. Such a view is not without its difficulties, but it is not obviously incorrect. Accepting it implies that it is irrational to deny that friendship and esthetic experience enrich one's life. This seems plausible. Imagine people who sincerely assert that they see no reason to care for their friends, family, or children, or who refuse to accept that they would have reasons to regret living a life entirely devoid of any esthetic experience. Few would deny that such people exemplify a certain sort of irrationality.

Does irrationality of this kind consist in a failure to appreciate certain facts about art or friendship? This is a peculiar way to put it. Surely it is not that people who are irrational in this way fail to grasp certain inert facts or lack certain sorts of information. It seems better to say that they lack an appropriate sensitivity or attunement to goods that might enhance their lives, goods like friendship, beauty, love, and so forth. This sensitivity, one might say, is a precondition for any rational appreciation of the ends that ought to guide one's choices and conduct and of the likely contours of a successful life.

If this is right, it is misleading to say that the soundness of judgments about what we have reason to do or choose (i.e. our practical reasoning) is a function of whether they conform to, or are derived from, certain "facts" about goods. Rather, such judgments are sound to the extent that they reflect a proper appreciation of, and give due consideration to, the goods and values at stake in the decisions we face. Those goods and values give us reasons for and against acting in particular ways. Practical rationality is a matter of recognizing and responding appropriately to these reasons.

By appealing to an account of practical reasoning along these lines, proponents of the common-good approach can disavow any suggestion that their arguments move illegitimately from facts to norms. Common-good justifications, on such a view, rest ultimately on certain basic assumptions about the goods constituting human well-being, assumptions whose acceptance defines what it is to choose and act rationally. No doubt these evaluative assumptions themselves imply certain conclusions about "human nature." But that is not equivalent to saying that these assumptions are *grounded* on or *derived from* facts about human nature. We can instead regard them simply as basic nonfactual presuppositions of practical reasoning. Insofar as this view of practical reasoning makes sense and is available to their proponents, common-good arguments can be cleared of the charge that they are unsound because they make invalid inferences from facts to norms.[12]

The subordination of the individual?

Another perennial concern about common-good arguments is that they impose undue sacrifices and burdens on the individuals in the name of "social welfare." The worry is that by postulating a collective good that defines the ultimate ends of political organization, common-good arguments set up an antagonism between the welfare of the collectivity and that of its individual members. They then typically resolve that conflict in favor of the former, usually with unacceptably oppressive consequences for individuals and their freedom, or so the objection runs.

This complaint seems plausible because common-good theorists have very often drawn an analogy between individuals' rational pursuit of their personal ends and political communities rationally pursuing their collective ends. We noted in the previous chapter that Plato's argument in the *Republic* turns on just such an analogy between the rational ordering of the individual psyche and the social organization of a state. Thus many twentieth-century critics depicted Plato's ideal state as a totalitarian nightmare, within which individuals realize their true selves only when they are merged into the larger collective projects pursued by the state and its politburo of philosopher-guardians.[13]

Utilitarianism is subject to a related criticism. The utilitarian injunction to maximize aggregate welfare requires that the welfare of the few be sacrificed for the sake of the welfare of the many. But according to one of its most influential critics, John Rawls, utilitarianism does not take sufficiently seriously the "separateness of persons."[14] According to this Rawlsian objection, the utilitarian drive to maximize overall welfare makes sense only if we think of the collectivity of all human beings as a kind of aggregate person that seeks to maximize its own welfare. On this analogy, just as individuals sometimes sacrifice some of their own desires

---

[12] See Finnis (1980).

[13] Popper (1966), vol. I.

[14] Rawls (1999a), pp. 19–24.

in order to satisfy more of their other desires, so collectivities may sacrifice the welfare of some of their members in order to secure the happiness of a greater number of others. But, the objection runs, this analogy is mistaken. Collectivities are not super-persons whose welfare conflicts with and takes priority over the welfare of the individuals comprising them. Rather, they are made up of separate, individual persons, each with his or her own life to lead.

These objections conjure up the specter of society as having a kind of collective life apart from and superior to the life and interests of its members. It seems absolutely right to insist, against any such view, that collectivities are not conscious selves that can suffer, whose prosperity competes with and trumps that of individuals. But is it clear that sophisticated versions of the common-good approach must deny this?

Of the various possible common-good theories, utilitarianism seems most vulnerable to this line of criticism because, as we noted earlier, its classical formulation favors aggregate welfare rather than mutual advantage. Thus it does not require that, for something to be justified, everyone be shown to benefit from it, or even that no one suffer harm. Utilitarianism implies that we are justified in imposing great suffering on the few whenever this is necessary to maximize utility. Even on this austere version of the doctrine, though, it is misleading to say that utilitarians must assume that society *as such* is a kind of collective person with interests in its own right. The utilitarian claim rests, rather, on the commonsensical thought that, all else equal, it is better that fewer suffer and more prosper. Surely this does not commit us to thinking that collectivities are persons in their own right or themselves feel pleasure or pain.

Of course, this will not clear utilitarianism of the substantive charge that it could impose unacceptable sacrifices on the few under certain circumstances. To this charge hard-line utilitarians can only reply that there is in the end no better way to determine what sacrifices are acceptable and unacceptable except by asking whether their imposition would minimize overall costs and maximize overall benefits. After all, they might point out, most political actions and institutions inevitably impose sacrifices of one sort or another on somebody. And we can all think of cases in which the overall value of some goal seems to justify imposing even very serious costs on others. For example, we were prepared to kill many thousands of innocents in World War II in order to rid the world of the Nazis. Many would also be prepared to shoot down the innocent passengers of a civil aircraft hijacked by terrorists intending to fly it into a densely populated area. Utilitarians ask: If we are prepared to think this way in such crisis situations, why not in all?

Clearly, this unrepentant utilitarian view remains very controversial and requires further defence. (Are there not important differences between crisis situations and ordinary social and political life?) But however matters stand with regard to utilitarianism, common-good arguments more generally are far less vulnerable to the charge that they unacceptably subordinate "the individual" to some overriding collective goal. For, in contrast to utilitarianism, many of these theories insist on mutual advantage, not aggregate welfare. Once we keep this point firmly in view, the claim that common-good theories must somehow privilege the claims of collectivities over those of "the individual" starts to look confused.

To see why, consider again the Platonic objection to Auden's "two atlases" model. As we saw in the previous chapter, Plato claimed that the enforcement of collective rules that give individuals the freedom to pursue their own good as they choose will predictably cause many individuals to lead unhappy, unfulfilled lives. Now we may reject this argument on empirical grounds; we may disagree with the particular perfectionist criteria by which Plato judged individuals' lives to be fulfilled or unfulfilled; and we may agree with Mill and other modern liberals that his judgment rests on an over-optimistic perception of the alternatives. But it is unfair to object that Plato's argument assumes that patterns of collective organization are somehow valuable for their own sake, apart from their contribution to individual welfare. Plato's whole project is to show how justice benefits (each of) its (individual) possessors. This betrays a commitment to the well-being of individuals that is neither more nor less "individualist" than that of modern liberals like Mill.

Indeed, one can go further and suggest that this Platonic critique of democratic conceptions of justice has exactly the same *form* as the anti-totalitarian arguments that so many critics have leveled at Plato. In both cases the worry is that the relevant views fixate on certain patterns of collective organization but are blind to the likely suffering of individuals enmeshed within them. Far from suggesting that the real disagreements among these views are about whether to accept the common-good approach itself, this suggests rather that they occur within that approach. All sides seem agreed in principle that any adequate account of the common good must show impartial concern for the well-being of every individual sharing in it. The disagreement is over how best to do so.

Radical disagreement again

As we saw in chapter 1, the presence of seemingly unadjudicable disagreements between rival interpretations of complex ethical ideals like justice encourages skepticism about rational justification in politics. Plato thought he could cut through these disagreements, and put such skepticism to rest, by asking whether organizing political associations around different conceptions of justice would promote or hinder the well-being of everyone living within them. In this way, Plato effectively reduced the quest for justification in political life to the quest to uncover the collective conditions of individual flourishing. This is the organizing intuition of the common-good strategy, later renewed and updated by the utilitarians, notwithstanding their many disagreements with Plato. For common-good theorists, political arrangements are justified to the extent that they promote human flourishing and well-being and unjustified insofar as they retard it.

However, this strategy can succeed in overcoming skepticism only if inquiry into human well-being and its implications for the social good yields conclusions that are themselves relatively uncontroversial. Perhaps the most troubling objection to the common-good approach contends that few uncontroversial conclusions about these matters are to be found. On this objection, claims about the constituents of individual and collective well-being turn out to be no less contestable than claims about how best to interpret a complex ethical ideal like justice. If this is true, rather than overcoming radical disagreement the common-good strategy only confronts it elsewhere.

The discussion in the previous two chapters lends support to this objection, for we have seen that proponents of the common-good approach have disagreed among themselves about how best to understand human flourishing and its social conditions. We noted, for example, that while Plato and Mill agreed that the promotion of human happiness is the ultimate end of political organization, they differed radically on the appropriate political means for achieving it. While Mill claimed that individuals should pursue their own good in their own way, Plato insisted that this is likely only to subvert the goal of securing well-being to as many individuals as possible. Theorists of the common good have also advanced very different views about how to understand human well-being. Some, as we have seen, have defended a perfectionist account of human fulfillment; others have understood happiness in hedonistic terms. There are also deep disagreements about whether the "welfare of everyone" means mutual advantage or aggregate welfare.

There are also many possible perfectionist positions, each organized around a slightly different ideal of human flourishing. For example, religious belief-systems are characteristically perfectionist. This is why they often focus on the lives and actions of particular individuals, like Jesus Christ or the Buddha, whom their adherents exalt as models to emulate. But notoriously different religious traditions endorse quite incompatible perfectionist ideals. Many secular and strongly anti-religious belief-systems are also perfectionist. For example, there is a widely accepted ideal of human flourishing that regards the development and full realization of our capacity for critical thinking as a central aspect of the human good. Some atheists who subscribe to this perfectionist ideal complain that most, if not all, forms of religious faith involve the surrender of this ideal of open-minded self-criticism to manifestly implausible superstitions, often for psychologically suspect reasons.

Whatever the merits of such objections, it is important to acknowledge that they pit one perfectionist ideal against another. The fact that these ideals can conflict in this way reveals a serious difficulty facing perfectionist approaches to political justification. Claims about human flourishing and about what counts as a genuinely "good life" seem to be as controversial as claims about the proper interpretation of ethical ideals like justice. The same seems true of claims about how we should properly integrate these claims about individual well-being into an appropriately impartial account of the social good.

Conclusion

The outstanding worry about the common-good approach, then, concerns the controversy its operative notions of individual well-being and of impartial collective benefit tend to provoke. These notions seem too unstable and equivocal to serve as a basis on which to draw determinate conclusions about which political arrangements deserve our support or opposition. This objection represents the most powerful challenge facing the common-good approach, in both its classical and its modern utilitarian guises. If we are persuaded by it, we may lose confidence in the idea that the quest for justification in political life can be advanced by philosophical inquiry into the nature and conditions of well-being. Those impressed by this objection have often suggested that, rather than looking to ambitious and endlessly contestable claims about happiness and our real interests, we might instead look to more modest and tractable judgments about what agents would voluntarily agree to under defined conditions. This attempt to reformulate the grounds of justification in politics in terms of agreement, consent, and choice resulted in the development of the social-contract theories we consider in the next chapter.

4   The social contract

In chapter 1, we discussed two imaginary countries, Atlantis and Pacifica, committed respectively to egalitarian and inegalitarian conceptions of justice. Suppose that, for a time, Atlantis and Pacifica go to war. After several years of bitter fighting, the war ends in stalemate. There is a peace conference at which both sides, keen to end hostilities, make various concessions and eventually agree on the terms of a treaty to regulate their future interaction.

Some years later, after the horrors of the war have faded from popular memory, a new Altantan government starts making bellicose denunciations of Pacifican "tyranny," "injustice," and "oppression." Influential voices in the Atlantan government start calling for "regime change" in Pacifica: this is justified, they claim, because it is important to eradicate "evil" from the world. The Pacificans respond by calling the Atlantans "arrogant imperialists" whose political society is "degenerate" and morally "corrupt." The Pacifican regime threatens to roll back the concessions it made earlier. War again looms; but it is eventually averted thanks to the efforts of groups in both societies to remind their governments that they are already bound by the terms of an agreement to which they were themselves parties.

The most important thing to notice about this story is the way in which the existence of an agreement allows proponents of peace to change the topic of conversation. We can imagine the peace parties in both societies arguing along similar lines: "Look, we can argue until the cows come home about whether Atlantis or Pacifica more closely approximates true justice, furthers human well-being, or realizes the common good. Not only will we never reach final agreement, but these arguments are only likely to inflame animosities. But the question of how our respective governments ought to be acting is in any case controlled by considerations that are not in dispute: we know that Atlantis agreed to respect the territorial integrity of Pacifica and we know that the Pacificans agreed to make certain permanent concessions. So instead of fighting vainly over the correct interpretation of justice, we can resolve our differences and live in peace simply by living up to our own commitments." This argument appeals to the voluntary commitments of the parties involved as a way to preempt further discussion of the merits of the two countries' moral causes.

The apparently preemptive potential of claims about agreement and voluntary commitment led the pioneers of the social-contract approach to hope that certain of our political arrangements could be justified on a similar basis. As a matter of history, the classical theorists of the social contract focused in particular on the justification of the state itself. Thus, writing in the seventeenth century, Thomas Hobbes and John Locke argued that state authority can be thought of as the product of a certain kind of voluntary agreement among the individuals who submit to it.[1] They thought that by appreciating the likely terms of this social contract, we can explain why the state is justified, and why its citizens have reasons to support and submit to political authority. But, as we shall see, more recently philosophers have employed social-contract arguments to defend a wider array of ethical judgments about social and distributive justice.[2] This chapter considers the character, strengths, and weaknesses of these contractualist approaches to political justification.

Politics as conflict resolution

As I have already hinted, the kinds of agreements in which Hobbes and Locke were interested differ in an important respect from the Pacifica–Atlantis peace treaty. The latter is an agreement between already existing states. But Hobbes and Locke understood the social contract as an agreement between *individuals* to institute the state in the first place. Clearly, in order to make sense of such an agreement, we have to postulate a situation in which individuals interact prior to the institution of a state. In the jargon of classical social-contract theory, this initial situation is usually called a "state of nature". The burden of the theory is then

---

[1] Hobbes (1994); Locke (1993), pp. 261–387.
[2] Rawls (1999a); Scanlon (1998).

to explain how and why individuals in a state of nature would find it rational to make mutual agreements that bring the state into being on certain terms. On most versions of the theory, these terms define the legitimate scope of state authority and answer the question of whether and when state institutions of various sorts are justified.

Voltaire famously said: "If God did not exist, it would be necessary to invent Him." The early modern theorists of the social contract asserted just such a claim with regard to the state. By explaining why individuals in a state of nature would find it necessary to invent the state by agreeing among themselves to set it up, these philosophers hoped to provide a justification for the state. We shall have to think carefully about exactly why one might think that a story about *others* agreeing to something explains why *we* ought to regard it as justified. But for now, it is important to note only that underlying the social-contract approach is the assumption that the state and other political institutions are best analyzed as artificial creations of human will and choice.

While they thought of the social contract as an agreement between independent individuals rather than between states, Hobbes and Locke nonetheless understood its function, like the Pacifica—Atlantis peace treaty, in terms of the resolution of conflict. For both philosophers, the state of nature is a situation of instability and violence. Of the two, Hobbes's depiction of the state of nature is notably bleaker in this respect. Hobbes asserted that the state of nature would be equivalent to a war of all against all. Even when individuals in the state of nature are not openly fighting, he thought, they would operate with the (self-fulfilling) presumption that they harbour aggressive intentions toward each other.

Contrary to a popular misconception, Hobbes did not take this view because he believed that humans are inherently wicked or "evil." Rather, he thought these conflicts would be endemic because of the particular circumstances in which individuals in a state of nature find themselves. While not naturally motivated to harm others for its own sake, individuals are, he thought, naturally partial to their own interests, and are rarely altruistic. They are also prone to resent and respond angrily to slights, insults, and other perceived assaults on their pride. Hobbes contended that when these natural predilections (not in themselves symptoms of wickedness) are placed in the context of the competition for scarce resources that would characterize a state of nature, a spiral of violence and mutual suspicion is inevitable. According to Hobbes, the resulting conflicts give individuals strong reasons to band together to set up some institution capable of settling these conflicts peacefully. That institution is of course the state, which Hobbes thought of as essentially a mechanism of authoritative dispute resolution, using coercive power to enforce peaceful cooperation among citizens. Although Locke's depiction of the state of nature is more pacific, he agreed with Hobbes that it would be marked by conflict, and that the main purpose of the state is to adjudicate these conflicts authoritatively.

This underlying focus on dispute resolution, which is characteristic of the entire social-contract tradition, reflects features of the historical context within which these theories were first extensively developed. At the time that Hobbes and Locke were writing, modern centralized states, sovereign within their own territory, were not yet fully entrenched in any region of Europe. Partly for this reason, European politics was marked by endemic and violent conflicts between and within states. These conflicts were exacerbated by the bitter religious division that followed the Reformation, and by the complete failure of the Christian tradition to provide a settled account of secular authority and its relation to the divine authority claimed by the church.

Hobbes and Locke both understood that states could never hope to settle these conflicts unless the parties to these disputes could all be brought to recognize its authority as legitimate on some relatively uncontentious basis. They thought the notion of a social contract could fulfill this role. They believed it could explain why all citizens – notwithstanding their religious and ethical differences – ought to reconcile themselves with state authority on similar terms. Although much more complex, then, their arguments were intended to have the same sort of effect as the arguments of the peace parties in Pacifica and Atlantis. In both cases, claims about voluntary commitment are mobilized to bypass intractable disagreements, and to establish an uncontroversial basis from which political justification can proceed, one on which all can and should agree.

The simple-consent model

But why suppose that arguments about a supposed social contract have the power to justify anything? What can speculation about the likely terms of such a social contract tell us about the attitude we ought to take to state authority?

We can begin with a *bad* way of understanding the social-contract argument. Perhaps Hobbes and Locke were primarily interested in making descriptive claims about how states either did, or must have, come into being. On this tempting interpretation, Hobbes and Locke were trying to convince us that we ought to acknowledge the authority of the state because as a matter of fact people have already consented to it.

However, this simple-consent model (which seems more in the spirit of Locke's arguments than Hobbes's) is an extremely unpromising strategy and is open to obvious objections. Even if it is true that *others* have consented to a government in the past, why should that give *me* any reason to believe that its claims to authority are justified? Nor could this fact, if it is one, by itself explain why I ought to consent myself. The bare fact that others have done something is no reason for me to follow suit. Furthermore, it is very hard to believe that such claims are true in any case. At least in the case of the Pacifica–Atlantis peace treaty, one can point to an actual agreement signed by the representatives of the two governments. But no one remembers ever having signed any sort of social contract before being expected to submit to the authority of the state, and recorded history reveals no trace of any such agreements. Some suggest that the social-contract theorists hoped to rescue the simple-consent model by arguing that, whether or not we recall having consented, we have "tacitly" given our consent simply by going about our business, using state-maintained roads, not emigrating, complying with the law most of the time, and so on.

But this move, if it is indeed one that Hobbes and Locke meant to make in exactly this crude form, seems hopeless. Citizens presumably have no choice − if they want to get around − but to use state-maintained roads. But it seems grotesque to suggest that we can interpret this readiness to use the roads as signaling any sort of *consent* to the way they are governed: "We may as well assert, that a man, by remaining in a vessel, freely consents to the dominion of the master; though he was carried on board while asleep, and must leap into the ocean and perish, the moment he leaves her."[3]

---

[3] Hume (1985), p. 475.

Natural rights

It is not clear, however, that the classical theorists of the social contract ever intended their argument to be taken in this very crude way. The simple-consent model assumes that the social contract is simply an aggregation of separate individual acts of consent. But this misses the sense in which, for both Hobbes and Locke, the social contract is already a form of collective action, a joint act involving different individuals who nonetheless share a view of what they do collectively in participating in the contract. These individuals understand, for example, that in making the relevant agreements, they are bringing the state into being; their agreement constitutes a new thing — a collective agency claiming legitimate authority over them all. It is not for nothing that the sorts of agreements Hobbes and Locke discussed have traditionally been described as *social* contracts.

What makes it possible for separate individuals in the state of nature to share this vision of what they do in joining together in a social contract? How do they know that they have the power to bring a state into being in this way? The answer is that Hobbesian and Lockean contractors do not merely agree to something; they also *do* something. They participate in a transaction in which they exchange certain "natural rights" that they originally possess in the state of nature. In surrendering or transferring these rights in particular ways, Hobbesian and Lockean contractors understand themselves to be bringing the state into being on certain terms. For Hobbes and Locke, then, the rights and powers that the state acquires through the social contract are to be analyzed in terms of certain primitive rights and powers that individuals allegedly possess in the state of nature.

Hobbes and Locke thought of these rights as "natural" in that individuals in the state of nature would recognize that they have them even before an institutionalized system of authority has been set up. Unlike conventional legal rights, such as my right to vote, these rights are not conferred upon individuals by specific laws in force in their particular jurisdictions. They are conceived in something like the way that people today understand "human rights": as pre-legal entitlements that individuals should recognize as valid independently of any institutionalized system of rules.

The Hobbesian contract

The early theorists of the social contract differed on the precise scope of these natural rights, although all agreed that the right of self-defense or "self-preservation" was central. To explain the role they play in the theory, however, I will for the moment focus on Hobbes's account. Hobbes claimed that individuals in a state of nature would recognize not only a right of self-defense but also a right to act on their own judgments about how best to defend themselves. But he argued that the shared recognition of this natural right guarantees that life in the state of nature will be appallingly insecure. As long as individuals retain it, everyone must feel vulnerable to predation at the hands of everyone else. For, in a Hobbesian state of nature, just as you have a right to judge me to be a potential threat and therefore to take preemptive action against me, so I am liable to form exactly the same judgment of, and have the right to take similar action against, you. The possession of these rights thus creates the self-fulfilling mutual suspicion and "war of all against all" mentioned earlier. In such a situation, individuals face "continual fear, and danger of violent death."

According to Hobbes, the nightmarish quality of the state of nature stems directly from the fact that individuals reserve the right to defend themselves as they choose. The naturally rational thing for individuals in this position to do is therefore to seek terms of peace, by signing some sort of collective treaty under which all lay down their rights to defend themselves as they choose, on condition that everyone else does the same. Hobbes argued, however, that in a state of nature individuals will be unable to assure themselves that others will follow through on such agreements even if they *say* that they are prepared to do so.

On his account, even if two individuals with guns pointed at each other are willing to agree *in words* to put their weapons down on condition that the other puts his down as well, in a state of nature neither party is likely to feel confident enough to put this verbal agreement to the test by actually putting *his* gun down first. In the absence of such trust, such agreements will never actually be put into effect. What is needed in situations like this is some independent enforcement mechanism capable of providing agents with a general assurance that others can be trusted to keep their word.

But Hobbes's own argument implies that such a mechanism cannot itself be put in place through direct agreement, since any simple bilateral commitment would suffer from exactly the debility we have just described. In order to be able to trust other parties enough actually to enact any such agreement, there would already need to be some enforcement mechanism capable of forcing others to keep their promises. Hobbes concluded, therefore, that to set up such an enforcement mechanism some special, nonbilateral agreement is required. This special agreement is the social contract, and the state it brings into being becomes the guarantor of all subsequent mutual commitments among members of a society.

Hobbes argued that if it is to succeed in bringing the war of all against all to an end, the social contract can have only *one* possible form. This is an agreement in which all members of a society agree, jointly, to lay down their natural rights and instead to follow the judgment of a third party about how best to preserve themselves collectively. This third party agency is designated the "sovereign". In the simplest case, the sovereign will be a single individual − giving rise to a monarchical regime. According to Hobbes, however, sovereignty may be also be aristocratic in form (if exercised by several individuals) or democratic (if exercised through procedures involving the participation of all citizens).

It is important to understand the precise structure of the resulting agreement. Hobbes's contract is an understanding among members of a society that each accepts the judgment of a third party − the sovereign − as authoritative for all of them. All members abandon their right to decide for themselves how best to preserve themselves on condition that all submit to the sovereign's decisions about the best means of their *collective* self-preservation. This is a nonbilateral undertaking because there is no reciprocity between the people and the sovereign. The sovereign does not surrender any natural rights in return for citizens' abandoning theirs, or even on condition that they do so. The sovereign, rather, retains its natural rights but, as a result of the agreement, now *exercises* them, not simply in his or her own name, but in that of the whole community.

According to Hobbes, this is the correct way to understand the institution of the state and our relation to it. Whereas in a state of nature individuals have the right to use force to preserve themselves as they see fit, a Hobbesian sovereign retains the (unlimited) right to use force − in the

form of coercive sanctions, punishments, and other mechanisms of enforcement – but now deploys it to coordinate the activities of its citizens in
ways that it judges to be required for their security. On Hobbes's view,
the state's right to determine rules of property, rights, and entitlements,
to establish court systems to enforce these legal rights and entitlements, to
identify and punish offenders, and indeed to perform all its traditional
functions (national self-defense, health-and-safety regulations, the provision
of important public goods, etc.), is simply an echo of the basic natural
right to self-preservation individuals would otherwise retain in the state
of nature.

It is important to stress that under the terms of the Hobbesian contract,
this right is absolute. Once sovereignty is set up on these terms, citizens no
longer possess any right to second-guess the judgments of the state about
how force is to be used for the sake of collective self-defense. For Hobbes,
acknowledging any such right would immediately return us to the state
of nature and the war of all against all. A state claiming absolute and
unlimited authority is, for him, the sole condition under which peace is
possible.

The rational will

It is hard to believe that Hobbes mobilized this larger theoretical apparatus
just in order to acquaint us with certain facts about the genesis of political
societies or to establish that I am or must have been a signatory to an actual
social contract that brought the state into being, as the simple-consent
model would have it. A better way to characterize Hobbes's argument, on
the more complex account just laid out, is to see it as a kind of hypothetical
"thought experiment" intended to demonstrate the *rationality* of accepting
state authority, given the alternatives.

One can think of that thought experiment as inviting us to consider
a series of hypothetical questions. In the absence of a state, would we
presume that individuals have the right to seek their self-preservation as
they (individually) choose? If so, would we want to remain in a situation
in which everyone retained this right? Assuming that we would not, given
the resulting insecurity, on what terms would we be willing to abandon
this right for the sake of peace? When we reflect on this, Hobbes thinks
that we must eventually grant that the only formula likely to do the trick

will be a social contract with the structure he recommends. The particular shape of this formula is important for Hobbes, not because he thought it accurately represented the way in which states were historically founded, but rather because it properly describes the relationship between state authority and our rational will.

Understood in this way, Hobbes's thought experiment attempts to reveal something about our own rational dispositions that is not at first obvious. As we normally experience it, submission to the authority of the state seems to involve recognizing constraints on our ability to act as we would want, that is, constraints on our own will. For example, in recognizing speed limits as authoritative legal requirements, I recognize that I am not free to drive at whatever speed I like in (say) built-up areas. But if it succeeds, Hobbes's argument enables me to see these apparent limitations on my choices as something that I should rationally will for myself, given the alternative.

Thus, in the absence of a state with the authority to enforce rules about safe driving, each of us would retain the right to drive in whatever ways we judge necessary to our self-preservation. This would likely be very dangerous for all of us: a Hobbesian state of nature equipped with cars would give new meaning to the term "aggressive driving." When we imagine the likely results of each of us retaining the right to drive our cars in whatever ways we judge necessary for our self-preservation, the irrationality of each trusting to our own wills in this way becomes vividly apparent. So it seems rational for us to defer to the judgment of a will other than our own in deciding where, how, and at what speeds to drive, as long as everyone else is disposed to do so as well. For Hobbes, surrendering judgment in this way represents the rational attitude to take to state authority, and the purpose of his thought experiment is to induce this realization in his readers. If it works, the argument makes it possible for us to think of acceptance of state authority, not as a limitation on our rational will, but actually as conforming to it at a deeper level.

Before assessing it, it may be helpful to notice the contrasts and continuities between this revised version of the social-contract argument and the structure of the common-good arguments we met in previous chapters. The two sets of arguments resemble each other in that they hinge more on judgments about rationality and rational action than on the truth of empirical or factual claims. As we saw in the previous chapter,

Plato and Aristotle did not build their theories around facts about what individuals desire or what they are actually interested in; rather, their arguments rest crucially on an account of agents' *real* interests — that is, an account of the goods that it is rational for agents to seek, whether or not they are in fact interested in them. Similarly, Hobbes was not very concerned to uncover *facts* about what people have chosen or willed in the past. Rather, he hoped to bring to light what we ideally *ought* to will for ourselves, once we properly perceive the alternatives we actually face.

But whereas the common-good approach is organized around conceptions of our *real interests* in achieving various forms of well-being, the social-contract argument is organized around a conception of our *rational will*. Clearly, these two notions are not sharply distinct. After all, if we are rational we presumably will our well-being. But there is a crucial difference in the way in which these two theories access these assumptions about our interests and our wills. On the common-good approach, we understand our real interests by reference to some substantive ideal of human well-being and happiness. But on the social-contract theory, there is no need to construct an elaborate account of human well-being, or for a perfectionist account of the good life. The question of what we ought rationally to will for ourselves is settled simply by reflecting on an imagined choice between pertinent alternatives.

Since, as we saw in the last chapter, disagreements about the correct conception of well-being are extremely difficult to settle, the ability of social-contract arguments to bracket this whole issue seems to count strongly in their favor. By isolating the narrower and more immediate choices at stake in the decision to accept or reject state authority, the social-contract theorists hoped, like the peace parties in Pacifica and Atlantis, to change the subject and to proceed with political justification on a less contentious basis.

Empirical issues

As we have reconstructed it, Hobbes's argument turns crucially on a claim about the *alternative* to voluntary submission to the state. Only if we agree that Hobbes has correctly described the alternatives can we conclude that his thought experiment establishes the rationality of accepting the state and the authority it claims. Should we? This is partly an empirical question. If we are not convinced that life in the state of nature would be as insecure and as devoid of trust as Hobbes claimed, or we doubt whether the alternatives he described are exhaustive, the rationality of embracing the state will seem correspondingly less clear.

But it is only partly an empirical question. This is because Hobbes's argument does not only hinge on empirical predictions about individuals' likely behavior and motivations in a state of nature. It also hinges crucially on the assumption that individuals in the state of nature would recognize certain "natural" rights. As we have seen, the shape of these rights conditions both the problem faced by individuals in a Hobbesian state of nature and the solutions available to them. So one might question Hobbes's account, either by challenging his empirical description of life in the state of nature, or by questioning his normative assumptions about the natural rights individuals should recognize in the absence of a state.

The question of whether the empirical assumptions of Hobbes's thought experiment are plausible could be debated indefinitely and cannot be decided here. Still, it is important to see that there is much counting in favor of Hobbes's hypothesis. Hobbes himself defended it by inviting his readers to consider the behavior of states in the international arena. The international case is pertinent because, like individuals in his state of nature, states interact with each other in the absence of any overarching global authority. Thus Hobbes noted that

> at all times kings and persons of sovereign authority, because of their
> independency, are in continual jealousies, and in the state and posture
> of gladiators, having their weapons pointing, and their eyes fixed on one
> another; that is, their forts, garrisons, and guns upon the frontiers of their
> kingdoms, and continual spies upon their neighbours, which is a posture
> of war[4]... What would be the point of this if they had nothing to fear from
> their neighbours?[5]

It is worth noting that a still widely influential school of international-relations theory, known as "realism," is predicated on a version of this Hobbesian hypothesis. Realists accept Hobbes's view that states interact under conditions of anarchy. They argue that states are therefore inevitably

[4] Hobbes (1994), p. 78.
[5] Hobbes (1998), p. 10.

locked into a perennial struggle for power and scarce resources and recognize no constraints on their conduct other than strategic ones. This, Hobbesian realists say, is why the history of international relations is a story of *raison d'etat*, preemptive attack, broken promises, mistrust, violence, and war (both cold and hot).[6] The resilience of this realist view, which we will meet again in chapter 10, hardly shows that Hobbes's empirical assumptions about the likely terms of individuals' interaction in a state of nature are correct. But it does lend them circumstantial plausibility.

The Lockean critique

At first glance, it seems much easier to find fault with Hobbes's normative assumptions about rights in the state of nature. The obvious suspicion is that the scope of Hobbesian natural rights is implausibly wide. Hobbes himself admitted that the effect of individuals retaining their natural rights as he understood them "is almost the same as if there were no right at all. For although one could say of anything, *this is mine*, still he could not enjoy it because of his neighbour, who claimed the same thing to be his by equal *right* and with equal force."[7] But it is tempting to object that this misses the point of having rights at all: we ordinarily think of rights as protecting us *against* the predations and assaults of others, not as permitting others to commit them. In other words, Hobbes's account of natural rights seems perverse because it lacks an account of natural *wrongs*. Very little, if anything, is decisively forbidden by Hobbesian natural rights. Even the killing of innocents is permitted in principle, as Hobbes explicitly admits.

Locke attempted to correct this seeming defect in Hobbes's account of the social contract. He agreed with Hobbes that self-preservation would be the overriding concern of individuals in a state of nature, but he denied that this would lead individuals to recognize a general permission to take *whatever* steps they deem necessary to further their self-preservation. Locke insisted, rather, that in a state of nature, individuals would recognize important limits on their rights to defend themselves. They would not

---

[6] For a recent statement of the realist view, see Mearsheimer (2001).

[7] Hobbes (1998), p. 29.

assume that they are permitted to destroy each other on mere suspicion alone. Thus, for Locke, the state of nature is already regulated by a law of nature, appreciable by everyone, that prohibits individuals from wantonly depriving innocent others of life or property. These natural prohibitions serve as independent limits on the means individuals may select to preserve themselves. They also license the use of force against individuals who violate the law of nature; for, on Locke's view, individuals possess a natural right to punish those guilty of offenses against the natural law.[8]

One objection that one might make to this Lockean revision is that if the state of nature is *already* governed by a recognized body of enforceable rules that protect individuals against preemptive attack at the hands of others, it is no longer obvious that one needs a state at all. Anticipating this objection, Locke argued that private enforcement of the law of nature would be patchy, frequently unjust, and fraught with conflict. Violators need to be apprehended and punished; but in a state of nature victims and other interested parties would have trouble identifying the culprits, and be over-zealous or unduly timid in meting out punishment. Locke predicted that this will only create further resentments and conflicts. These will be hard to settle definitively because in a state of nature there is no impartial judge that all recognize as authorized to arbitrate these disputes. It is therefore rational for individuals to establish a neutral "umpire" with the right to adjudicate them, and this institution is of course the state. Individuals can do this, according to Locke, by surrendering to a third party – the state – their natural right to punish those who violate the law of nature. This is the substance of the Lockean social contract.

For Locke, then, the state is a means to settle conflicts about how to enforce an already recognized and independently authoritative body of rules. It is *not* – as in Hobbes's theory – the ultimate and unique source of *all* authoritative rules and obligations. This implies, again in contrast to Hobbes's position, that on Locke's account the state's authority is limited. For, as Locke cogently argued, if the authority of the state derives from a transfer of individuals' natural rights, the state could not acquire rights more extensive than those originally possessed by individuals in the state of nature. Since, on Locke's view, individuals' natural rights are already

---

[8] Locke (1993), pp. 263–9.

limited by the natural law, the state's authority must be similarly limited. Thus the Lockean state cannot have the authority to kill innocents preemptively, take their property without their consent, inflict unjust punishments, and so forth. And when the state exceeds this authority, citizens retain *in extremis* a right to overthrow the current regime and replace it. It is easy to understand why these Lockean arguments were so congenial to the American colonists in their struggle against the British Crown in the eighteenth century.

Problems with Locke's account

This Lockean view is much more attractive than Hobbes's, but it is problematic nonetheless. Is it clear that individuals in a state of nature *would* recognize the authority of a law of nature that constrains their actions in the way Locke describes? On what basis would they recognize this more extensive schema of rights and duties as authoritative? Locke's answer to this question was unclear. Although the tradition of natural-law theory on which Locke drew is predominantly a Christian one, Locke often claimed that the natural law is known to us independently of revelation. Thus he sometimes suggested that it is sufficient for individuals simply to consult their natural reason; this will reveal to them immediately that killing innocents and stealing from others is wrong, forbidden by a natural law that is written on their hearts.

On the other hand, much of what Locke actually wrote about the law of nature and its basis contradicts this claim. For example, he argued that individuals would recognize the authority of the law of nature because they are "all the workmanship of one omnipotent, and infinitely wise maker; all the servants of one sovereign master, sent into the world by His order, and about His business; they are His property, whose workmanship they are, made to last during His, not one another's pleasure."[9] Locke also argued that the state ought not to tolerate atheists, claiming that "the taking away of God, though but even in thought, dissolves all" motivation to act morally: "promises, covenants, and oaths, which are the bonds of human society, can have no hold upon an atheist."[10] These claims

[9] Locke (1993), p. 264.
[10] Locke (1993), p. 426.

suggest that Locke's understanding of the law of nature is inextricably linked to the assumptions of a Christian worldview.

Taken literally, then, these claims would imply that as long as there are atheists and other nonChristians in a state of nature, not everyone would recognize the authority of the natural law. But is it reasonable to suppose that in a state of nature everyone would already embrace Christianity? This seems rather an extravagant assumption, not likely to satisfy a skeptic. No doubt Locke's seventeenth-century audience would have been prepared to grant this, but it is difficult for us to take seriously.

What of Locke's alternative suggestion that his law of nature is self-evident to the light of natural reason independently of revelation? At this point it is open to the Hobbesian to retort, drawing on a long tradition of skeptical argument, that if there is any conception of rationality that would be self-evident to individuals in a state of nature it would be the logic of self-interest and self-preservation. However, it is doubtful whether compliance with a Lockean rule proscribing preemptive attacks against others should always strike individuals as rational in this sense. For, in a Hobbesian state of nature, strict compliance with such a rule will often expose one to a very high risk of attack. In what sense is it "naturally rational" for individuals to accept such risks for the sake of an abstract moral principle? Doesn't honest introspection compel us to admit that, were we faced with such a choice, we would regard compliance with the rule as self-evidently foolish rather than "naturally" rational?

By contrast, Hobbes's assumption that individuals would recognize a right to use whatever means necessary to defend themselves accords much better with this self-interested sense of rationality. Perhaps there is some richer form of "natural reason" that individuals in a state of nature would apply to their decisions; but the burden seems to lie with the Lockean to convince a skeptic that this would be the case. Locke's gestures in the direction of Christian theology are hardly encouraging in this regard. In contrast, Hobbes's position does not require any controversial theological backup. Whatever else they disagree about, atheists and Christians might (upon reflection) agree that, if they found themselves in a state of nature and faced a choice between compliance with some moral rule and taking action they deemed necessary to their self-preservation, they would recognize a right to do the latter. Notice that this does not require agreement that violating the relevant rule is morally ideal; it requires only an acknowledgment that agents at least reserve the right to take otherwise morally questionable action when they judge that their own survival is at stake.

Doubts about natural rights

So despite the greater attractiveness of Locke's theory, we may still conclude that Hobbes's more austere and rigorously secular account of natural rights is more realistic. But in the last analysis it remains unclear that Hobbes's pared-down version of the argument is better able to answer the question with which we saw Locke's theory struggling. For in the end he, too, has to convince us that individuals in a state of nature would recognize certain "natural" rights. But is it clear that there are any "natural" rights at all?

For suppose one countered that all rights are social artifacts, in the sense that individuals recognize them only relative to some preexisting set of conventional rules or institutional arrangements. On this sort of view, it makes sense for me to claim that I have a property right in my car only because there exists in my society an accepted framework of rules and conventions that confers this right on me. If anyone doubts that I have property rights in my car, they can consult the relevant deeds and apply the pertinent legal provisions. But in the absence of such background conventions or institutional arrangements, it may seem senseless to imagine individuals being in a position to recognize that they have certain rights. On this sort of view, the notion of "natural" rights is – as Bentham put it – "nonsensical."[11] The shared recognition of rights is possible only after certain social conventions, legal and political arrangements, and so forth, have come into being. We cannot assume that individuals would be in a position to recognize any rights beforehand.

This line of argument led eighteenth-century critics like David Hume and Jean-Jacques Rousseau to ridicule the arguments of the seventeenth-century social-contract theorists.[12] They thought the notion of a "natural" right confused, for the reasons just given, and concluded that classical social-contract theories are therefore caught in a dilemma. On the one

---

[11] See Bentham (2002).
[12] Hume (1969), p. 542; Rousseau (1987), pp. 141–7.

hand, if individuals in an alleged "state of nature" are indeed able to recognize and discuss certain rights, moral powers, and entitlements, then it must already be the case that they interact within the framework of some set of political institutions or legal conventions whose authority is accepted. This renders the notion of a social contract superfluous: by hypothesis, individuals already find themselves immersed within exactly the institutions for which the theory of the social contract was supposed to account. So it is difficult to understand, on this alternative, how talking about a social contract could help to justify such institutions. Whether or not particular systems of entrenched conventional rights should command our approval or disapproval will have to be decided on some other basis (according to Hume, at least, in terms of general utility).

On the other hand, we might try to imagine a genuine "state of nature," representing the likely condition of human life purged of any social conventions or political arrangements whatsoever. Rousseau undertook such an experiment in his famous *Discourse on the Origin of Inequality*.[13] But as he made clear in that text, individuals in such a situation could have no access to the concept of a "right" at all, for, in the absence of any such conventional arrangements, individuals would lack any basis for recognizing that they enjoy certain rights. This undermines the notion that individuals in a state of nature would be in a position to understand themselves to be jointly participating in a social contract of the sort envisaged by Hobbes and Locke. If individuals do not recognize any natural rights, then they will not be able to make sense of a social contract involving an exchange of such rights.

Does Hobbes have any response to this line of criticism? How might he convince us that individuals in his state of nature would recognize the natural rights that form the substance of his social contract? One answer sometimes suggested by Hobbes's own discussion is that in this area what agents *do* is more revealing and important than what they are able to *say*.[14] While agents in a state of nature cannot refer to any settled rules or conventions to establish through discussion what rights they have, their likely behavior will nonetheless tacitly betray a commitment to natural rights of the sort he described. Thus, like nations in the international

[13] Rousseau (1987), pp. 25—109.
[14] E.g. Hobbes (1998), p. 11.

arena, they will often find themselves driven to renege on their agreements, to seize others' possessions, and preemptively attack perceived threats, and in that way implicitly claim a right to do so.

But, as Rousseau later argued, this suggestion is confused. At best, we can say that agents in a Hobbesian state of nature tacitly *assert* a right to do whatever they find necessary to defend themselves. Thus we can say that, in preemptively attacking Snodgrass, Snidvong asserts a right to take action against a perceived threat. But it is one thing for Snidvong to *assert* such a right, and another thing for him to certify that he is *justified* in claiming it. Presumably, Snodgrass is not going to be convinced by Snidvong's merely arguing that he has the right to attack Snodgrass just because he has the power to do so. This does not seem to qualify as an adequate justification; as Rousseau pointed out, it is tantamount to asserting the principle that might makes right, which surely no one ought to accept. It would also imply, counterintuitively, that when we lack the power to do something it follows that we cannot really have a right to do it. But as Rousseau cogently asked: "What kind of right is it that perishes when the force on which it is based ceases?"[15]

These considerations suggest that force alone cannot be sufficient to justify rights claims; there needs to be some independent standard such as a set of conventionally accepted and authoritative rules that confer these rights upon us. But again this implies — against the current of social-contract arguments — that rights must be the *products* of political and legal institutions, not, as both Locke and Hobbes supposed, the primitive raw material from which they are made.

The resilience of contractualism

One might think that these objections are fatal to the contract approach. That was certainly Hume's verdict and, under his influence, that of the subsequent British utilitarian tradition. Rousseau, however, took a different view. He believed that the core idea behind social-contract arguments could be salvaged. As our discussion of Hobbes suggested, that core idea

---

[15] Rousseau (1987), p. 143; here Rousseau anticipates H. L. A. Hart's classic criticism of the Hobbesian conception of law advocated by the nineteenth-century jurist John Austin. See Hart (1997).

was the effort to ground political authority in the rational will of its subjects. Rousseau realized that this effort relies on an extremely compelling principle of political justification: to justify themselves, political institutions must vindicate themselves before the tribunal of each and every subject's rational will. By the lights of this principle, political institutions that are imposed on individuals against their rational will must be illegitimate.

Rousseau saw that Hobbes's and Locke's efforts to explain the rationality of accepting political authority in terms of a hypothetical decision to retain or (on certain terms) to transfer certain natural rights implicitly appealed to this principle. But Rousseau denied that the problematic doctrine of natural rights was needed in order to explain how political institutions might meet this contractualist standard of legitimacy. Indeed, he thought that, once we understand that rights are purely conventional artifacts, the social-contract idea can be turned around to test the legitimacy of the conventional arrangements that define and allocate them.

To appreciate how Rousseau proposed to rescue the social-contract argument, consider again the Snodgrass/Snidvong example. Suppose Snidvong attacks Snodgrass in order to steal something from him — a weapon, say. As we saw before, it is possible to view Snidvong as asserting a right to attack Snodgrass and to take his weapon. However, as we also saw, merely asserting such a right on the basis of force is not sufficient to justify it, and in this case we have a strong intuition that Snidvong's claim cannot be justified. But, once we abandon the idea that rights are "natural," our misgivings about Snidvong's claim cannot specifically be misgivings about whether he has a "natural right" to attack Snodgrass. They must, rather, be misgivings about the legitimacy of any conventional schemes of rules conferring such a right upon him. In questioning the justifiability of his claim, then, we are simultaneously questioning the legitimacy of some conventional scheme — call it the Snidvong Convention — that confers upon Snidvong the right to attack Snodgrass at will.

What accounts for our strong intuition that the Snidvong Convention is illegitimate? Rousseau's answer was that it would permit Snidvong to force Snodgrass to do things against his will. The point here is not merely that Snodgrass does not *want* to part with his weapon and therefore that Snidvong prevents him from getting what he wants. It is rather that, quite apart from his desires and wants, Snodgrass is being forced to submit to a will other than his own. The Snidvong Convention simply requires Snodgrass to submit to Snidvong's superior force. But, as Rousseau put it, "to give in to force is an act of necessity, not of will."[16] Rousseau suggested that no set of conventional rules requiring agents to submit to force in this way could satisfy the contractualist test of legitimacy. For that test requires that political institutions and conventions be in accord with the rational wills of all those subject to them. But the Snidvong Convention effectively bypasses Snodgrass's will entirely; it permits Snidvong to treat Snodgrass as if he has no will of his own that needs to be taken into account. It is difficult to see how any scheme of rules that would deny Snodgrass any say *at all* in this transaction could be regarded as conforming to Snodgrass's own rational will. We can be confident, then, that on Rousseau's analysis the Snidvong Convention cannot be reconciled with the rational wills of all those subject to it: Snodgrass, at least, must have a reasonable objection.

At a minimum, then, Rousseau's contractualist test requires that legitimate political institutions and conventions respect every individual's independence and autonomy, their capacity to act in accordance with their own will. Submission to legitimate conventions must be such that, in submitting, citizens "obey no one but their own will alone."[17] As Rousseau also saw, this automatically presumes certain notions of equality and impartiality. For, on this view, the autonomous will of one individual deserves no greater or lesser consideration than the next: if even *one* person is unable to reconcile some conventional scheme of rules with his or her rational will, the whole scheme is thereby rendered illegitimate.

The general will

What would an ideal set of conventions, impartially respecting each individual's autonomy in this sense, look like? Rousseau left his own

---

[16] Rousseau (1987), p. 143.

[17] Rousseau (1987), p. 158. In this, Rousseau anticipates Kant's imperative that we always treat ourselves and others as "ends in themselves" and never merely as means to our own ends. To be an "end in oneself" in Kant's sense is to be a self-determining, autonomous, agent.

answer to this question tantalizingly vague, but its outlines are clear enough to have exerted a continuing influence on political philosophy down to the present. According to Rousseau, conventional allocations of rights and obligations can be legitimate only if two conditions are met: first, the rules and principles governing their allocation must actually be approved by the full assembly of citizens to whom they apply; and second, the decision procedure by which this assembly endorses those rules must itself be of a very particular kind. In Rousseau's language, the "social contract" (or sometimes: "social compact") refers, not to an exchange of natural rights by which agents leave a state of nature, but to the design of this ideal legitimacy-conferring decision procedure in which all citizens participate. The purpose of this decision procedure is to reveal the authentic will of the political community as a whole, what Rousseau called the "General Will." Rousseau distinguished the General Will from the particular wills of partial associations and specific individuals. These private groups and individuals are oriented toward their narrowly sectional interests and so cannot claim to embody the will of society as a whole.

The terms of the "social compact" that defines Rousseau's favored decision procedure are roughly as follows. All citizens agree to submit to the General Will and in return receive equal privileges as colegislators of the laws and constitutional principles in their society. In this capacity, citizens are expected to vote on the basis of a sincere consideration of what the General Will ought to be, rather than on the basis of their own personal preferences. They are also to make up their minds on their own, and not to vote in organized blocs, parties, or coalitions. Citizens must also understand that, if this General Will is to emerge at all, it must be articulated in the form of general laws (as opposed to particular executive decisions, edicts, declarations, and actions) that apply impartially and equally to all members of the relevant political community. The General Will is revealed only in rules that apply to all those who enact them.

This last provision was particularly important for Rousseau, for it implies that, in participating in the process by which the General Will is articulated, individuals enact rules that will apply equally to themselves as to others. Rousseau supposed that as long as this is true, citizens would impose on each other only those requirements they would be prepared to endorse for themselves, since "in this institution each person necessarily submits himself to the conditions he imposes on others."[18] Under these conditions, Rousseau hoped that political institutions might genuinely embody a "form of association which defends and protects with all common forces the person and goods of each associate, and by means of which each one, while uniting himself with all, nevertheless obeys only himself and remains as free as before."[19]

This, at any rate, was Rousseau's general thought. Unfortunately, Rousseau's discussion is mired in obscurity and it is extremely difficult to extract from his texts a detailed account of what, once properly articulated, the General Will would actually require in practice. Still, it is important to notice that, under this Rousseauan revision, the aims of the social-contract approach have broadened. As we saw, Hobbes and Locke deployed social-contract arguments primarily in order to justify the authority of the state. Rousseau shared this goal, but he also described the General Will as an independent "rule of what is just and what is unjust."[20] As well as telling us when political institutions can command citizens' obedience, then, Rousseau's General Will also defines the terms on which individuals justly enjoy legal rights, civil liberties, private property, and other economic entitlements and opportunities.

There is a sense, then, in which our discussion has come full circle and we find ourselves addressing once again questions that resemble those that Plato faced in the *Republic* – questions about what rules, roles, rights, and other social arrangements we ought to recognize as ideally just. But whereas Plato and the philosophical tradition we considered in chapter 2 tried to answer these questions in terms of elaborate theories of well-being, Rousseau proposed to do so by asking what social principles free and equal individuals who are concerned to maintain their autonomy could rationally impose upon themselves. It is important, therefore, not to exaggerate the contrast between the social-contract approach and the common-good arguments we looked at in the previous chapter. Rousseau helps us to see that contractualism is not so much an abandonment of the ideal of the common good as an alternative way of identifying and conceiving it. Rather than justifying claims about the common good by

---

[18] Rousseau (1987).
[19] Rousseau (1987), p. 148.
[20] Rousseau (1987), p. 114.

reference to fully fleshed out (and often controversial) conceptions of human flourishing or welfare, contractualists seek to do so on an independent, and less controversial, basis, by considering what free and equal agents would be prepared to impose upon themselves in some appropriately defined choice situation.

The theory of Rawls

As I have said, Rousseau failed to develop this project with much clarity or rigor. But in his seminal work *A Theory of Justice*, first published in 1971, some 200 years after Rousseau's death, the American political philosopher John Rawls took it up with as much rigor as anyone could wish. Like Rousseau, Rawls's book invites us to think of the principles regulating an ideally just society as validated by a decision procedure involving the participation of all those to whom the principles are to apply. Unlike Rousseau, however, Rawls did not conceive of this decision procedure as a regularly convened public assembly through which citizens of an actual political community exert direct and ongoing control over the laws under which they live. Rather, he proposed to reformulate it as a purely imaginary meeting at which free and equal agents choose in advance, and once and for all, principles of justice to govern their interaction in some future scheme of association. Rawls's argument therefore harks back to (what I have suggested is) the more Hobbesian conception of the social-contract argument as a kind of thought experiment.

Rawls called this hypothetical meeting, in which agents preselect the "foundation charter of their society," the *"original position."* In words Rousseau might have penned, Rawls suggested that a society governed by principles chosen in his original position would come "as close as a society can to being a voluntary scheme, for it meets the principles which free and equal persons would assent to under circumstances that are fair. In this sense its members are autonomous and the obligations they recognize self-imposed."[21]

Rawls introduced another important twist on this Rousseauan idea. If, as Rawls suggested, the original position is part of an imaginary and hypothetical thought experiment, its design is entirely within our control.

---

[21] Rawls (1999a), p. 12.

Philosophers can therefore tinker with the various features of the original position (the motivations of the individuals in it, their understanding of the task before them, the amount of information available to them, and so forth) until they reach a specification of it that seems most appropriate given its aim of definitively recommending a set of principles of justice. Rawls's design of the original position is therefore guided by a search for a truly fair and impartial benchmark from which to assess the justice of social institutions and practices. Simplifying considerably, Rawls's original position has the following three features.

First, the individuals in it understand themselves to be deciding how the "basic structure of society" (its laws, conventions, constitutional documents, institutional ground rules, etc.) makes available to citizens what Rawls called "social primary goods." Rawls's list of social primary goods comprises rights, liberties and opportunities, income and wealth, and the "social bases of self-respect."[22] These goods are "primary" in that every rational person can be presumed to want them whatever else they want — without them, our ability to pursue virtually *any* activity in which we might have an interest will be impaired. They are "social" in that, unlike certain "natural" primary goods like health or intelligence, their availability is mainly a function of the basic institutional principles around which political communities are organized. Such principles directly allocate such social primary goods as rights, freedoms, and economic advantages, but have only indirect effects on people's share of natural primary goods. For example, institutional rules of this kind clearly will not determine how intelligent I am, or any genetic susceptibility to chronic or life-threatening diseases.

Second, individuals in the original position are motivated by the desire to obtain as many social primary goods as possible. They will therefore favor principles of justice likely to secure for themselves the best possible share of these goods. So, although not positively motivated by a desire to outdo or harm others, Rawls's contractors are nonetheless essentially self-interested rather than altruistic. Like the individuals in Hobbes's state of nature, they are neither saints nor monsters.

Finally, and most importantly, Rawls's hypothetical contractors are deprived of any particular information about the society they are about

---

[22] Rawls (1999a), pp. 54–5.

to enter, about the precise social positions they occupy within that society, and about their own identifying attributes. The individuals in the original position deliberate behind a "veil of ignorance."[23] Behind this veil, individuals have access only to generic information about human life, societies, and their historical modalities. That is, they will know *that* societies are often stratified into groups enjoying different economic advantages, but they will not know to what extent this will be the case in their society, or their own economic position or prospects; they will know *that* societies often treat individuals with different religious and ethical beliefs (what Rawls calls "conceptions of the good life") differently, but they will not know what their own "conception of the good life" is; they will know that individuals are endowed with different needs, preferences, talents, and abilities, but they will not know their own specific endowments, and so on.

The purpose of the veil of ignorance is to prevent individuals in the original position from adopting the standpoint of particular individuals with specific interests and biases. In a way that recalls Rousseau's distinction between the General Will and particular wills, Rawls's individuals act from a point of view purporting to represent society as a whole, not particular groups or individuals.

Rawls argued that individuals in the original position would select several basic principles of justice to allocate social primary goods. According to Rawls, these principles are likely to be correct because we have independent reasons to believe that the original position in which they would be chosen represents a fair and impartial standpoint from which to evaluate social institutions in terms of justice.

Reflective equilibrium

In later chapters we will consider in detail the particular distributive principles that Rawls believed would be chosen in the original position. I conclude this chapter by considering a more general question raised by Rawls's overall strategy of justification. Suppose we were convinced that the particular principles Rawls recommended would indeed be chosen by individuals in his original position. So what? Why should the decisions of

---

[23] Rawls (1999a), pp. 11, 118–23.

hypothetical people in an imaginary situation determine our own judgments about what sorts of social arrangements we ought to support and
value as just?

Rawls offered a subtle answer to this question. It turns on the assumption that we should test theories of justice against widely shared
"intuitions" or "considered convictions" about fairness and justice.
According to Rawls, such beliefs include (among others) the thought that
the requirements of justice have a certain priority over considerations
of mere expediency or advantage; the notion that it would be unfair for
social arrangements to impose punitively high costs on some merely to
further the welfare of (even many more) others; the idea that justice
involves notions of impartiality and equality; and that to treat people
justly means respecting their freedom and independence in some sense.
So Rawls took himself to be addressing readers already predisposed to
take such intuitions seriously, people moved by what he called a "sense of
justice." He argued, however, that, as it stands, this pre-reflective sense
of justice is too vague to settle detailed questions about exactly how social
institutions ought to be arranged so as to be fully just. People moved by
these same convictions about justice may still disagree about which
specific political principles and patterns of wealth distribution they require.
To settle these disagreements we need some way to bring our blurry general
intuitions about justice into sharp focus on matters of detail.

Rawls thought the original-position device provides a way of doing
just this. Because the original position is a completely imaginary situation,
there are many possible designs for it, in each of which different principles
of justice will be chosen. According to Rawls, this feature allows us to
test different theories of justice against our settled intuitions at two
independent points. We can ask, first, whether the particular principles
of justice a theory recommends mesh with our intuitions about what just
societies ought to look like. Second, we can consider whether the choice
situation in which those principles of justice would be chosen fits our
intuitions about how an appropriately fair and impartial original position
ought to be designed. It is possible that particular designs for the original
position that strike us as intuitively fair nonetheless produce principles
that seem intuitively unfair. And vice versa: intuitively fair principles might
be chosen only in original positions whose design may seem intuitively
unfair in important respects. By mutually adjusting the principles and the

design of the original position, Rawls believed he had arrived at a theory in which both sides of his account mesh seamlessly with our intuitive beliefs about justice.

Rawls referred to this happy outcome as a state of "reflective equilibrium."[24] The virtue of a theory of justice displaying reflective equilibrium is that it taxes our intuitive sense of justice as little as possible. At the same time it systematizes our intuitions about justice and pins down their precise implications for the proper ordering of social institutions. So, on Rawls's view, we ought to pay attention to the choices of the individuals in his original position because they help us to understand the mutual relations and specific repercussions of assumptions about justice that already move us. Rawlsian contractualism is, in this sense, a sophisticated exercise in self-understanding and self-clarification.

Intuitions and their status

Rawls's reflective-equilibrium strategy thus treats our intuitive assumptions about justice as fixed points around which we then construct a coherent theory. But do they deserve this status? One reason to doubt it is that such intuitions have been historically and culturally highly variable. As the example of Pacifica and Atlantis illustrates, our intuitive beliefs about justice often reflect our socialization into particular kinds of societies, organized around diverse social practices. Rawls himself recognized this. In his later writings, Rawls explicitly renounced any suggestion that his theory is based around intuitions about justice accepted at all times and in all places. Instead, he argued that it should be understood as constructed from assumptions about justice that are peculiar to the liberal democratic culture of the United States and the European nations in the late modern period.

But this acknowledgment of the historical contingency of our intuitions about justice, which dramatically narrows the scope and ambition of Rawls's theory, raises at least two troubling questions for the reflective-equilibrium strategy. First, why assume that intuitions and convictions about justice we inherit from our political environment can be reconciled systematically without distortion? It seems equally plausible, if not

---

[24] Rawls (1999a), pp. 18–19.

more so, to expect that these intuitive beliefs are fragments of inconsistent social ideals reflecting the influence of quite incongruous historical sources and political practices. In that case, we might legitimately worry that the effort to impose seamless coherence on our intuitions about justice will succeed only in misrepresenting both them and the political cultures from which they are drawn.

Second, even if they do naturally fall into a consistent theory of justice displaying reflective equilibrium, why should that establish that we have reasons to value social arrangements meeting its requirements? Here, it is helpful to recall some of Plato's qualms about democratic conceptions of justice. As we saw in chapter 2, Plato feared that individuals socialized into democratic conceptions of justice will predictably make unnecessary and harmful mistakes about their own interests; their lives may be gravely damaged as a result. That is why Plato saw few redeeming virtues in democracy and democratic conceptions of justice.

For present purposes, it does not matter whether we think Plato's allegations about democracy ultimately have merit. The important point, rather, is that Rawls's reflective-equilibrium approach seems powerless to address concerns of this general form. If we are worried that prevailing beliefs about justice (democratic or otherwise) inevitably inflict damage on the lives of those socialized to accept and act upon them, it simply seems beside the point to claim, in response, that the relevant beliefs can be worked up into an elaborate theory exemplifying reflective equilibrium in Rawls's sense. Beliefs and ideas whose acceptance is toxic to human well-being will not cease to be toxic just because they can be formulated as a philosophically systematic, self-consistent, conviction-accommodating package. This is not to say that the beliefs and intuitions from which Rawls argued *are* toxic in this way. But whether or not they are does not seem to be an issue that a reflective-equilibrium approach is by itself competent to settle.

This suggests that, without some independent analysis of their relation to human well-being, we cannot safely assume that our intuitive convictions about justice form solid bedrock on which to construct satisfactory theories of justice, and to explain their capacity to justify various political arrangements. But since, as I have emphasized here, contractualist arguments proceed precisely by *abstracting* from particular theories of well-being, and by bracketing the controversies to which they give rise, it is doubtful that they have sufficient resources to provide such an analysis. This weakness in the general approach partly explains why Rawls and his contractualist followers today face strong criticism from a perfectionist direction. Echoing the concern just articulated, many of Rawls's acutest critics insist that the contractualist attempt to justify political institutions and arrangements without a systematic account of the conditions of human flourishing is doomed to fail.[25]

Conclusions

In this chapter we have considered the nature and evolution of a distinctively modern idea in political philosophy, that of the social contract. We saw how the approach originated in the effort to sidestep interminable disagreement about the correct view of human well-being. But we have also seen that, despite their ingenuity, the advocates of contractualism have not succeeded in showing that political philosophers can avoid having to face these difficult questions about the conditions of human well-being.[26]

Still, contractualism remains a live option within the field,[27] and the long dominance of social-contract theory during the modern period has in any case profoundly shaped the agenda of contemporary political philosophy. The social-contract theorists bequeathed to political philosophy a special concern with the justification of authority, with the protection of individual liberty and autonomy, and with the question of how economic goods ought justly to be allocated among free and equal citizens. As we turn away from the larger theoretical questions about political justification that have occupied us in Part I, the four chapters that open Part II consider these specific topics in more detail; we will begin by turning directly to questions about the proper distribution of wealth and property.

[25] Haksar (1979); Finnis (1980); MacIntyre (1984); Williams (1985); Raz (1986); Sher (1996); Wall (1998).

[26] The so-called "Capabilities Approach" being developed by Martha Nussbaum and Amartya Sen represents an attempt to confront these questions. See the account in Nussbaum (2006), esp. pp. 69–97.

[27] See, for example, Gauthier (1986); Scanlon (1998).

Part II

Topics in political philosophy

5   Property and wealth

If you should see a flock of pigeons in a field of corn; and if (instead of each picking where and what it liked, taking just as much as it wanted, and no more) you should see ninety-nine of them gathering all they got, into a heap; reserving nothing for themselves, but the chaff and the refuse; keeping this heap for one, and that the weakest, perhaps worst, pigeon of the flock; sitting round, and looking on, all the winter, whilst this one was devouring, throwing about, and wasting it; and if a pigeon more hardy or hungry than the rest, touched a grain of the hoard, all the others instantly flying upon it, and tearing it to pieces; if you should see this, you would see nothing more than what is every day practised and established among men.

Among men, you see the ninety-and-nine toiling and scraping together a heap of superfluities for one (and this one too, oftentimes the feeblest and worst of the whole set . . .); getting nothing for themselves all the while, but a little of the coarsest of the provision, which their own industry produces; looking quietly on, while they see the fruits of all their labour spent or spoiled; and if one of the number take or touch a particle of the hoard, the others joining against him, and hanging him for the theft.[1]

These words were written in 1785. Over 200 years later, Paley's challenging analogy has lost little of its force. Although the worst-off members of the Western liberal democracies do much better, absolutely speaking, than the worst-off inhabitants of Paley's England, disparities in economic advantage among citizens in these societies remain quite stark and seem to be widening.

And if we consider the distribution of wealth across the globe, the picture is in some ways worse than the one painted by Paley: while affluent Americans and Europeans preoccupy themselves with seemingly trivial

---

[1] Paley (1828), pp. 80–1.

luxuries, in the "developing world" a child dies of a preventable waterborne disease every 15 seconds. That is around 6,000 deaths, the equivalent of 20 unsurviveable jumbo-jet crashes, per day. In 1999, the United Nations calculated that the three richest people in the world at the time, Bill Gates, Warren Buffet, and Paul Allen, held total assets greater than the *combined* GNP of the 43 least developed countries. At the time of writing, half of the world's population survives on less than $2 a day, and the richest one percent of the world receives as much income as the poorest 57 percent.[2] Some have speculated, on the basis of UN figures, that a 4 percent tax on the richest 225 individuals in the world could raise enough money to provide healthcare, food, clean water, and safe sewers for every person on the planet.[3]

These inequalities strike many as perverse and even obscene. They seem very difficult to justify. Can they be justified? If not, which distributions might we consider justifiable? These questions form the topic of the next two chapters.

Property, equality, merit

Surprisingly, despite openly acknowledging its direct responsibility for the "evil," "paradoxical and unnatural" consequences he has just described by means of his famous pigeon analogy, Paley goes on to defend the institution of private property. Paley's case hinges on claims about its efficiency in generating wealth. The system of private property, he argues, best realizes the productive potential of the earth's resources. It does so by encouraging humans to exploit those resources efficiently, by promoting a productivity-enhancing division of labor, by giving agents incentives for taking responsibility for the preservation and improvement of the earth's assets and resources, and by providing an effective and peaceful way to settle conflicts over who is entitled to control what.

These claims about the advantages of private property were not original with Paley, and he was not the last to articulate them. But Paley's discussion is nonetheless valuable and quite distinctive for the way in which it sets these familiar pro-property arguments against an especially vivid

---

[2] For more depressing statistics, see Pogge (2002), pp. 97–8.
[3] Yates (2003), p. 57.

acknowledgment of the potential costs of a free market constrained only by respect for private-property rights. On the one hand, we have the traditional line that the system of private property is to be valued for its capacity to increase wealth and productive capacity. On the other, we have (in the pigeon analogy) a frank admission of its seeming costs: the fact that it is propped up by the often brutal use of force against those it seems to dispossess; its tendency to distribute rewards without regard to merit or desert; its wastefulness; the fact that it condemns many people to lives of drudgery and alienation; and the often extreme inequalities of wealth it brings with it.

Paley expresses confidence that when we consider these pros and cons, "the balance . . . upon the whole, must preponderate in favour of property with a manifest and great excess." And yet his own discussion ends with an enigmatic concession: "If there be any great inequality unconnected . . . [with its tendency to promote the secure and efficient pursuit of wealth], it ought to be corrected."[4] How much of the inequality we see in the world today is strictly necessary in order for us to obtain the advantages of private property that Paley cites? If little of it is, then Paley's closing remark implies that the rules governing ownership should be adjusted so that, as far as possible, they prevent or mitigate the "unnecessary" inequalities. A similar question arises, though Paley does not mention it, about another major concern expressed in the pigeon analogy – the question of desert. For one might suggest, as Paley does in connection with equality, that when departures from a principle of remuneration in accordance with desert are not required in order to secure the overall advantages of a system of private property, they too should be corrected.

Paley's discussion is therefore less conclusive than he suggests. At the very least, it indicates that more is at stake in our assessment of private-property regimes in particular, and distributive arrangements more generally, than simple considerations of efficiency. Apart from the issue of whether schemes of property rights promote the efficient expansion of wealth, they also raise questions about justice, about whether people are receiving their due, relative either to some standard of equality or to some (probably conflicting) notion of what they deserve or merit. It seems, then, that in order to decide whether distributive arrangements are justified,

---

[4] Paley (1828), p. 83.

we need to judge them by a complex set of standards, combining (suitably balanced) considerations of both justice and efficiency.

Distributive justice?

Libertarians and other defenders of largely unrestricted rights to accumulate personal wealth often try to preempt this whole discussion at the outset. In their view, emphasizing what economic rewards are due to people makes sense only if we accept an entirely unrealistic picture of the way in which wealth is produced and distributed. When we complain about some individual(s) not receiving "what they deserve," or the equal share that is (allegedly) their due, we seem to assume that there is some agency responsible for doling out the relevant goods in accordance with some principle of desert or equality, to whom our complaints are directed.

But this, libertarians argue, is not normally a reasonable assumption. Economic wealth is not initially held by some benevolent, wise, impartial, and central agent and then doled out as parents might divide up a cake equally among guests at their child's birthday party, or as teachers allocate grades for their pupils' performances in accordance with merit. Rather than being centrally controlled and consciously distributed, wealth is extracted from the raw materials to be found in nature in a radically decentralized way, through the efforts of uncountable millions of individuals investing time and energy in productive projects of one sort or another, and then competing with other producers to exchange their products in ways they hope will benefit them. This complex system of production, competition, exchange, and mutual advantage is essentially blind: its distributive consequences for particular people are largely unintended, not under the control of any overarching central agency. There is therefore no one to whom one can reasonably complain when one believes that one has not received one's due.

So, according to this line of argument, it is a mistake to suppose that, when we are considering how economic wealth should be allocated, principles of meritocratic or egalitarian distribution have the salience they enjoy in other contexts, like those of assigning grades or dividing up birthday cakes. In the absence of a relevantly responsible agency of distribution, our assessments of distributive arrangements must depend largely on judgments about their efficiency in increasing wealth.

It is tempting to resist this libertarian argument by condemning the very blindness and seeming arationality of capitalist economic exchange and urging that the state step in to plan the economy in a more rational way. Nineteenth- and twentieth-century socialism was partly inspired by this thought. While they granted that capitalism massively enhances our productive capacity, socialist critics deplored the way in which it then unleashes this capacity as an uncontrolled force of nature, indiscriminately exposing people, especially the poor and defenceless, to the unplanned and sometimes highly adverse effects of market competition. In response, socialists argued that the state should assume responsibility for protecting those most vulnerable to these adverse consequences, and for securing more equitable distributions of the fruits of economic growth. They suggested that, through effective planning informed by the latest economic theories, states might satisfy these distributive standards without sacrificing economic efficiency. And once states' responsibilities are understood in these terms, the question of whether (and how far) they should be sensitive to principles of equality or merit in controlling distributive outcomes becomes salient once again.

Hayek and spontaneous order

But this socialist argument faces two formidable and complementary libertarian objections. The first derives from economic considerations, although its most able and influential exponent, Friedrich Hayek, transformed this specifically economic claim into a provocative thesis about the limitations of social planning more generally. Following other economists (especially his mentor Ludwig von Mises), Hayek argued that individuals can make rational economic decisions only if they have reliable information about supply and demand in the particular sector of the economy within which they are operating. According to Hayek, however, their ability to access this information depends crucially on the undistorted operation of what economists call the "price mechanism." In a free market, prices fluctuate in relation to changes in the supply of and demand for different goods and services. In this way, market prices communicate information about supply and demand and facilitate rational economic decision-making on the part of individuals and firms. Hayek claimed, however, that when states intervene in the free market in order to influence distributive outcomes, they distort the price mechanism. As a result, it becomes harder for firms and individuals to make rational economic decisions. Socialist economic planning, he concluded, is thus a self-defeating project: central planners aiming at certain distributive ideals must inadvertently sabotage the wealth-creating properties of the free market.

This argument struck Hayek as merely one illustration of several deeper truths about rational social organization, all of which (in his view) the socialists misunderstood. For one thing, he argued that if they are honest, would-be central (economic) planners must confront their overwhelming ignorance of the needs, wants, and purposes of the multifarious individuals and organizations engaged in economic and social cooperation of various sorts. Such knowledge of these purposes as can be obtained is widely dispersed and available only to particular agents with close knowledge of the various locales within which they interact with specific others. But it is hubristic, claimed Hayek, to believe that this knowledge could somehow be assembled, apprehended, and then rationally acted upon by a single, central agency, as (perhaps) the socialists had thought in the context of economic planning.

For another, Hayek suggested that the forms of rational social coordination that use this local knowledge best typically exemplify what he called "spontaneous order." The price mechanism itself provides a paradigm example of what Hayek meant by this. In producing and exchanging goods, no-one *intends* to generate prices, and yet the unintended result of economic competition turns out to be an extremely elaborate and sensitive mechanism for signaling information about supply and demand. And as we have already seen, Hayek believed that this spontaneously arising mechanism of economic coordination in practice must outperform any artificial or consciously planned alternative. Hayek held that what goes for economic planning goes for centralized social organization more generally. Such (as Hayek called them) "rationalist" or "constructivist" ideals of political order are typified in the ambitious vision of Platonist perfectionism, in which a group of wise and benevolent rulers organizes society in accordance with an intelligently planned conception of society's common good. But for Hayek, this notion of intelligent planning from some position of central insight is a delusion: social organization is centerless, and the information and knowledge needed for rational cooperation are widely dispersed and recoverable only by agents adapting to the particular locales within which they operate.[5]

Such observations led Hayek to conclude that the state should play a far more modest and minimal role in regulating social and economic cooperation than the socialists and other "rationalists" had advocated. At most, states should assume responsibility for formulating and enforcing a framework of open-ended ground rules or principles likely to encourage those forms of spontaneous order that alone constitute rational social coordination in pursuit of individual ends. Hayek regarded ground rules of this sort as "device[s] for coping with our constitutional ignorance." Such rules, he wrote, "can never be reduced to a purposive construction for known purposes." Instead, they constitute an "abstract order" that does not "aim at the achievement of known particular results, but is preserved as a means for assisting in the pursuit of a great variety of individual purposes."[6] Clearly, adopting this conception of the state's role threatens the view that it should be responsible for securing distributions in accordance with principles of equality or merit.

Liberty and patterns

The second, and complementary, libertarian objection to the ideal of centralized distributive control concerns the connection between private property and personal liberty. Robert Nozick provided a particularly elegant formulation of this objection. Nozick referred to conceptions of justice that require wealth to be distributed according to some standard of equality or merit as "patterned" theories, because they demand that particular distributive patterns ("to each in accordance with their . . . due, desert, need, equality, talent, effort") be maintained. According to Nozick, however, no patterned conception can be implemented without "continuous interference in people's lives." In order to preserve the required distributive pattern, governments must frequently and objectionably intervene "to stop people from transferring resources as they wish."[7]

---

[5] Hayek (1937).
[6] Hayek (1976), pp. 5, 8, 136.
[7] Nozick (1974), p. 163.

The force of this objection derives from an observation to which philosophers since Aristotle have drawn attention: private ownership gives us control over our assets and resources and is therefore intimately bound up with our sense of ourselves as free agents. When others claim the right to determine for us how we should dispose of these assets, we will feel, and arguably are, less free than we would otherwise be. Such rights have implications for my ability to view myself as in charge of my own destiny, and for my ability to invest in projects of personal significance and to plan for the future on my own terms. Conversely, respecting individuals' freedom to make and pursue their own plans seems to preclude the preservation of particular distributive patterns. As Nozick succinctly put it, liberty upsets patterns.

The entitlement theory

This argument has clear affinities with Hayek's claims about spontaneous order. But it adds an important dimension. Like Paley's defense of private property, Hayek's argument for the free market is, in the first instance at least, a claim about the preconditions of economic efficiency. But Nozick's argument about liberty suggests a more principled basis for rejecting patterned ideals of distributive justice in favor of a free market. Accordingly, Nozick elaborated a challenging theory of distributive justice to bring out the freedom-based rationale for a largely unfettered free market. The resulting conception of justice – the "entitlement theory" – combines Hayek's notion of a social order constrained only by certain open-ended ground rules with an emphasis on respect for the freedom of individuals to form and pursue their own personal projects.[8]

Nozick's entitlement theory is "unpatterned," in that it does not require that distributive shares approximate any standard of merit, desert, or equality. But it is also (what Nozick called) a "historical" as opposed to an "end-state" theory of justice. An end-state theory assesses the justice of particular distributions at particular moments by reference to some set of criteria that specify what a just distribution ought to look like.

[8] Nozick (1974), pp. 150–82.

For example, a utilitarian might insist that, in order to be just, distributions of wealth must be shown to maximize utility. It is not clear (for reasons explored in chapter 2) what such a principle of utility maximization could possibly mean, or what it requires by way of distributive shares (though it is worth noting that some utilitarians, citing the diminishing marginal utility of income, have argued that only quite egalitarian distributions are likely to satisfy the utilitarian standard). But however utilitarians settle these details, this view clearly involves an "end-state" conception of justice in Nozick's sense. To determine whether a distribution is just, we here ask whether the current distribution meets a particular standard: Does it maximize utility? If so, it is just; if not, changes are required. Importantly, on this sort of view, the question of how the particular distributions we observe at specific times *came about* is immaterial.

In contrast, "historical" conceptions of justice like Nozick's entitlement theory assess the justice of present distributions by looking at the sequence of past transactions that led to it and asking whether they satisfied appropriate desiderata along the way. In Nozick's case, the relevant desiderata – again following Hayek's cue – require conformity to certain ground rules defining and protecting individuals' rights to own private property. These rules

regulate the terms on which agents may fairly acquire property ("justice in original acquisition");

determine what counts as a legitimate transfer of property from one owner to another ("justice in transfer"); and

mandate certain forms of restitution when owners' rights have been violated ("justice in rectification").[9]

As long as the entitlements defined under these rules are upheld and not violated by any of the participants in the transactions leading up to a particular distribution, the resulting distribution is *ipso facto* just, under Nozick's theory.

Although Nozick did not develop the entitlement theory in great detail, its broad requirements are clear enough to provide a challenging counterpoint to the socialist view. Most importantly, it seems to reconcile the system of private property with our intuition that justice requires that

[9] Nozick (1974), pp. 150–3.

individuals receive their due. For while it refuses to postulate some central agency of distribution responsible for giving people "their due," the entitlement theory does not dispense with the notion of people's receiving their due entirely. Rather, in keeping with Hayek's conception of social cooperation as radically centerless, it reinterprets that notion in a decentralized way, requiring that, over the course of their mutual dealings, individuals respect each others' rights to own, invest, and transfer their property as they choose. Responsibility for giving people "their due" is displaced from the center and left to individuals to fulfill in their direct mutual encounters.

So the entitlement theory replaces the question "What does the state owe me, as a matter of justice?" with the question "What do we owe each other, as free, property-owning individuals, in the course of economic exchange?" It answers that we owe each other respect for our rights as owners of property and for the freedom these rights bring. As long as private-property holders engage in transactions that do not violate these rights (i.e. through force, fraud, or theft), the patterns of wealth distribution that result are, on Nozick's view, entirely just, no matter how unequal or undeserved they may be.

Despite this seemingly anti-egalitarian feature of the Nozickean view, there remains a sense in which it incorporates a notion of equality in the context of distributive justice. While it obviously rejects any requirement that individuals receive equal *shares* (this would presuppose both a patterned and an end-state conception of justice), the entitlement theory does require that agents recognize and treat each other as equals, in that individuals are to be regarded as independent and free, with their own lives to lead, and entitled to invest their personal assets and property in pursuit of their personal projects as they choose. It is also at least possible to maintain that free-market outcomes actually remunerate roughly in accordance with merit more effectively than any feasible alternative. True to his rejection of patterned theories of justice, however, Nozick did not advance this claim himself.

Assessing the libertarian challenge

In the closing decades of the twentieth century, as the planned socialist economies of Eastern Europe collapsed, these Hayekian and Nozickean arguments became extremely influential and led to a resurgence of libertarian ideas, especially in Britain and the United States. They inspired hostility, not only to economic planning, but also to the welfare state and redistributive taxation more generally. These ideas are partly responsible for the gathering orthodoxy that the distribution of pre-tax income in a free-market society is presumptively just, such that when governments cut taxes, they are merely returning to individuals what they already own.[10] Indeed, some libertarians have argued that taxation for redistributive purposes is, morally speaking, a form of theft and – in Nozick's notorious exaggeration – "on a par with forced labour."[11]

There is no doubting the ingenuity and force of the libertarian arguments that underwrite these currently popular views. But we should not allow ourselves to be carried away. It is particularly important to distinguish the case *against* a full-scale socialist state, with central planning and public ownership in the means of production, from the case *for* an unfettered free market. These are not exclusive alternatives; even if we reject public ownership of the means of production, it hardly follows that the only remaining alternative is a largely unrestricted scheme of economic exchange of the sort required by Nozick's entitlement theory.

For example, it is entirely possible that participants in a scheme of exchange could respect each other's ownership rights with religious devotion and yet produce distributive outcomes in which significant groups of people find themselves stricken with crippling poverty through no fault of their own. Indeed, as the statistics given at the start of the chapter suggest, this looks like a pretty accurate description of our current global situation.

To illustrate, concede for the sake of argument that (as some speculate) a 4 percent tax on the income of the world's richest 225 individuals could yield funds sufficient (in principle) to provide adequate shelter, food, clothing, and healthcare for everyone on the planet.[12] Imposing such a tax hardly amounts to central planning. But such a tax would be forbidden by

[10] For a recent criticism of this view, see Murphy and Nagel (2002).

[11] Nozick (1974), p. 169.

[12] Whether or not this speculation is precisely accurate I am not competent to say; but surely it is generally plausible that relatively modest taxation of the affluent could provide adequate funds for these purposes. For further discussion see Singer (2002), ch. 5.

Nozick's entitlement theory, since it would violate the property rights of the 225 by coercively exacting a portion of their (let us assume) justly earned income. But can it make sense for an adequate a theory of justice to *prohibit* redistribution that might end the severe poverty and deprivation that we see around the world today, at such a modest cost to the affluent? This certainly runs counter to many people's intuitions about social justice. Why should we believe that the right of the richest 225 to control every last penny of their already vast incomes outweighs the seemingly more urgent claims of the global poor to assistance? There is surely ample room for a moderate middle position – neither central planning nor wholly unres- tricted free markets – that answers more effectively to these intuitions about distributive justice than the raw entitlement theory does.

Misfortune and injustice

To this, libertarian free-marketeers might offer two responses. First, they often insist that it is important to maintain and not blur the distinction between injustice and misfortune. We do not believe that the victims of earthquakes and other natural disasters are the victims of injustices or wrongs for which we can hold someone morally responsible. On this view, we can reasonably complain that the global poor are the victims of injustice only if we can identify some agent whom we can legitimately hold respon- sible for an injustice or wrong.

To be sure, if we find that particular individuals among the global poor have had property deliberately stolen from them, or have been the victims of fraud or aggression at the hands of identifiable others, we can then claim that they have been treated unjustly. (Recall that Nozick's theory entitles them to restitution under the rubric of principles of "justice in rectifica- tion.") But it is not clear that unforeseen aggregate effects of property- respecting economic exchange, even if very unfortunate, can by themselves legitimately count as instances of unjust treatment at the hands of respon- sible others. Such effects more closely resemble the unfortunate conse- quences of natural disasters, or so libertarians often claim.[13] This need not imply that agents have no duties of charity to both victims of natural

---

[13] Hayek (1976), pp. 70ff., 177.

disasters and those suffering from severe economic deprivation. But, libertarians claim, it is one thing to say that people ought to support such worthy causes as a matter of charity, and another to say that justice requires us to *force* others to contribute to them. According to the libertarians, such forcing is simply theft, and therefore unjust. Behind this response lies the assumption that justice is, and can only be, a property of individual actions, not of events, circumstances, or states of affairs.

The Lockean proviso

Second, one might argue that Nozick's position already has within it a mechanism for dealing with the problem of severe deprivation around the world. To understand this response, we need to look more closely at a technical feature of the entitlement theory: its account of how individuals may justly acquire private property in the first place. Following a suggestion made by Locke in his famous discussion of property in the *Second Treatise of Government*, Nozick's entitlement theory postulates that individuals come into the world with a primordial property right in their own person, a right of "self-ownership."[14] The idea here is simply that each of us enjoys a natural right to make use of our own bodies, our labor, our talents, and other personal assets as we choose. Leaving aside the issue of inheritance, which for Nozick would fall under the rubric of "justice in transfer," the acquisition of property in external assets is understood as a process by which individuals invest their self-owned energy in appropriating or improving those external assets ("mixing their labor" with them, to use Locke's phrase).[15] In so doing, agents come to own these external assets and acquire a right to profit from any improvements they make to them. In the simplest case, an individual self-owner in a state of nature "mixes her labor" with (for example) an apple tree (by investing energy in climbing up and picking apples) and thereby acquires a legitimate title to the collected apples.

But according to both Locke and Nozick, just acquisition must be subject to an important constraint: appropriation must leave "as much and as good in common" for others to use.[16] For Locke, at least, this proviso flows from

[14] Nozick (1974), pp. 171–2.
[15] Locke (1993), p. 274.
[16] Locke (1993), p. 277.

the assumption that the external resources of the world originally belong to humankind in common: everyone therefore has a residual entitlement to share in those resources and the wealth they contain.

This "Lockean proviso" is open to various interpretations. If it is interpreted too strictly, it becomes impossible to satisfy: If I take one apple from the tree, others are no longer free to appropriate *that* apple for themselves, and are in that sense worse off than before, and so there is no longer "as much and as good" in the tree for others to appropriate for themselves. But Nozick canvasses a more realistic, weaker interpretation, according to which appropriation is legitimate as long as no one is any worse off than they would be in a state of nature in which the fruits of the earth are as yet unowned, and each has free access to sufficient means of survival.[17]

Clearly, this revised interpretation of the Lockean proviso is fairly relaxed. It points toward a welfare baseline (something like "adequate resources for survival") whose satisfaction is nonetheless compatible with great inequalities of wealth. Still, Nozick admits that even this weaker version of the proviso must cast a "historical shadow" into the future, forbidding subsequent transfers of legitimately acquired property that would deny some individuals the required welfare minimum. Suppose for example that as a result of otherwise legitimate (by Nozick's lights) transfers, a small number of corporations legitimately acquire a monopoly in the entire world's water supply and thereby the right to exclude others from its use and to charge for it as they please. As Nozick himself conceded, this could well worsen the position of others in the sense prohibited by his proviso.[18]

The second response, then, is to point to this feature of the entitlement theory and maintain that it is sufficient to motivate a principled objection to the current pattern of global deprivation. Even if none of the parties involved in the sequence of transactions resulting in the current distribution of wealth is responsible for unjustly violating the property rights of anyone else, it might still be the case that some transfers fail to satisfy the Lockean proviso and its historical shadow. One philosopher has recently noted that "with average annual *per capita* income of about $85,

---

[17] Nozick (1974), pp. 176—8.
[18] Nozick (1974), pp. 179—80.

corresponding to the purchasing power of $338 in the US, the poorest fifth of humankind are today just about as badly off, economically, as human beings could be while still alive."[19] Not surprisingly, mortality within this group is catastrophically high. Clearly, these individuals fall significantly below the welfare baseline suggested by Nozick's interpretation of the Lockean proviso. Perhaps, then, Nozick's position would allow these severely deprived people around the world to claim a just entitlement to assistance in accordance with the Lockean proviso. If so, we would not need to abandon the libertarian view in order to accommodate that intuition.

Social responsibilities

However, these two responses actually work against each other and serve only to expose some deep problems in the libertarian position. It will be helpful to begin by asking: How are we supposed to apply the test of legitimate acquisition and transfer implied by Nozick's revised Lockean proviso? To establish that a particular appropriation or (in the case of the "historical shadow" claim) transfer of a piece of property violates the Lockean proviso, one presumably must show that it is by itself sufficient to worsen the position of others in the relevant way. This seems to be implied by the first response, which assumes that only individual actions can count as just or unjust. So an appropriation or transfer can count as unjust under the Lockean proviso only if we can hold some individual appropriator or transferrer responsible for objectionably worsening the situation of others.

However, in many if not all cases, it will be unclear that any *one* person's actions in appropriating or transferring property are in themselves sufficient to worsen the condition of others in the prohibited way. It may be that a very large number of transactions are jointly sufficient, but neither individually sufficient nor necessary, to cause serious economic deprivation. In such cases, we will be unable to identify specific culprits to hold responsible for causing anyone's deprivation, whether by violating their property rights or by infringing the Lockean proviso. Much of the severe economic disadvantage we observe in the world today is plausibly of this kind. Insofar as this is true, the entitlement theory will deny that such

[19] Pogge (2002), p. 203.

deprivation generates any just claim to organized assistance from those who are better off. It will tend to classify these outcomes as merely "unfortunate," like the regrettable results of a natural disaster.

Furthermore, taxing affluent individuals to provide assistance must itself be unjust under the entitlement theory. According to libertarians, this violates the rights of the affluent to dispose of their own justly acquired property as they choose. Since, in such cases, we cannot plausibly regard better-off individuals as responsible for *wronging* the severely disadvantaged, there is no basis for requiring the affluent to assume responsibility for assisting them, or so the entitlement theory asserts. While it gestures in the right direction, then, many will still suspect that this appeal to a Lockean proviso represents an insufficient response to the problem of global poverty and deprivation.

As we shall see, this suspicion points to serious shortcomings in the libertarian account of justice, but we must be careful to pinpoint exactly where that account goes wrong. The problem is *not* with its claim that we cannot fairly hold affluent individuals responsible for wronging the global poor just in virtue of their vast relative prosperity. The entitlement theory is on strong ground in maintaining that the bare existence of huge disparities in wealth does not show that the relatively prosperous have culpably wronged those who have next to nothing.[20]

The truly problematic feature of the libertarian view lies elsewhere, in its insistence that just claims to assistance from others can be grounded *only* on claims about those others' wrongdoing. But why assume this? Are there not other ways in which responsibilities to assist others can arise to which our conceptions of justice ought to be sensitive?

Consider here the following comments of economist Amartya Sen:

As people who live – in a broad sense – together, we cannot escape
the thought that the terrible occurrences that we see around us are
quintessentially our problems. They are our responsibility . . . As competent
human beings, we cannot shirk the task of judging how things are and what
needs to be done. As reflective creatures, we have the ability to contemplate
the lives of others. Our sense of responsibility need not relate only to the
afflictions that our own behavior may have caused . . . but can also relate
more generally to the miseries that we see around us and that lie within

---

[20] See Nozick (1974), pp. 191–2.

our power to help remedy. That responsibility is not, of course, the only consideration that can claim our attention, but to deny the relevance of that general claim would be to miss something central about our social existence.[21]

Here Sen identifies a notion of social responsibility that the entitlement theory seems unable to recognize. The sort of responsibility involved here clearly is not the sort of backward-looking culpability for wrongdoing on which the entitlement theory focuses. Rather, it involves the thought that we have a forward-looking responsibility for mitigating those "miseries" that result from human interaction and that lie within our collective power to remedy.

Justice and responsibility for others

The entitlement theory makes no room for responsibilities of this kind, or if it does, it does not regard them as institutionally or legally enforceable (for its proponents might allow that we have unenforceable responsibilities to provide charitable aid to the global poor, as we noted earlier). The entitlement theory thus assumes that the only forms of responsibility to others that justice permits political institutions to enforce are those that involve culpability for wrongdoing. Applied to the issue of global deprivation, this view implies that affluent individuals bear an enforceable responsibility to assist disadvantaged people only to the extent that they have culpably violated their property rights or the Lockean proviso.

But why should we believe this? Why should the scope of social and economic justice be restricted in this way? Since the entitlement theory assumes it, we cannot, without begging the question, use that theory to defend this view about the scope of justice. Libertarians must present an independent argument for their contention that claims to organized assistance may justly arise only when individuals are guilty of having wronged someone or of violating the Lockean proviso.

One suggestion that libertarians sometimes make here is that the only conceivable alternatives to their own view must appeal to problematic notions of *collective culpability*.[22] On such views, the affluent *as a group*,

---

[21] Sen (2000), pp. 282–3.

[22] E.g. Hayek (1976), p. 69.

or institutions like Western liberal democratic states that act in the name of affluent groups of people, are somehow collectively culpable for wrongfully harming the global poor. Marxists have sometimes advanced this argument with respect to the conditions of the working class. For example, Engels wrote:

> Murder has been committed if society places hundreds of workers in such a position that they inevitably come to premature and unnatural ends. Murder has been committed if society knows perfectly well that thousands of workers cannot avoid being sacrificed as long as these conditions are allowed to continue ... if a worker dies no one places the responsibility for his death on society, though some would realize that society has failed to take steps to prevent the victim from dying. But it is murder all the same.[23]

Engels's description of these purported wrongs as "murder" is clearly rhetorical. Still, we cannot simply dismiss the idea that these deaths might be collective wrongs of some kind. And, if sound, such considerations naturally apply to the relation between affluent and poor societies in the present global order.

But, as libertarians often insist, suggestions along these lines are open to two kinds of objection. First, they require that we treat failing to prevent certain harms as equivalent to directly causing them. But many are uneasy about collapsing this distinction between actions and "omissions." It undermines our ordinary intuitions about responsibility, according to which there is an important moral difference between directly injuring someone and failing to intervene to prevent harms that will take place but for one's intervention.

Second, these arguments assume that we can make sense of group responsibility, of the idea that collectivities *as such*, as opposed to the individuals who make them up, can be blamed for wrongful actions. But such notions of group agency and collective blame for wrongdoing are mysterious. We might worry that, when indulged, they indiscriminately and unfairly burden entirely innocent individuals with liability for "collective" wrongdoing.

It is not clear that these objections are decisive. Perhaps some suitably fair and discriminating theory of collective culpability can be worked out;

---

[23] Engels (1958), p. 108.

and perhaps – as utilitarians have often urged – we should on reflection abandon the intuitively attractive distinction between actions and omissions.

But even if these objections were decisive, this would not suffice to defend the libertarian view. Rejecting the "collective-culpability" argument would vindicate the entitlement theory only if these were the only two plausible views available. But this is manifestly false. There is at least one other alternative. According to this alternative, arguments for organized transfers of wealth from the affluent to the global poor depend *neither* on the claim that anyone (whether individuals or groups) is culpable for wrongdoing *nor* on the claim that such transfers are directly required by justice. But whether or not they are required by justice, there remains the possibility that such transfers should nonetheless not be ruled out as *unjust*. After all, we might want to insist, in the spirit of Sen's comments, that any adequate conception of justice ought at least to *permit* the enforcement of positive social responsibilities of the sort he identifies in that passage. I will call this the Permission View.

The entitlement theory excludes the Permission View. For as we have seen, that theory asserts that forced redistribution can be justified only when those forced to contribute can be shown to be culpable for wronging someone or violating the Lockean proviso. Otherwise, their rights to their own property preempt any further coercive transfers of wealth. In contrast, the Permission View denies that the claims of affluent property-owners enjoy this overwhelming priority over the urgent needs of the severely disadvantaged. Under the Permission View, whether or not affluent individuals have wronged anyone, there is no reason to regard requiring them to provide assistance to the global poor as itself unjust.

Again, on a Permission View, the case for imposing such enforceable obligations on the affluent need not assume that justice *mandates* them. The argument may simply rest on the – surely uncontroversial – claim that it would be a good thing if individuals and institutions assumed responsibility for eliminating severe poverty and deprivation around the world. Since few would dispute that claim, insisting that this is also something required by justice seems unnecessary anyway. So we do not need to embrace mysterious notions of collective culpability in order to oppose the libertarian view. Nor need we maintain that affluent individuals have wronged anyone. We need only point out that libertarians still owe us an argument for their contention that justice *prohibits* all efforts to relieve severe deprivation and poverty by coercive means except when required to rectify culpable violations of individuals' property rights or of the Lockean proviso.

Libertarianism rejected

Libertarians sometimes defend themselves against this sort of criticism by claiming that the right to private property is a *natural* right. As such, it enjoys a special sort of priority over other, purely conventional rights and preempts the sort of considerations that, the Permission View (dire need, responsibility to relieve suffering) assumes, otherwise justify redistribution. But we noted the difficulties of appealing to natural rights in chapter 4: Where do such "natural" rights come from? Are they dictates of God? What sense can be made of the claim that something is someone's right "by nature"? It seems far more straightforward to assume that legally enforceable property rights are conventional, the result of artificial and therefore in principle malleable human constructions. The burden of proof lies with the libertarian to defeat this simpler and less extravagant assumption.

Notice that in order to defeat that assumption, it is *not* sufficient to show that conventions of property ownership tend to evolve naturally and spontaneously, without anyone consciously creating them. Even if that is true, it does not entitle us to conclude that the resulting entitlements are sacrosanct and that we are forbidden to adjust them in any way in the light of their unwelcome effects. For by that argument we would be similarly forbidden from taking action to curb the unwelcome effects of many other spontaneously arising phenomena, such as venereal disease, halitosis, aggression, racial prejudice, domestic abuse, and short-sightedness. Even if property rights are in some sense "natural" or "spontaneously arising," then, we still need a further argument for the claim that they carry some special privilege over other considerations. "Natural" and "spontaneous" are not synonyms for "more important." So bare appeals to property rights as "natural" or spontaneously arising entitlements provide no reason for rejecting the Permission View.

Libertarians might still insinuate that indulging the Permission View must eventually require something like central socialist planning, and is therefore vulnerable to all the Hayekian criticisms we noted earlier. But this worry seems misplaced. There is nothing in the Permission View that commits one to the idea that the whole pattern of wealth-holding must be determined directly by central distribution. It is entirely compatible with Hayek's claim that rational social coordination rather consists in compliance with certain ground rules that guide and constrain individuals' conduct.

To be sure, the Permission View would tolerate more expansive ground rules. Whereas the entitlement theory requires only that agents respect private-property rights, conceptions of justice incorporating Sen's notion of social responsibility will, under specified conditions, limit the right to accumulate property by permitting forced adjustments to pure-market distributions under specified circumstances. Such rules would permit the imposition of legally enforceable obligations on individuals to contribute, in the form of taxation, to efforts to relieve severe economic disadvantage and deprivation. But this still leaves us far short of central economic planning and does not require that we abandon the Hayekian notion of justice as compliance with general rules constraining individual choices. It merely amends such rules so that they permit adjustments to pure-market outcomes under specified circumstances (e.g. as long as some individuals are suffering severe economic disadvantage).

It is important to notice here that proponents of the entitlement theory cannot claim in response that the very possibility of adjusting the results of property-respecting economic exchange must be ruled out in principle. For attention to the Lockean proviso and its "historical shadow" would itself require such adjustments under certain circumstances. So the issue cannot be whether *any* adjustment to market distributions is ever permissible. It is rather that of how far the appropriate adjustments can permissibly go. And this simply reinstates the question we originally raised against the Lockean proviso: why settle for rules that permit adjustments to market outcomes only when deprivation can be attributed to the wrongdoing of specific agents? To do so by embracing the entitlement theory represents a definite decision to ignore those forms of deprivation that cannot be attributed to wrongdoing. Libertarians claim that justice forbids us to enforce any responsibilities to contribute to efforts to relieve such deprivation. But it is not clear that they have given us any reason to endorse this counterintuitive and, in Sen's terms irresponsible, view.

The famine-relief argument

This conclusion can be buttressed by considering a famous argument advanced by Peter Singer. In an article first published in 1972, Singer argued that the relation between affluent individuals and victims of famine and economic deprivation around the world is exactly analogous to that between a person walking by a pond and a child drowning in it. In both cases, Singer argued, agents can prevent something very undesirable at modest personal cost. By wading into the pond, I may ruin my new suit, but in so doing I may save a child's life. Similarly, affluent individuals who contribute 10 percent of their income to overseas aid may have less money to spend on luxury items, but, in forgoing them, they may nonetheless save someone overseas from starvation. Singer concluded that, just as we would regard someone who chose to save his new suit rather than the drowning child as grossly negligent, we should regard affluent individuals' failure to contribute more than they currently do to overseas aid as similarly irresponsible.[24]

However, Singer overlooked some important differences between the two cases. In the first case, it is quite obvious who bears a responsibility to save the child, since in the example there is only one person passing the pond, and only one child drowning. The passer-by's assistance is here uncontroversially necessary for the child's life to be saved. She could not plausibly defend her inaction by saying, "How was I to know that the child would drown if I didn't jump in to save him?"

But this is not exactly how matters stand in the case of global deprivation. Consider a more closely (though perhaps still not exactly) analogous situation. Suppose there are X thousands of people passing a large lake, in which Y hundred children are drowning. Since X is greater than Y, it is not necessary for all of the individuals passing the lake to jump in to save the children: we need only Y hundred people to save one child each. For this reason, none of the passers-by can be sure that their jumping into the lake is strictly necessary to save any of the children. In the absence of information about what others are going to do, each may decide to leave it to someone else to save a child; but clearly, if they all reason along these lines, none of the children will be saved. Since none know that their assistance is necessary, they can cite this as an excuse for inaction; so here, it is not quite

---

[24] Singer (1972).

so easy to accuse anyone of negligence as in Singer's original, simpler example. The problem of global deprivation presents similar difficulties. In these cases, "How was I to know that my intervention was necessary?" looks like a more plausible (albeit still not wholly compelling) defense for inaction.

But even if Singer underestimates these differences, the lesson to draw is not that a libertarian conclusion follows, and that since no one has clearly wronged anyone it must be unjust to impose enforceable responsibilities on anyone to assist the drowning children or the global poor. For, as before, this line of reasoning overlooks the possibility of a response along the lines of the Permission View.

To appreciate this alternative response, note first that the situation we have described exemplifies what is sometimes called a "coordination problem." Such problems arise when agents are unable to coordinate their choices effectively without the guidance of some externally imposed rule or convention. Practices like queuing, and the expectations of others that they create, seem to have evolved as means by which we solve coordination problems of this sort. If there is no expectation that people will form a queue and abide by the rule that they await their turn, for example, everyone will rush to the ticket window at once, drowning out each other's requests, and making the efficient management of their inquiries impossible. Similarly, in the present case, the absence of any settled rule by which passers-by can recognize who is and who is not responsible for providing assistance means that individuals lack reasonable expectations about what others are going to do. This provides individuals with an excuse for evading responsibility for providing assistance (though I again grant that even in this case the excuse is a weak one).

What is needed, therefore, is some rule determining who bears responsibility for providing assistance in such cases. An obvious candidate would be a rule designating certain individuals as lifeguards. Such a rule would impose on them a recognized duty to assist anyone drowning in the lake and confer on them the authority to command the assistance of others in saving swimmers. It might also mandate sanctions against lifeguards who are derelict in their duties, and against those who ignore instructions to assist them. The costs of compensating lifeguards and of administering sanctions for noncompliance could then be shared out equitably among members of society.

Such a scheme is, in effect, a way of organizing a social responsibility when, despite a firm sense that *someone* ought to be responsible for providing assistance, agents cannot spontaneously settle the question of exactly who is answerable for doing so and on what terms. No doubt there is room for much debate about the detailed merits and demerits of alternative versions of such schemes. In the case of global deprivation, for example, we would still need to consider the further issue of how much relief is appropriate. And there also remain complex empirical questions about the most effective way to design and direct relief efforts. The important *philosophical* point, however, is that it seems perverse to settle for ground rules that would render these questions irrelevant by prohibiting in advance most forms of forced redistribution as unjust anyway. It is natural to say that the rules of justice should *facilitate* rather than *impede* the fulfillment of important social responsibilities. The entitlement theory seems to license just such impediments. But we should demand very strong arguments before concluding that justice actively prohibits the enforcement of schemes organizing important social responsibilities of the sort we have been considering, including the responsibility for relieving global deprivation. The libertarian arguments we have canvassed here do not meet this burden of proof.

Conclusions

This chapter has been largely critical of the libertarian account of economic justice. It is therefore particularly important to end by acknowledging an important virtue in the entitlement theory. As we have seen, the libertarian argument is motivated by a desire to correct the naïve assumption that there is some central agency responsible for directly allocating economic shares. Instead of viewing conceptions of distributive justice as directly recommending principles for the central distribution of economic goods, libertarians understand them as comprising various general rules and principles to guide agents' choices. Such rules specify and demarcate the responsibilities of individuals and institutions by, for example, directing agents to recognize certain rights and not interfere with them, authorizing others to fulfill various valuable or necessary social functions and to apply certain sanctions and penalties or require forms of compensation when the rules are broken. This is, of course, exactly how the rules comprising the entitlement theory should be understood. They require agents to abide by certain rules circumscribing spheres of personal control over possessions and defining individuals' and institutions' responsibility to respect and enforce these boundaries; as long as those rules are followed, the theory regards the particular distributive results as just.

This assumption that conceptions of distributive justice primarily require conformity with *general* rules allocating social responsibilities and entitlements and only derivatively with the *particular* distributions of wealth that result is a strength of the libertarian view. We should probably agree with Hayek that it is utopian to begin the discussion of economic justice by postulating an agency with an already recognized responsibility to allocate economic shares centrally. Economic exchange is too dynamic and complex, the preconditions of its well-functioning too delicate, for comprehensive central control to make much sense. We are likely to do better by formulating a general framework of rules defining an adequate "social division of responsibility," to use a helpful phrase from Rawls. On this more subtle approach, acting justly is a matter of making legitimate rather than illegitimate moves within such a settled scheme of rules, not a matter of doling out goods in accordance with some simple principle like "Equal shares for all," or "From each according to his ability to each according to his need."

This sound Hayekian insight also connects the present discussion with views about justice held by the classical Greek philosophers like Plato. Plato's understanding of justice is clearly very different from modern liberal and libertarian conceptions. Still, as we saw in chapter 2, it resembles them insofar as it primarily associates injustice with improper meddling and interference. But any notion of improper interference presupposes rules and principles determining appropriate spheres of control, freedom, jurisdiction, competence, and authority. By the lights of such rules, agents recognize that it is (say) none of their business to tell others how to dispose of their property, not their place to interfere in the activities of public officials, "above their pay grade" to assume certain responsibilities, beyond their sphere of competence to inflict punishment on wrongdoers, and so on. In this respect at least, the entitlement theory is at one with the classical assumption that the primary function of conceptions of justice is to settle questions about who should be responsible for what, to fix the terms on which we are entitled to dispose of our property as we choose, and to determine where our obligations to respect the entitlements and honor the claims of others begin and end.

The difficulties we have identified in the libertarian view, therefore, do not impugn its choice of starting point. They rather concern the way in which it moves from this sensible starting point to a premature optimism about the sufficiency of rules that primarily protect the privileges of private ownership. This assigns undue priority to the responsibility to protect the rights of property-owners over other social responsibilities that also command our attention, like the responsibility to mitigate extreme suffering and deprivation. As we have seen, libertarians have not adequately defended this ordering of priorities. Like Paley's arguments, their case is incomplete and question-begging.

If we have found the libertarian view wanting in this respect, however, this does not mean that we have vindicated any alternative. We are so far entitled to conclude only that the libertarians have not yet refuted the claim that we may justly tax affluent property-owners for the sake of poverty reduction alone, or indeed for that of any other worthwhile social goal. The larger questions of which division of roles and responsibilities with respect to the control and regulation of economic wealth is most adequate, and of how we might establish that this is the case, remain open. But we have at least clarified that this is a propitious way to frame the question of economic justice. In the next chapter, we will consider these questions more closely and focus on the answers to them provided by John Rawls. His writings remain the most comprehensive and influential recent effort to grapple with the problem on these terms.

6   Economic justice

The previous chapter concluded that the quest for economic justice is best understood as a search for some general framework of rules and principles regulating the terms on which individuals may claim and institutions adjust holdings of wealth. We saw that such rules, and their recognition and acceptance among members of a society, define a "division of responsibility" with respect to economic activity. Such rules will typically determine, for example, responsibilities to respect others' property, to acknowledge the right of specific agencies to tax individuals' wealth under certain conditions, to ensure that private and public organizations providing important social services have access to adequate resources, and the like. The question is how such rules should be configured if they are fully to realize the ideal of social justice among people who accept and live by them.

It is important to emphasize that, in formulating the question this way, we are not directly evaluating existing social institutions by the lights of some already settled criterion of justice. Rather, we are asking which set of rules and principles is *worthy* of serving as such a criterion among members of a political community. In our discussion of skepticism in chapter 1, we noticed that different societies and cultures have often differed over what counts as just and unjust conduct, which allocations of social responsibility ought to be recognized as just rather than unjust. To take a very vivid economic example, many human societies have practiced slavery. Such societies have therefore formulated and lived by sometimes very elaborate rules specifying the just responsibilities of slaves and those of their owners. In contrast, our own societies now operate with the understanding that *any* form of ownership of persons is to be prohibited as unjust, a violation of a very basic right enjoyed by persons as such. On this now happily dominant view, nobody has any business claiming other human beings as their property, and both individuals and institutions ought to recognize and uphold this general principle of just treatment.

Given these deep disagreements about how justice and injustice are to be conventionally recognized, we do not have the luxury of being able to point to some settled, natural, conception of justice to answer our questions about how economic responsibility ought to be divided. We must rather decide between different possible conceptions of economic justice, that is, between different possible schemes of rules that classify as just or unjust various ways of regulating, controlling, interfering in, and assuming responsibility for wealth and economic resources. Once we have somehow vindicated a preferred conception of economic justice of this form, we might *then* compare existing institutions against that social ideal. But at this stage the question is to determine which ensemble of principles regulating the holding of wealth makes the most sense as an ideal criterion of justice to apply.

Some initial leads

But what sort of question is this and how might we go about answering it? Our discussion of the libertarian entitlement theory in the previous chapter was largely negative, but it is possible to draw from it several positive clues about what we need to take into consideration in addressing it. Five points stand out.

First, we need to take account of the likely effects of different schemes of rules on the performance of the economy. The stock of productive assets in the world is not fixed, but may itself be augmented or diminished by the terms on which economic production is socially regulated. In particular, we need to organize the rules so as to give agents adequate incentives for productive economic activity. For example, if – as opponents of equality often contend – guaranteeing everyone roughly equal shares threatens productivity by undermining incentives to work hard, this surely counts against strongly egalitarian principles of distributive justice.

Second, the stock of productive assets is not simply "external" to human beings; it includes our own talents and capacity for labor. The fact that these personal resources constitute important economic assets creates worries about unacceptable exploitation and alienation. Our freedom and self-respect seem bound up with our ability to control these personal assets on our own terms; when others can override our own wishes in this particularly intimate sphere of concern, we are likely to feel dispossessed and alienated from ourselves. Such worries motivate the libertarian insistence that humans are "self-owners."[1] The idea is that agents should be thought of as coming into the world already owning their labor and assets and enjoying the right to exclude others from decisions about how they should be controlled and invested. The appeal of this notion of self-ownership derives from its ability to forbid involuntary enslavement and other forms of exploitation.

Third, we cannot assume that individuals are equally situated with regard to access to the means of economic prosperity. Individuals' talents and assets are highly unequal. Moreover, different schemes of social regulation may affect differently placed individuals in very different ways. These overall regulatory schemes are hard to change and difficult to escape, with effects on individuals' prospects that are "profound and present from the start."[2] Individuals are therefore potentially very vulnerable to these effects: they can make the difference between a successful and an unsuccessful life.

Fourth, schemes of social regulation are not themselves costless.[3] As we saw in the previous chapter's lifeguard example, they must be paid for, and this raises questions about how these burdens ought to be fairly divided. This question arises even in the case of the pared-down scheme of rules constituting the entitlement theory. For even that theory requires the provision of legal services to adjudicate disputes about property rights and restitution for injury. These services do not come for free: someone must pay to maintain the courts and to remunerate the judges and other legal officials.

Fifth, as a general principle, rules of justice ought to facilitate, not impede, the fulfillment of socially necessary tasks and responsibilities.

The philosopher who has made the most sustained and influential recent attempt to synthesize these considerations into a single, ideal conception

---

[1] See the discussion in the last chapter.

[2] Rawls (1999a), p. 7.

[3] See Holmes and Sunstein (1999).

of justice is John Rawls. The rest of this chapter considers and assesses Rawls's remarkable contribution to this discussion.

Rawls on social justice

Each of the five considerations listed above raises questions about costs and benefits. According to Rawls, the point of a theory of justice is to tell us how we should ideally allocate these benefits and burdens. Translating into his distinctive terminology, the subject of justice is "the basic structure of society," by which Rawls meant the institutionalized framework of publicly accepted principles that regulate the "terms of social cooperation." Such cooperation, Rawls thought, is marked both by identities and by conflicts of interest: "There is an identity of interests since social cooperation makes possible a better life for all than any would have if each were to live solely by his own efforts. There is a conflict of interests since persons are not indifferent as to how the greater benefits produced by their collaboration are distributed, for in order to pursue their ends they each prefer a larger to a lesser share."[4] Rawls's theory of justice is intended to identify the best set of rules for dividing these benefits and burdens, the most rational basis for settling the terms of social cooperation.

It is natural to see this problem as inviting a utilitarian analysis. After all, if the question boils down to judgments about the costs and benefits of social cooperation, surely the obvious way to proceed is to ask which set of rules would maximize the benefits and minimize the costs. However, Rawls rejected this view in favor of the version of contractualism we described in chapter 4. Thus he invited us to think of his recommended principles of justice as the outcome of an agreement reached at an imaginary meeting – the original position. The purpose of this imaginary meeting is to decide in advance, and once and for all, on a set of principles organizing the basic structure of a political association that the persons in the original position will later share with each other.

Readers will recall that individuals in Rawls's original position deliberate behind a "veil of ignorance." The veil ensures that they have access only to general facts about human society and the modalities of social and economic reproduction. They lack specific information about themselves

---

[4] Rawls (1999a), p. 4.

and their position in the society they are to enter after their deliberations are complete. They do not know, for example, how talented they are, or what talents are highly valued in their society. As we saw in chapter 4, Rawls defended the veil of ignorance because he thought that it guaranteed procedural fairness and impartiality. It is worth noting, however, how well it fits in with Hayek's notion that rules of justice ought not to "aim at the achievement of known particular results" but rather to define an "abstract order" to be "preserved as a means for assisting in the pursuit of a great variety of individual purposes" of whose details we must remain ignorant. As Rawls wrote of his own proposal: "no attempt is made to define the just distribution of goods and services on the basis of information about the preferences and claims of particular individuals."[5]

Rawls preferred this contractualist approach over utilitarian derivations because in his view it better captures our considered conviction that "each person possesses an inviolability founded on justice that even the welfare of society as a whole cannot override." The intuitive problem with utilitarian conceptions, Rawls feared, is that they might recognize as perfectly just the imposition of sacrificial burdens on the few in order to promote the welfare of the many. Thus, although various utilitarian principles are considered in Rawls's original position, all are rejected. Rawls reasoned that individuals would not risk endorsing principles under which such catastrophic personal sacrifices could count as just. In this way, the design of the original position captures and guarantees individuals' "inviolability" by giving them a veto over principles that would expose them to the risk of such sacrifice or unreasonable exploitation, or so Rawls maintained.

Although Rawls's individuals choose among various possible rules and principles, they understand that in doing so they are determining the terms on which they are entitled to certain fundamental goods – the "social primary goods." As we saw in chapter 4, Rawls's list of primary goods comprises rights, liberties, opportunities, income and wealth, and "the social bases of self-respect." The two principles of justice that Rawls recommended, therefore, represent an agreement to make these basic

---

[5] Hayek (1976), p. 5; Rawls (1999a), p. 42.

goods available to members of society on certain terms. Those two principles read as follows:

1. Each person is to have an equal right to the most extensive total scheme of equal basic liberties compatible with a similar system of liberty for all.
2. Social and economic inequalities are to be arranged so that they are both
    (a) to the greatest benefit of the least advantaged (the "Difference Principle"), and
    (b) attached to offices and positions open to all under conditions of fair equality of opportunity.

The "Difference Principle" (2.[a], above) is the part of this proposal with the most distinctive and controversial implications for the regulation of economic holdings. But before we consider that principle and some of the criticisms it invites, it is important to note two aspects of Rawls's first principle that bear indirectly on the question of economic justice.

First, Rawls argued that the first principle should be "lexically prior" to the second. This simply means that on his theory, citizens' first responsibility is to secure to each other certain basic liberties. This they must accomplish *before* they contemplate redistributing wealth under the terms of the Difference Principle. To put it another way, citizens who associate under Rawlsian principles recognize *no* possible combination of economic advantages as compensating for the loss of the basic liberties protected under the first principle. Giving liberty this overriding priority over material prosperity is characteristic of the liberal tradition of political thought with which Rawls is often associated. Whether it deserves this strong priority over other social goods and values is an issue to which we shall return.

Second, while the right to hold personal property (in some form) is included in the list of liberties protected by Rawls's first principle, other economic liberties are conspicuously absent. Rawls's first principle protects the "political liberties" (the right to vote and run for office), freedom of speech, assembly, conscience, religion, and freedom from physical assault and theft. But it does not protect freedom of contract, rights to inherit wealth, or the right to ownership in the means of production. This does not mean that such freedoms could receive *no* protection in a Rawlsian society.

It means, rather, that Rawls did not regard them as fundamental liberties. Rawls's decision to exclude these privileges of private ownership from the list of liberties deserving the most urgent protection reflects a determination not to allow the rights of property-owners to block the fulfillment of other important social responsibilities. In the last chapter, we criticized the libertarian entitlement theory for doing just this. Rawls's proposal builds on that criticism.

It is important to emphasize, however, that Rawls agreed with the libertarians that personal liberty trumps other social values. Both accept, moreover, that individuals' self-respect is crucially at stake in these judgments about the relative importance of liberty. But they disagree over whether the *kinds* of freedom crucial to individuals' sense of self-respect are essentially economic and proprietary in character. While Rawls denied this, libertarians insist on it.

The Difference Principle

Rawls's Difference Principle requires that inequalities in income and wealth must be shown to secure the highest possible benefit to the least advantaged members of society — that is, those whose access to the social primary goods is most limited. Under this principle, when citizens find that their least-advantaged fellows could enjoy better economic prospects by *either* improving *or* diminishing those of better-advantaged groups, they must recognize that justice requires those adjustments. Three points will help to clarify this requirement.

First, it has a complex relation to notions of equality. On the one hand, the Difference Principle is itself justified as a requirement of political equality. Rawls's thinking was that any society that fails to do the best it can for its least-advantaged members cannot claim to be treating them fully as equals. Moreover, the principle assumes a presumption in favor of equal shares in that it permits departures from an equal distribution of income and wealth only under certain conditions — that is, when we are sure that inequalities will work to the greatest benefit of those with the meagerest holdings in primary goods. On the other hand, the Difference Principle might in practice very often prohibit as unjust efforts to enforce a strictly egalitarian distribution. For whenever a policy of strict equality would *worsen* the situation of the least-advantaged members of society, the Difference Principle would reject it. For example, if the least-advantaged will do as well as possible only if already affluent groups receive even more than they currently do (perhaps in order to provide them with incentives to greater productivity), the Difference Principle will require that we accept the resulting inequalities.[6]

Second, the Difference Principle is anti-utilitarian. It disallows any economic distribution that leaves the least-advantaged worse off than they could be under some sustainable alternative, whether or not it maximizes utility. Thus a Rawlsian society recognizes no responsibility to maximize wealth as such. As we have seen, Rawls argued that maximizing principles leave people, especially those least advantaged, unacceptably vulnerable to exploitation for the sake of marginal utilitarian gains. Behind the veil of ignorance, individuals in the original position are uncertain of their relative position in the society they are about to enter. Given the possibility that they may turn out to be in socially disadvantaged positions, they will regard utilitarianism and any other maximizing principle as too risky, or so Rawls reasoned. In contrast, the Difference Principle minimizes these risks. Even if they turn out to be the least-advantaged members of their society, individuals will nevertheless do as well as possible as long as that principle is enforced.

Third, the Difference Principle represents a clear and explicit repudiation of desert-based conceptions of distributive justice. Rawls recognized that, if left unregulated, economic exchange will be powerfully affected by the natural distribution of talents and abilities. Those who are more talented, or whose talents happen to be highly valued in their generation, will tend to do much better than others. Those naturally disposed toward hard work, too, will tend to be more successful. Common sense says that such inequalities are just because they are deserved. But Rawls rejected that view. He insisted that personal endowments of such character traits are as much a matter of luck as the social status into which one is born. Permitting distributive shares to be determined by factors so "arbitrary from the moral point of view" is therefore "improper," or so Rawls concluded. Accordingly, the Difference Principle is justified independently of, and its application insensitive to, considerations of personal desert or merit.

---

[6] For a critical discussion of incentives and the Difference Principle, see Cohen (2000), chs. 6–9.

Rawls's decoupling of social justice from desert has proven very controversial. Many critics have challenged Rawls's suggestion that because individuals do not deserve the good fortune of being naturally rich in abilities and talents, they cannot be said to deserve any economic rewards these traits command. We will consider these and other criticisms of the Difference Principle below. But before we do so, it is important to forestall a common misunderstanding of Rawls's views about desert and luck.

Some have been tempted to identify Rawls's stance with a position today dubbed "luck-egalitarianism."[7] Luck-egalitarians object to inequalities of wealth that reflect "brute luck." Jones's being a "giftless bastard" (as Tchaikovsky once described Brahms) is a function of her ill-fortune in the "natural lottery" for talents. Luck-egalitarians argue that insofar as her comparatively low income can be attributed to this undeserved raw deal, it is unjust. As a matter of justice, therefore, such inequalities must be eliminated or compensated for as far as possible. Once this is accomplished, however, luck-egalitarians have no further objection to economic inequalities that reflect individuals' subsequent choices. So according to luck-egalitarians, it is reasonable to regard individuals as responsible for disadvantages resulting from their *chosen* behavior, but not for those that reflect unchosen and undeserved ill-fortune.

Luck-egalitarianism deserves consideration in its own right, but the relevant point here is that Rawls's own view differs importantly. Luck-egalitarians assume that brute ill-luck is already an injustice that calls for compensation or mitigation. But Rawls expressly denied this, insisting that that the distribution of natural talents "is neither just nor unjust; nor is it unjust that persons are born into society at some particular position. What is just and unjust is the way that institutions deal with these facts." Unlike the luck-egalitarian, then, Rawls did not regard the Difference Principle as a device for compensating for some injustice in the genetic and social lotteries. Instead, he thought of it as a reasonable and fair basis on which citizens "agree to avail themselves of the accidents of nature and social circumstance only when doing so is for the common benefit."[8]

---

[7] See Anderson (1999).

[8] Rawls (1999a), pp. 87–8.

The desert objection

I now consider several objections to Rawls's Difference Principle. As already noted, many have been unhappy with Rawls's decision to exclude considerations of merit or desert from his theory of justice. One such critic, John Kekes, complains that, as a result of this decision, Rawls's Difference Principle has "numerous counterintuitive consequences":

> Suppose that a man and a woman are both among the least advantaged members of society. The man is a hitherto unapprehended mugger; he has never held a job; he is vicious when he can get away with it; he had moderate native endowments, but he has made no effort to develop them. The woman is the mother of several children; she and the children have been abandoned by her husband and their father; she earns meager wages by working part time at a menial job; she is doing her best to raise the children well; she has the same native endowments as the mugger but, unlike him, has used them to make great, although unsuccessful, efforts to improve her situation. According to the difference principle, the mugger and the mother are entitled to the same treatment. Their positions of inequality are due to contingencies that are arbitrary from a moral point of view ... They are entitled [for Rawls] to the same distributive shares.
>
> Changing the scenario a little illustrates another [counterintuitive] consequence of Rawls's position. The mugger continues as before, but the mother is no longer unsuccessful. Through her efforts ... she now has a moderately comfortable and secure ... middle class position. She has a good job, she bought a house, the children are doing well in school, and they can even afford the occasional family vacation. According to the difference principle, the contingencies of life, among which are counted the mugger's lack of effort and the mother's successful effort, are to be redressed in the direction of equality. Thus on Rawls's view, some of the mother's resources should be taken from her and used to support the mugger.[9]

But Kekes overestimates this objection. One initial point to notice is that he pursues his point by comparing a conscientious mother with someone — the mugger — whose conduct is not merely vicious but also criminal. We are likely to agree with Kekes that muggers do not deserve to have their criminal activities subsidized by taxpayers, but our immediate reaction

---

[9] Kekes (1997), pp. 132–3.

to such people is surely that they should be apprehended and punished, something that Rawls's theory very clearly supports. Moreover, the further issue of whether those convicted of crimes should or could permissibly be disqualified from receiving welfare benefits is not one that Rawls explicitly addresses, since he brackets the "nonideal" question of how social institutions ought to deal with "partial compliance" with fair and reasonable social expectations (like rules prohibiting violent theft). Because it overlooks these complications, Kekes's example is misleading and his conclusions about the counterintuitive implications of Rawls's position rather hasty.

Moreover, even if we accept that Kekes's example has counterintuitive features, it is not clear why *single* counterintuitive cases should be allowed to count against a principle that is offered as a *general* rule to follow. To take a parallel case, we all know that under the rule of law, guilty persons often go free. We also know that we could reduce the number of such injustices by relaxing the burden of proof that the state must satisfy in order to secure a conviction. But one obvious reason to resist this solution is that it runs the graver risk of the state unjustly convicting (and punishing) the innocent. Surely in most cases the guilty going free seems the lesser evil. Citing specific cases in which guilty parties have been freed and pointing out that this offends against widely held intuitions about justice would not (and should not) shake our confidence in this judgment.

Kekes's citation of a single counterintuitive case against the Difference Principle seems similarly beside the point. Individuals in the original position might know perfectly well that the Difference Principle could permit seeming injustices of the sort Kekes describes. But they might still think this a reasonable price to pay for insuring themselves against the greater evil of severe economic disadvantage and its attendant indignities. Kekes's counterexample would be decisive only if we can assume that the likely beneficiaries of a Difference Principle are all or mostly as reprehensible as the mugger he describes. But this assumption would be at best empirically questionable, and at worst gratuitously insulting.

Two final points about desert also count in Rawls's favor. First, judgments about what people deserve are notoriously controversial and hard to justify. This is partly because taking all relevant factors into consideration requires extremely complicated comparative assessments. (How shall we weigh one person's superior but effortless attainments against another's heroically effortful mediocrity?) But these judgments are also difficult to justify because people often disagree about what substantive standard of merit we should apply. One person's merit is another's demerit; one person's virtue is another's vice.

A clear advantage of Rawls's rejection of desert as a general criterion for just economic shares is that it avoids the need to resolve these extremely difficult questions publicly. Kekes obscures these difficulties by focusing on a case in which our attitudes to someone (the mugger) are partly predetermined by the fact that he is a criminal. This *just means* that there already exists a well-recognized (and in this case uncontroversial) public standard by which we are licensed to think ill of him. But such cases are not really representative. The tougher cases for Kekes and other proponents of desert-based conceptions of justice are ones in which we cannot appeal to generally recognized and uncontroversial rules of conduct like those constituting the criminal law to dictate of whom we should disapprove and to specify how we should do so (by applying certain punishments, for example). Perhaps I consider the otherwise law-abiding Snodgrass to be a worthless emptyhead, unacceptably unorthodox in his religious beliefs, lacking in important social graces, vulgar, pathetic, or sinful. But how would I convince others (who may quite like him) both that these judgments are correct and further that Snodgrass is *therefore* less deserving of economic rewards than others whom I deem more worthy?

Second, it is important to remember that Rawls's principles distribute social primary goods. But these are not the only goods there are. Consider ("secondary"?) social goods like gold medals, Nobel prizes, Oscar statuettes, professional recognition, promotions, academic grades, beatification, and fame. There are also goods (and bads) that consist in the personal attitudes we adopt and express towards each other. Approval and disapproval, love and hatred, attention and neglect, or respect and disrespect are obvious examples. The distribution of these goods is controlled by private organizations and individuals, often in accordance with distinctive personal or cultural standards. Rawls's two principles do not impinge on these private forms of distribution. Indeed, not only do they leave people free to apply merit-based assessments in their decisions about whom to reward, promote, respect, ignore, dismiss, and hate; they actually *protect* the rights of individuals and organizations to do so in accordance with their own conceptions of what people deserve. For example, freedom of association and of religion, protected under Rawls's first principle, guarantee the rights of religious communities to govern themselves by their own lights, and to apply distinctively religious conceptions of personal merit in recognizing and celebrating the character and achievements of some of their members. Rawls's rejection of desert therefore needs to be kept in proper perspective. It would be quite misleading to suggest that he left absolutely *no* room for conceptions of personal desert ever to influence any decisions about the distribution of goods in a just society.

The common-assets objection

Rawls claimed that the Difference Principle "represents ... an agreement to regard the distribution of natural talents as a common asset," to be exploited to the benefit of the least fortunate members of society.[10] Many critics have taken Rawls to task for seeming in this passage to introduce some sort of collective ownership in individuals' personal assets and talents. Leading this charge have been the libertarians, for whom Rawls's infamous remark about talents as "common assets" represents a repudiation of their cherished principle of self-ownership and hence an unacceptable concession to socialism. For, libertarians complain, if "society" has the right to redistribute the fruits of some people's labor and talents to others without their consent, the latter can no longer be said to be unqualified owners of these personal assets. Such assets would instead form a common pool of resources that society may allocate as *it* chooses. Those entitled to benefits under the Difference Principle in effect acquire a right to some portion of others' earnings and the labor and talents that produced them. This institutes "ownership by others of people and their actions."[11] Once we see this, we must conclude that the redistribution required under the Difference Principle is "on a par with forced labor," or so libertarians like Nozick contend.[12]

This criticism seems powerful because it raises the same concerns that led Rawls himself to reject utilitarian conceptions of social justice. As we have seen, Rawls's worry about utilitarianism was precisely that it would

[10] Rawls (1999a), p. 87.
[11] Nozick (1974), p. 172.
[12] Nozick (1974), p. 169.

objectionably permit individuals to be treated merely as means for maximizing aggregate welfare. According to Rawls, individuals who accept such a permission must think of themselves as in principle reducible to little more than fodder for the mill of utility maximization. Believing oneself exploitable in this way, Rawls reasoned, precludes a proper sense of self-worth and self-respect. But if that is true, is it not the case that treating individuals' talents as a common asset, to be exploited to maximize the benefits of the least-advantaged members of society, is a comparable threat to individuals' self-respect? As Nozick charged, individuals' sense of self-worth seems safe under this arrangement "only if one presses *very* hard on the distinction between men and their talents, assets, abilities and special traits. Whether any coherent conception of the person remains when the distinction is so pressed is an open question. Why we, thick with particular traits, should be cheered that (only) the thus purified men within us are not regarded as means is also unclear."[13]

Although many contemporary philosophers seem to regard this objection as extremely powerful, even devastating, I find it hard to understand why. The objection alleges that the way in which successful individuals' assets are used to benefit others, under Rawls's proposal, is comparable to the kinds of personal sacrifice that utilitarianism could permit or even require. But when one actually thinks about the kinds of cases that led Rawls to reject utilitarianism, this comparison loses much of its plausibility. Rawls was worried that utilitarianism might permit very extreme personal sacrifices for the sake of overall utility. Perhaps the abject impoverishment of the few is a condition of the freedom and prosperity of the many; perhaps overall utility requires that some surrender any claim to basic liberties, such as the right to freedom of speech and association, or to practice one's religion in accordance with one's conscience; perhaps it requires that some be enslaved so that many more others enjoy greater well-being. Given these possibilities, Rawls thought that individuals who embrace utilitarian principles would be stalked by anxiety that at any moment the "calculus of social interests" might require them to forfeit their freedoms, basic well-being, and even their lives merely to secure marginal increases in overall welfare.

But the predicament of those liable to taxation under the Difference Principle is surely less dire in several important respects. First, they need not

[13] Nozick (1974), p. 228.

worry, as denizens of a utilitarian society might, about their basic liberties being sacrificed. For these basic liberties are already guaranteed under Rawls's lexically prior first principle and they are explicitly *not* subject to the "calculus of social interests." Notable among these liberties is what Rawls called "freedom of the person," in which he included "freedom from psychological oppression, and physical assault and dismemberment (integrity of the person)."[14] These entitlements, which would categorically rule out any sort of enslavement or privation of basic liberties, the Difference Principle leaves wholly untouched.

Second, those liable to taxation under Rawls's proposal are in socially advantaged positions, abundant in social primary goods. They are thus assumed to be already rich in "the social bases of self-respect," which for Rawls comprise the most important primary good of all. The question is whether these reserves of self-respect are likely to be in any significant way depleted by redistribution of some of their earned income to less-advantaged citizens. In this context, comparisons with "forced labor," which evoke images of chain gangs, labor camps, manacles, and dangerously arduous physical effort, seem ludicrously indiscriminate. *Real* forced labor − of the Burma Railway variety − *is* a form of servitude. Its victims are forced to work under the most degrading of conditions, without regard to their physical safety, with little or no compensation, and without recourse to complaint or protest. *Maybe* utilitarianism might sometimes require that some individuals submit to such miserable conditions. But even so, why suppose that the Difference Principle could require anything so drastic? To suggest that when compelled to forgo a portion of their presumptively ample income to support those less fortunate than themselves, successful professionals (say) undergo treatment that is comparably degrading or corrosive of their self-respect seems on its face quite ridiculous.

So obvious are these differences that it is only natural to speculate about why those impressed by this objection to the Difference Principle seem so willing to overlook them. Why are people in our culture tempted to think that their self-worth is closely bound up with their ability to retain every last penny that their talents and personal assets can command in a market economy? Why do they resent redistributive taxation to the point where

[14] Rawls (1999a), p. 53.

they are prepared to take implausible comparisons with forced labor seriously?

One possible answer, deserving closer scrutiny than we can give it here, draws attention to the way in which post-industrial societies create new demand for goods and services, and thus fuel economic growth, by encouraging certain false needs. I mainly have in mind here demand for luxuries, and especially those goods that serve as tokens of the social status, peer-recognition and self-definition to which many people, driven by the fads of modern commercial culture, today aspire. These phenomena may explain – though would not justify – the tendency to associate redistributive taxation with a loss of self-worth. If taxation threatens agents' ability to afford the badges of honor and recognition they seek, it becomes easier to understand why they might resent it as potentially degrading. On this view, widespread resentment of redistributive taxation by wealthy individuals is a symptom of a narcissistic anxiety about status and inclusion characteristic of the more affluent sectors of contemporary society.[15]

This suggestion is obviously speculative. Whatever its plausibility, however, we have yet to be given any convincing reason to reject the Difference Principle on the grounds that it necessarily injures the self-respect of advantaged individuals. And if the principle at the same time combats those forms of economic disadvantage that *do* tend to erode self-respect, one could conclude – vindicating Rawls's original contention – that considerations of self-respect support rather than impugn the Difference Principle.

The relevance of coercion

Those sympathetic to libertarian views will insist that I have missed the point of the forced-labor analogy. They will say that it is a mistake to make too much of an exact correspondence between forced labor and redistributive taxation. The crucial overlap between them, rather, is that both extract resources from people by *coercive* means. "Coercion," writes one philosopher, "... reduces the will of one person to the will of another; [it violates] autonomy not simply in virtue of that fact, but because of the

---

[15] See Frank (1985); Milner (2004).

symbolic gesture this fact represents. In subjecting the will of one otherwise autonomous agent to the will of another, coercion demonstrates an attitude of disrespect, of infantilization of a sort inconsistent with respect for human agents as autonomous, self-creating creatures."[16] Importantly, coercion remains objectionable in this way even when used to promote valuable ends. We would still resent a mugging even if perpetrated by a Robin Hood who intends to "redistribute" his ill-gotten gains to the deserving poor. This suggests that redistributive taxation is, after all, at least on a continuum with other degrading forms of coercion. Forced labor is simply another, albeit more extreme, example.

It is true that taxation involves coercion. But that does not mean that there are no relevant differences between submitting to taxation under the terms of Rawls's proposal and being the victim of a well-intentioned Robin Hood. Here, it is vital to remember that Rawls assumed that his two principles are willingly endorsed by members of his ideal well-ordered society as settled public criteria determining just entitlements and fair treatment. Indeed, Rawls argued that individuals in the original position would reject principles that, when publicly recognized in this way, they could not willingly endorse, given general knowledge of the limits of psychological tolerance and the typical circumstances of political association. His contractualist thought experiment thus purports to test whether it is fair and reasonable to expect individuals to submit to different possible schemes of social rules and principles. On the strength of his contention that his two principles of justice survive this test, Rawls felt entitled to conclude that individuals in a well-ordered society indeed *would* willingly accept and fulfill the responsibilities those principles impose upon them and can reasonably expect that others do so as well.

Clearly we are not entitled to dismiss these claims until we have fully assessed the cogency of Rawls's overall contractualist approach. In chapter 4 we expressed some reservations on this score, but suppose we give Rawls the benefit of the doubt in the meantime. Doing so exposes two important differences between submitting to redistribution under his proposal and being mugged by a Robin Hood. First, a Robin Hood has *no idea* and *does not care* whether his victims are themselves disposed to contribute to whatever worthwhile social causes he intends to subsidize by stealing. His direct

---

[16] Blake (2001), p. 268.

resort to coercive threats testifies to his willingness to proceed *without regard* to his victims' own wishes. It is this assumption that the victim's own will is simply irrelevant that makes the coercion of a Robin Hood offensive and contemptuous of his victims' autonomy.

But, at least in theory, Rawls envisaged a very different situation. For, as Rawls conceived it, a well-ordered society *just is* one in which there exists willing acceptance of the responsibilities imposed by the two principles and in which it is publicly known that citizens are disposed to fulfill them. Rawls's contractualist argument is intended to determine what principles individuals concerned to reconcile their own autonomy with their sense of justice would be prepared to accept as a fair account of their own responsibilities to each other. So unlike Robin Hood, a Rawlsian state has at least some reason to think that its expectations of those it coerces are ones that citizens themselves acknowledge as fair and reasonable.

Second, and relatedly, it is Robin Hood's coercion that gives his victims their primary reason for complying with his demand for their money. If Robin Hood were not threatening them, they might see no reason at all to give him any of their money. But as we have just seen, individuals in Rawls's well-ordered society already acknowledge that they have a responsibility to assist their least-advantaged fellows. The purpose of legal coercion in Rawls's view is therefore *not* to supply a reason to do something where previously none existed. Its purpose, rather, is to provide agents who already recognize good reasons to fulfill their responsibilities with an assurance that, once they have done so, others will also do their part in accordance with a fair and reasonable principle for sharing out the costs.

The sufficiency objection

Rawls's Difference Principle seems more vulnerable to another criticism, this time one aimed at egalitarian conceptions of justice more generally. According to this line of argument, pioneered by Harry Frankfurt, egalitarianism is a confused version of a better principle of economic distribution – the principle of *sufficiency*.[17] What matters, for "sufficientarians" (with apologies), is not that everyone's shares approximate to equality, but rather that everyone receive *enough*. Imagine a society in which everyone has access

---

[17] Frankfurt (1988).

to sufficient economic resources for personal fulfillment and contentment. No one is impoverished in, or deprived of, the material goods they require to meet their needs. Still, there remain large disparities in income between individuals working in different sectors of the economy. Sports stars and computer whizzes make a lot more than teachers and nurses. But again, even the latter have enough. Sufficientarians claim that, as long as this is true, there is nothing objectionable about these inequalities. Egalitarians, of course, must claim that there is; to them there is something inherently offensive about departures from equal shares. But why? If everyone really has enough, why complain about those who have more than enough? Aren't such complaints simply motivated by envy, a seedy emotion with no place in dispassionate assessments of economic justice?

Rawls's Difference Principle is vulnerable to this criticism because – like stricter egalitarian views – it could require redistribution well beyond the point of sufficiency (whatever that is). For it requires, not merely that the least advantaged members of society have enough in an absolute sense, but that they do as well as economically feasible relative to other members of society. Citizens who embrace the Difference Principle therefore recognize an important social responsibility, based upon justice, to insure that people have more than enough under certain conditions. But does Rawls give us any reason to agree that, beyond guaranteeing that everyone has enough, this is an important social responsibility that conceptions of justice must recognize? This is not clear.

Sufficientarian views are not without their own difficulties, of course. We need in particular to explain what counts as enough, and this is a potentially very complicated matter. Here, it is important to stress that Frankfurt himself did not interpret sufficiency as any sort of *minimal* requirement, like the Lockean proviso we discussed in the last chapter. He thought, for example, that it requires that individuals have not merely enough *to survive* but enough for a decent life.[18] So a principle of sufficiency might still require quite radical forms of redistribution. But however these details are settled, the sufficiency argument represents an important challenge to conceptions of distributive justice that pay attention – like Rawls's Difference Principle – to agents' *relative* as well as *absolute* economic shares.

[18] Frankfurt (1988), pp. 152ff.

Rawls's decision to make his theory sensitive to considerations of relative deprivation remains a puzzling and undermotivated feature of his theory; more so, since in his later work Rawls himself defended a sufficientarian view in the international arena. As we shall see shortly, Rawls denied that the Difference Principle applies globally. Instead, he argued that our responsibilities to the economically deprived overseas are exhausted by a "duty of assistance." This duty requires that affluent states transfer sufficient funds to allow societies "burdened" by unfavorable economic conditions to solve their problems by themselves. However, once affluent states have discharged this duty, they have no further responsibility to insure that the recipient states succeed in relieving poverty and deprivation within their own borders: if the latter fail, they have only themselves to blame and no legitimate complaint against the affluent states.

But, as many have pointed out, applying this same logic to the domestic case undermines the Difference Principle.[19] One might well ask: If we have supplied all our fellow citizens with resources for an adequate life, why impose a *further* responsibility to improve the condition of the least-advantaged *as far as possible*? What more do we really owe them? Does not justice require that at that point *they* assume responsibility for themselves?

Global distributive justice?

I now return to an issue we introduced in the previous chapter, and consider the implications of Rawls's theory for the global distribution of wealth. The discussion in that chapter suggested that global inequalities of wealth are, if anything, of more urgent concern than disparities between rich and poor within existing states. But Rawls rejected this view. As he conceived them, his two principles apply only within states, but not beyond their borders. This view reflects Rawls's assumption, latent in his theory from the start, but more pronounced and explicit in his later writings, that only states possess the sort of "basic structure" to which his theory was supposed to apply. But many now think that, in an increasingly interdependent world, this assumption that distributive justice is almost exclusively an *intranational* concern is mistaken.

[19] E.g. Singer (2002), p. 178.

Commentators have been consistently puzzled by Rawls's views about justice between nations. Many of his early readers took his decision to focus on the just configuration of national institutions to be a residual prejudice that Rawls inherited from the philosophical tradition. They assumed that, once fully acquainted with the growth of international legal regulation since World War II, and with the magnitude and density of economic interdependence between nations today, Rawls would not hesitate to extend his principles of justice beyond the borders of states. Some of his "cosmopolitan" followers, indeed, blazed this trail themselves, though without Rawls's own blessing.[20]

They argued that there already exists a global basic structure whose effects on individuals' life prospects are no less "profound and present from the start" than those imposed by domestic institutions. They also claimed that Rawls's avowed hostility towards allowing "factors arbitrary from a moral point of view" to affect distributive shares requires international redistribution. For without it, individuals' economic prospects will often be determined by their place of birth. But what could be more arbitrary than permitting people's economic prospects to be determined by (for example) whether they are born in the United States or Bangladesh? These authors therefore suggested that Rawls's original position be mobilized to determine principles of planetary justice. One might expect that a strong case for a global Difference Principle could be mounted on this basis, and this is indeed what some Rawlsians have advocated.

But, in his own later writings, Rawls opposed this cosmopolitan extension of his theory, and did so, moreover, on principled grounds. While he accepted that global principles ought to be ratified through an international version of his original-position argument, he denied that the parties to such a hypothetical planetary agreement should be conceived as individuals, as in his main theory. Rather, he argued, the parties should be representatives of nation-states, or (as Rawls preferred to call them) of "peoples." Thus the outcome of Rawls's own international contractualist theory is not a rich conception of distributive justice for a global order of planetary equals, but rather a "Law of Peoples" to govern the terms on which independent, self-sufficient, and putatively self-governing states

---

[20] Beitz (1999); Pogge (1994); Pogge (2002).

might live together in peace.[21] As Rawls conceived it, the Law of Peoples comprises a familiar set of rules recognizing (among others) the equality and political independence of "peoples," their right to go to war in self-defense, and a minimal list of human rights. The only economic proviso that Rawls added was the aforementioned "duty of assistance" under which economically successful "peoples" are required to supply enough aid to "burdened" societies to allow them to achieve "decent" social institutions by themselves.

Not only does it reject a global Difference Principle, but Rawls's Law of Peoples does not even expect that all "peoples" themselves endorse the Difference Principle as a requirement of justice within their own borders. This particularly puzzling feature of the Law of Peoples reflects Rawls's later concession (noted at the end of chapter 4) that his theory cannot be defended as true for all societies at all times, but should be conceived more narrowly as specifying the dominant understanding of social justice characteristic of modern liberal democracy. Given this revised under-standing, the cosmopolitan temptation to write into the Law of Peoples expectations deriving from a specifically *liberal democratic* conception of justice became, for Rawls, a potentially imperialist impulse to be resisted. So while Rawls continued to insist that the Difference Principle is an appropriate principle of justice for societies (like ours) already locked into the project of liberal democracy, he denied that we can dogmatically impose it upon societies elsewhere. Their public cultures, he argued, may be quite reasonably inhospitable to liberal democratic ideals. Accordingly, the Law of Peoples embodies a principle of international toleration that resembles the "diff'rent strokes for diff'rent folks" principle we discussed (and rejected) in chapter 1.

Particularism and cosmopolitanism

Few find this account of global distributive justice satisfactory. There are real difficulties squaring it with Rawls's original articulation of his theory. It is therefore extremely unfortunate that Rawls died before having had an adequate opportunity fully to clarify his own view of these matters. However, while most remain perplexed by his own defense of it, many insist

---

[21] Rawls (1999b).

nonetheless that Rawls's conclusion that the requirements of distributive justice are weaker at the global level than within domestic political society is essentially sound.

Some defend it on strongly "particularist" or "communitarian" grounds that Rawls himself could not have accepted.[22] "Communitarianism" or "particularism" here refers to the view that ethical standards, principles, obligations, responsibilities, and duties, and our conceptions of them, make sense only in the context of some shared cultural framework, anchored in actually realized forms of community or association. In other words, effective ethical norms require some strong and rich set of bonds, loyalties, and affiliations (e.g., kinship, culture, friendship, nationality, ethnicity). This "social thesis" promotes skepticism about cosmopolitan justice and the ethical universalism on which it seems to rest. The crucial particularist allegation is that the global community is too large and attenuated to provide a fertile soil for any framework of ethical principle.[23]

In its purest version, this view implies that the very notion of universal or impartial ethical values is incoherent, like the idea that someone could speak a language without *any* accent at all, as if there were some "impartially" correct way of pronouncing words that is not itself just another accent. On such a view, all ethical standards and understandings of justice must be inherently local and partial, and so-called "global justice" an oxymoron. On the strength of such assumptions, some claim that only when people share the appropriate cultural and civic affiliations can they owe each other significant economic assistance as a matter of justice. While this assumption holds among citizens of the same nation, they claim, it does not hold at the global level.

There is no doubt that strong bonds of affective or cultural affiliation can make a difference to our obligations to others. Few would deny that we owe more to our friends, family, and cultural intimates than we do to those outside these circles of concern. It is not clear, however, that cosmopolitans or universalists must deny any of this, or that it makes ethical particularism

---

[22] For communitarian views, see Sandel (1982); Taylor (1985); Taylor (1995); Walzer (1982); and the excellent discussion in Kymlicka (1989).

[23] E.g. Walzer (1983), pp. 28ff., 312–21; for a recent defense of a modest particularism, see Miller (1995).

a plausible view. But, however we decide these larger questions, a more immediate doubt hangs over this argument. Does *citizenship* credibly belong in the category of those affiliations that intensify our sense of obligation to others, particularly with regard to economic justice?

This is far from obvious. In complex modern societies, the bond of citizenship is not necessarily a particularly close one, and not only in the sense that one does not know one's fellow citizens very well. The more telling point is that, even when one *does* know them, one all too often finds their ways of life, beliefs, experiences, and emotional responses largely incomprehensible, alien, reprehensible, and even repellent. In some cases, citizens of the same state may not even speak the same language (think of Canada, Belgium, or Switzerland). One reason to be suspicious of this argument, then, is its unwelcome implication that, whenever shared understanding and cultural intimacy are lacking among citizens (as they very often are), domestic redistributive justice may be as hard to justify as it claims it is in the global case. To adapt the aphorism about Russians and Tartars, scratch a fellow citizen and you will find a stranger. It is doubtful, then, that these particularist arguments can justify Rawls's view that justice imposes more extensive obligations to provide material assistance to economically deprived fellow citizens than to similarly disadvantaged foreigners.

Coercion and autonomy (*again*)

Others have, however, defended this conclusion in a different way, more congenial, perhaps, to Rawls's own approach. They deny that the salient difference between the domestic and the global case is that there exist cultural ties in one that are absent or too weak in the other. Rather, they suggest that the crucial difference lies in the presence — in the domestic case — of the coercive apparatus of the state itself. These powerful reserves of coercion, they argue, potentially warp the relations between citizens, leaving them especially vulnerable to abuse at each other's hands. For, unlike foreigners, one's fellow citizens enjoy ready access to these coercive resources and so represent an immediate danger to one's own autonomy. Association within the framework of a state thus creates distinctive problems that do not arise between humans operating in the wider global environment. Most important, wealthier groups may be able to use their domestic political institutions and their coercive capacity to dominate and take advantage of less well-situated groups of citizens. We need therefore to ensure that disadvantaged groups have adequate resources to counteract this risk that better-situated groups will convert economic advantage into political oppression. This requires that we attend to the relative economic position of the two groups and create pressure towards a more egalitarian distribution of resources within states. These dangers thus lend relative economic shares, and perhaps the Difference Principle, a special significance in the domestic case that they do not enjoy in the global one, or so these authors contend.[24]

One attraction of this argument is that it seems compatible with the cosmopolitan or universalist assumption that all humans *as such* are to be respected as *planetary equals*, regardless of their nationality, ethnicity, or other particularist affiliations. Some of its proponents therefore allow that, at the global level, universal respect for the moral equality of all humans requires that we guarantee everyone in the world sufficient economic resources to live as autonomous, independent individuals.[25] Still, while conceding this much to the cosmopolitan, they nevertheless argue that this same principle of moral equality gives rise to additional redistributive obligations among those who routinely coerce each other through political institutions they share. Call this the coercion argument. If sound, it partly vindicates Rawls's instinct that global standards of economic justice ought to be sufficientarian, concerned only with individuals' absolute shares, while domestic ones ought to be concerned as well with relative shares.

Problems with the coercion argument

Ingenious as it is, however, the coercion argument faces several serious objections. First, insofar as it purports to establish that a concern for relative shares *cannot* be motivated beyond state borders, the argument is fallacious. For it does not follow from the claim that the terms of domestic association might trigger such a concern that there are no features of the international order that might do so with comparable or even greater urgency.

[24] Variants on this argument can be found in Miller (1998); Blake (2001); and Nagel (2005).
[25] Blake (2001).

Indeed, surely it is quite plausible to think, as cosmopolitans vigorously argue, that wealthy Western states and corporations often use their position of global economic and political advantage to coerce and exploit the globally disadvantaged. Clearly, showing that such exploitation justifies a concern for relative shares when it occurs within a state does nothing to falsify the claim that it also does so when it occurs between parties interacting across states. At best, the argument shows only that any exploitation or objectionable coercion that does occur across states will not be imposed on victims directly through legal institutions they share. But surely objectionable coercion and exploitation can often exist between agents who do not share citizenship in the same legal order. Why lower the burden of justification for nonlegal coercion that occurs under these conditions?[26] The coercion argument gives no answer.

Second, like Rawls's Difference Principle itself, the coercion argument remains vulnerable to a version of the sufficiency objection. Its proponents are prepared to assert that at the global level everyone has an entitlement to sufficient economic resources to permit autonomous functioning. But if the distinctively *economic* conditions for personal autonomy are already guaranteed by this global-sufficiency principle, it becomes unclear why additional monetary forms of redress like the Difference Principle are needed to forestall any efforts by better-situated groups to take political advantage of their less-privileged compatriots. Under the proposed global-sufficiency principle, everyone is guaranteed sufficient economic resources to live autonomously. If less-advantaged groups are still menaced with oppression and privations of freedom at the hands of their wealthier compatriots, the obvious solution is to fortify the political procedures guaranteeing them their basic liberties and rights. But increasing their relative share of the national wealth is hardly an appropriate response to this problem. For good Rawlsian reasons, buying citizens off with economic benefits seems poor compensation for any losses of personal freedom and political liberty to which they remain vulnerable.

Of course, guaranteeing citizens their basic liberties itself costs money, and presumably the financial burden of providing them will, and probably should, fall more heavily on better-advantaged groups at home and abroad.

---

[26] I am very grateful to Ryan Pevnick for many illuminating conversations about these matters.

But that is not the same as saying that a concern for relative shares of wealth enjoys a special significance within groups of citizens that it does not enjoy between them. Rather, it amounts simply to a global expectation that, regardless of where they live, citizens are entitled to a fully adequate bundle of basic liberties. Once again, this implies a global entitlement to an adequate threshold of a primary good, not the application of a principle sensitive to relative shares of such goods.

Finally, the argument assumes that the forms of legally sanctioned coercion that exist within states create a stronger burden of justification than those that hold the international order together. But why? That the international order *is* held together by legal coercion cannot be seriously disputed, as anyone who has been turned away at gunpoint by border guards well knows. Perhaps, as some proponents of the coercion argument maintain, the coercion involved in (say) immigration restrictions is different from that involved in the ongoing regulation and adjustment of property-holding by domestic legal institutions, and thus raises different issues.[27]

Remember, though, that all of these authors, including Rawls, require some organized redistribution across state borders. Rawls's "duty of assistance" is admittedly a rather modest redistributive requirement. But guaranteeing all persons in the world sufficient economic resources for personal autonomy, as entertained by some proponents of the coercion argument, could require very extensive redistribution. Presumably the funds for these transfers are to be gathered by coercive taxation across states, enforceable through international legal instruments. But if this amounts to the routine coercive regulation of property rights, the coercion argument turns out to have paradoxical consequences. For in calling for such coercive adjustments, it seems to require at the international level *exactly* those measures that it claims trigger a concern for relative economic position in the domestic context. But, if that is so, the argument plausibly undermines its own intended conclusion.

Conclusions

The position we have reached mirrors the current state of the debate about global justice. On the one hand, few would deny that the current

---

[27] Blake (2001), p. 280 n. 30.

distribution of wealth across the globe is seriously unjust. And, as we have just seen, it is difficult to find *principled* reasons for believing that criteria of international distributive justice differ from, or are less urgent than, those that apply to the assessment of domestic economic arrangements. A cosmopolitan perspective seems to be an inescapable implication of an impartial commitment to respect all individuals as equals.

On the other hand, the lack of principled grounds against cosmopolitanism does not mean that there are no valid *political* reasons to be cautious about global redistributive justice. We currently lack adequate institutional means to effect such redistribution and to guard against the possible abuses that such transnational economic authority might invite. While it may not be defensible on grounds of high principle, then, Rawls's position may still win on points.[28]

Here it is helpful to remember the predicament of individuals in the Hobbesian state of nature. As we noted in chapter 4, Hobbes was quite clear that rational individuals in a state of nature could see that the solution to their problems lies in agreeing mutually to lay down their rights to preserve themselves as they choose. Indeed, he derived an extensive further list of quite specific rules that ideally it would be rational for peace-seeking individuals to recognize and follow, including rules prohibiting the ridicule of others, requiring that every person acknowledge every other person as an "equal," and prescribing a willingness to be accommodating to others.[29]

So the problem confronting individuals in Hobbes's state of nature does not lie in their inability to perceive, even in some detail, the provisions of a workable and effective mutual peace treaty to put an end to their endemic conflicts. Rather, for Hobbes the difficulty is that, in order for such a treaty to come into effect, individuals would have to trust each other's word to abide by its terms. But Hobbes thought such trust must be absent in the state of nature. In his view, it can be cultivated only through the artifice of a sovereign state, deploying legal coercion to assure citizens that their fellows will make good on their undertakings. To put Hobbes's point in more contemporary terms, individuals in a state of nature have access to the

---

[28] Rawls's cosmopolitan critics concede that, in our nonideal world, the application of even an ideal cosmopolitan vision of redistributive justice may result in conclusions that tally with Rawls's. But this still leaves the outstanding question of why Rawls defended those modest conclusions as the correct account at the *ideal* level.

[29] Hobbes (1994), pp. 94–9; Hobbes (1998), pp. 47–57.

software of peace — they have access to an algorithmic list of rules the following of which will reliably result in peaceful cooperation. But they lack the *hardware* capable of actually running the programme. This, for Hobbes, can be provided only by the distinctive institutional powers of a sovereign state.

Something similar seems true of our current situation with regard to criteria of global distributive justice. Suppose we concede for the moment that Rawls has given us a reasonably compelling set of ideal criteria for economic justice. Even if we grant this, and moreover that these criteria are not *inherently* national or statist, it remains unclear that we possess the political hardware to actually run this programme at the planetary level. In contrast, we have such hardware ready to hand in our domestic political institutions, and it is not too difficult to see how these institutional resources might be adapted so as to run the Rawlsian software (assuming it to be sound). For the time being, then, criteria of distributive justice will continue to seem most salient within the domestic political arena.

Still, it is important to remember that this reflects contingent facts about available political resources, and about the limits of our current ability to imagine and defend with conviction the sort of planetary institutional hardware needed to apply them on a global scale. It does not amount to a principled objection to cosmopolitan distributive justice as such. There is therefore every reason to follow Hobbes's example and to seek, with as much ingenuity as we can muster, a compelling rational account of the global agencies that might enable us better to live up to our responsibilities to each other.

7   Authority

We saw in the previous chapter that Rawls's theory of justice presupposes the existence of a state, with the legal apparatus to implement and enforce just terms of social cooperation. In this respect, Rawls's theory differs from the older social-contract theories expounded by Hobbes and Locke. Whereas the latter deployed contractualist arguments to justify the state itself, Rawls takes the state for granted and deploys them instead to specify and defend criteria of social justice that should ideally guide, and be integrated into, its daily operation. But this seems to skip a step, for one might question whether the authority claimed by states is legitimate in the first place. Is it?

The challenge of authority

So far we have mainly focused on political *ideals* like justice and the common good, but inquiring into the legitimacy of political authority raises a different sort of question. Authority is not an ideal but an existing social practice, one that we confront rather directly on a daily basis, when courts order us to pay a fine, when police officers pull us over, or when tax authorities command us to cough up. Does the state really have a right to our compliance with these expectations, and, if so, how far does it extend and how much weight does it carry?

Reflection on these questions is most likely to be prompted by cases in which states order us to do something of which we disapprove, or which seems wrong. May states require citizens to risk their lives in military operations to which they conscientiously object? But in some ways the deeper puzzles about political authority emerge when we consider cases in which states make demands of us in the context of doing something that seems fairly clearly morally desirable. Suppose we agree that X would promote the common good, or is required by justice. Does it follow that states have the right to compel us to participate in schemes providing X, even when we accept that X is a good thing? For example, organizations like Oxfam, the Church of England, trade unions, etc., all perform uncontroversially valuable social functions, at least some of the time. But this does not mean that we acknowledge their right to force us to give them money, to attend church, or to provide assistance to striking workers. Why should it be any different in the case of the state?

Addressing these questions seems not to require freestanding speculation about the nature of the common good, about how best to promote human flourishing, or about how to realize ideals of economic fairness and distributive justice. It requires, rather, that we think about the actual claims made by states on their citizens and whether these claims can possibly be vindicated. We begin, then, by asking how much authority modern states claim, and of what sort it is.

The claims of states

Four important features of the authority claimed by modern states as we know them stand out. First, states claim special authority over their own citizens. To be sure, those temporarily resident within their borders are expected to obey and to refrain from subverting the laws. But beyond this, states do not demand of them the special allegiance they require of citizens. Apart from import duties, for example, visitors are normally exempt from general taxation, and are usually explicitly disqualified from requirements to serve in the armed forces, or to perform other public duties such as serving on juries. So we normally associate political authority with special obedience or loyalty to one's own state. Political authority, and the special obligations it imposes upon its subjects, are in this sense "particularized."

Second, states recognize no limitations on the *content* of the requirements they may impose on their citizens.[1] It is important to be clear here, since this Hobbesian suggestion that modern states always claim unlimited authority may seem to conflict with the practice of "limited government"

---

[1] Raz (1986), p. 76.

central to the public culture of liberal democracy. One thinks, for example, of the various constitutional checks in force in the United States preventing governments, both State and Federal, from infringing on certain basic legal rights like the right to free speech. But it is important to remember that these limits on the legal powers of particular branches of *government* are themselves authorized by constitutional law. The rights enshrined in the American Bill of Rights claim authority as part of the state's constitution, but not for any other reason. And, since (like most constitutions) the American one allows for its own amendment, it is in principle possible to imagine US law authoritatively repealing the Bill of Rights. So it is misleading to think of these limits on the powers of government as having some authority independent of the state; one cannot therefore cite them as evidence against the assertion that states claim unlimited authority.

Note, though, that this is not the same as saying that states are in any sense *omnipotent*. From the fact that states claim the authority to require obedience to laws with virtually any content it does not follow that states must always succeed in actually enforcing these expectations. For example, when laws strike citizens as deeply morally offensive, they may rebel, refuse to comply, and eventually thwart the state's intentions.[2] But even so, that would not falsify the state's claim to be acting within its authority, any more than the fact that speed limits on motorways and freeways are routinely ignored tells against the claim that the state has, and is generally recognized to have, the authority to impose them.

Third, and relatedly, the authority claimed by states is not equivalent to political power. In claiming authority, that is, states do not claim an infallible capacity to bring things about by threatening and coercing people. Indeed, as the earlier example of speed limits illustrates, states claim authority even when they lack the power to guarantee widespread compliance.

Authoritative directives purport to differ from exercises of naked coercion or power in that the mere utterance of an instruction by a recognized authority is supposed to be a sufficient reason for compliance apart from any threats or other forms of influence. To illustrate, a mugger exercises power over her victims but neither claims nor has any authority

[2] See Atiyah (1995), pp. 84ff.

over them. It is a mugger's threats, not her demands themselves, that supply her victims with a reason to comply. But, while police officers may eventually resort to the use of force (and, again unlike muggers, are authorized to do so), those who recognize their authority regard their instructions ("Pull over!", "Hands behind your back!") as already giving them a reason to comply. One should pull over, and put one's hands behind one's back, when instructed to do so by a police officer, simply because he is exercising his authority to direct your actions. Those who lack such authority can only give people reasons to pull over or to put their hands behind their backs by threatening them, manipulating them, or persuading them with arguments.

Finally, state authorities claim to supply "content independent" reasons for compliance. That is, not only do authoritative instructions command our obedience apart from any threats of force, they also do so apart from our own judgments about what should happen. For example, I may strongly believe that a court decided a legal case wrongly, and that it made a mistake in ruling for the plaintiff (perhaps I am the defendant). But insofar as the court claims authority over me in this matter, my own opinions become irrelevant to the question of how I am to act in this case: I am expected to pay damages regardless of my personal judgment on the merits. In other words, authoritative directives *preempt* our own judgments about how we should act.

This final feature of the practice of modern institutional authority creates a double puzzle, partly formal and partly substantive. The formal problem is this. If authorities give us reasons to do things, but those reasons are independent of any threats of force, and also distinct from the soundness of beliefs or arguments about what ought to happen, they seem to have the form, "Do X *just because* we say so." But what sort of reasons could these possibly be? When is someone's mere say-so ever *any* sort of a reason to do something?

The more substantive issue concerns freedom and autonomy. If compliance with authority involves allowing someone else to preempt my own sincerely held views about what ought to happen, it seems to require agents to surrender their own judgment. But this conflicts with our sense of ourselves as autonomous moral agents, entitled to act on our own judgments about what ought to happen rather than on judgments substituted by outsiders.

Political obligation

The claims made by states are thus both expansive and puzzling. Among philosophers, these puzzles have elicited two broad patterns of response. Some view them as an intellectual challenge, and have canvassed arguments and theories purporting to legitimate the authority claimed by actually existing states. Those who take this project seriously have established a small subfield within political philosophy devoted to inquiry into the "problem of political obligation."[3] As we shall see, these theorists of political obligation disagree about which arguments provide the most propitious basis for establishing the authority of states over their subjects. But they share the common assumption that an adequate theory of political obligation must succeed in vindicating the right of at least decent states to impose on their citizens obligations to provide support for a variety of familiar and conventionally uncontentious public goods and services (national defense, law and order, and social insurance).

The second response views the quest for a "theory of political obligation" as a vain endeavor: the very extensive claims to authority actually made by states on this view far outrun their possible legitimacy. Proponents of this view thus contend that citizens of modern states are often socialized into habits of obedience that are not actually warranted: in most cases citizens lack the political obligations that are conventionally assumed to exist.[4]

These self-described "philosophical anarchists," however, stop short of the more radical anarchist conclusion that states are not merely illegitimate but also irredeemably immoral institutions that must be actively subverted and eventually abolished. Philosophical anarchists are more circumspect. They often acknowledge, for example, a "natural duty" to support just political institutions, and they allow that, when and where such institutions actually exist, agents have good reasons, and may even stand under an obligation, to support them. But such concessions, insist philosophical anarchists, do not fully vindicate political obligations, nor do they come close to redeeming the claims made by actual states.

[3] Beran (1987); Gans (1992); Green (1990); Horton (1992); Klosko (1992); Klosko (2005).
[4] Simmons (1979); Simmons (2001); Wolff (1970).

For instance, a natural duty to support just institutions applies to just institutions *wherever we find them*, but clearly this cannot support the characteristic particularity of political obligations, the claim that citizens owe a special allegiance to their own states. It would also fail to justify the supposed "content-independence" of authoritative commands. Acknowledging a natural duty to support just institutions is quite compatible with the view – recommended by philosophical anarchists – that individuals ought to weigh the question of their obedience on a case-by-case basis. But part of the point of claiming authority to direct someone's actions is precisely to deny their right to weigh their options for themselves and act accordingly. As we have noted, this is what gives authority its preemptive quality. Appealing to a natural duty to support just institutions thus fails to explain this puzzling aspect of authority, and so seems insufficient as an account of political obligation.

Four theories

Philosophical anarchists have had little difficulty in exposing grave difficulties with all the main arguments favored by theorists of political obligation.[5] Apart from arguments based on duties to support just institutions, whose limitations we have already noted, discussion has centered on four main grounds for political obligation.

The first, which founds political obligations upon the consent of the governed, is at once the most natural and yet most obviously flawed option. It seems initially promising because personal consent is often a very simple way to establish that agents have certain obligations. Suppose, for example, there is dispute about whether I owe X a sum of money for a service he has rendered. Debate would be quickly ended if a valid written contract came to light establishing that I agreed to pay X the relevant amount for his services. But it is hard to believe that we can resolve questions about our purported *political* obligations in this way, for the simple reason that very few if any citizens have signaled their consent to political rule. And, as we noted early in chapter 4, the idea that

---

[5] For a fuller discussion see Simmons (1979).

we can infer citizens' "tacit" consent from their continued residence within a jurisdiction seems equally implausible.[6]

A second sort of argument, often dubbed "associative," appeals to the sort of communitarian or particularist arguments we encountered in the previous chapter.[7] Immersion within rich cultures, associative theorists suggest, both powerfully shapes members' sense of identity and characteristically socializes them into complex webs of obligation. Under these conditions of rich association, a commitment to meeting these communal obligations becomes inextricably bound up with fidelity to one's sense of self and maintaining the integrity of one's culture. The associative approach to political obligation attempts to legitimate claims to political authority by arguing that socialization within national political cultures automatically generates communal obligations of this sort. According to its proponents, citizens who shirk the political obligations conventionally recognized within their national culture can do so only by denying who they really are.

An attraction of associative arguments is that, if sound, they might explain the particularity of our purported political obligations. But despite this advantage, arguments along these lines nonetheless seem extremely unpromising. Even if we grant its premise, and accept that socialization into rich, culturally self-aware associations entails the acknowledgment of a web of obligation, it is very unclear, for reasons discussed in the previous chapter, that citizens of modern states share any such rich cultural matrix. For these same reasons, the argument is also hard to reconcile with the bureaucratic character of modern state authority. It may be plausible to claim that a lapsed Muslim who no longer prays five times a day in the direction of Mecca is somehow denying a core element of his identity. But it seems bizarre to say the same of someone who objects to having his car inspected annually, as required by the local department of transportation. (Perhaps he is a mechanic himself and is competent to make his own judgments about the roadworthiness of his car.)

The premise of this associative argument, too, is shaky. Our discussion of Pacifica and Atlantis in chapter 1 established that appeals to conventional moral beliefs, even widely accepted ones, raise the question of justification.

---

[6] Hume (1985).

[7] Dworkin (1986), pp. 186–215.

Pointing out that members of a political community recognize such-and-such as an obligation, a duty, a requirement of justice, or whatever, is the beginning, not the end, of the discussion. At best, such reports establish that certain expectations *purport* to be genuine obligations; but they cannot by themselves vindicate these claims. Simply asserting that agents socialized into particular associations already recognize a web of obligation similarly raises the crucial question of whether ultimately they *should* recognize and conform to its expectations.

A third argument appeals to debts of gratitude. States provide benefits (security, law and order, national defense, social insurance schemes, etc.). In return, we owe them obedience as a matter of gratitude. But this suggestion also seems hopeless. While receiving benefits may require some gesture of gratitude, it is quite unclear why submission to the authority of the state should be an appropriate gesture of gratitude for any benefits it confers upon us. You have me over for dinner, and no doubt this obligates me to write a thank-you note, and perhaps to reciprocate at some future date. But it seems very strange to predicate political obligation on such points of etiquette. And anyway, surely your kindness in this case does not give you the right to expect that I cook you dinner *upon demand*, though that seems more closely analogous to the sorts of rights actually claimed by political authorities.

A deeper problem with this proposal is that it assumes a wholly unrealistic picture of the relation between recipients and conferrers of public benefits. It is misleading to suppose that states start out with a bundle of "benefits" that they then, out of the kindness of their hearts, choose to confer benevolently upon their citizens. Apart from the questionable assumption that *institutions* can be said to have motives like generosity or benevolence, this view overlooks the crucial complication that the state has these benefits to confer only because of *prior* sacrifices it has imposed on citizens. The state would not be in a position to supply a system of law and order, national health care, and the rest, had it not already taxed its citizens to raise the necessary revenues. This suggests that the gratitude argument conceives the problem in an upside-down way. The question should not be why the state's largesse obligates me, but why it has the right to expect me to participate in its benefit-conferring projects in the first place. But far from resolving it, this simply reintroduces the original problem.

The fourth and certainly most promising argument turns on an appeal to fairness.[8] Suppose that everyone in some group accepts certain benefits from a cooperative arrangement, but that the provision of these benefits requires that participants in the scheme assume certain burdens. For example, everyone in our neighborhood freely uses the pleasant scenic lake around which it is built, but it will remain scenic and pleasant only if members of the community contribute to funds to cover the costs of keeping it clean and tidy. The Snidvong family frequently swims in the lake, but refuses to pay the maintenance fee that everyone else pays. This seems unfair: the Snidvongs are accepting a benefit but unfairly failing to do their part in maintaining it. Proponents of the fairness argument contend that our political obligations can be accounted for in this way. Having accepted the benefits of public association with their fellows (national defense, systems of law and order, democratic representation, welfare programs, etc.), citizens have obligations to assume a fair share of the burdens necessary to their provision.

But while it seems clear that obligations of fairness can arise in this way, doubts center on the question of whether citizens can normally be said to have "accepted" the benefits provided by the state.[9] It is not as if they usually have much choice in the matter. And it hardly seems fair simply to thrust benefits on people and then demand that they contribute their fair share of the costs. After all, this is not how things stand in the case of the Snidvongs, for they freely choose to take advantage of the lake and thus clearly accept benefits directly attributable to the sacrifices of their neighbors. But it is unclear that this is true with respect to publicly provided benefits.

Consider, for example, systems of democratic representation. These schemes (an electoral apparatus and the institutions of representative democracy) are quite expensive to provide and maintain, and so citizens of democratic societies are required to make significant contributions to covering their costs. Can we plausibly regard any obligations I have to make such contributions as analogous to those borne by the Snidvongs? Do citizens accept the "benefits" of representative democracy as do the

---

[8] See Hart (1967); Rawls (1964).

[9] For further discussion see Nozick (1974), pp. 90–5; Simmons (1979), ch. V.

Snidvongs those of the scenic lake? Presumably the relevant "benefit" is the opportunity to voice one's political preferences in elections. But suppose Snodgrass has no interest in voting. Perhaps he regards the democratic process as a corrupt farce and wants no part of it, or there are no political parties that represent his political opinions, or he believes that his vote is so unlikely to have any effect on the outcome that it is not worth the bother. Surely it is difficult here to maintain that Snodgrass has "accepted" the benefits of representative democracy, and correspondingly hard to believe that he has obligations of fairness to cooperate in its provision. Moreover, since many citizens choose not to participate in democratic elections, it cannot be argued that Snodgrass is in any sense strange or unusual. Nor does the Australian practice of requiring citizens to vote provide any solution. For in this case that would amount simply to thrusting an unwanted "benefit" on Snodgrass and then demanding payment for it. This seems a parody of fairness rather than its realization.

Unfortunately for the fairness argument, it is at least reasonable to think that the situation of citizens who receive public benefits from states more often resembles Snodgrass's predicament than that of the Snidvongs and their neighbors. Notwithstanding its relevance in other contexts, then, it is not clear that a principle of fairness gets us very far towards vindicating citizens' obligations to contribute to the provision of many familiar public benefits and services.[10]

Efforts to overcome these objections and resuscitate one or other of these grounds for political obligation will doubtless continue. But it is difficult not to agree with the philosophical anarchists that all face very serious obstacles.

A misguided debate?

On the strength of this result, philosophical anarchists draw the seemingly striking conclusion that the authority claimed by most existing states is illegitimate. But we need to keep such claims in perspective. This conclusion will seem newsworthy only if we take seriously the ambition, embraced by the theorists of political obligation, of vindicating (most of) the authority

---

[10] But see Klosko (1992) for the best recent defense of the fairness view.

claimed by actual states. ("A satisfactory theory should explain why citizens of existing societies ... have moral requirements to obey the laws of their societies."[11]) Philosophical anarchists are, in their own way, as committed to this ambition as their opponents, for they make their stand on this same turf. Their objections presuppose that theories of political obligation bear this burden of proof and claim to identify obstacles blocking efforts to meet it. Underlying the whole debate, then, is the implicit assumption that purported theories of political obligation fall short, and perhaps fail completely, to the extent that they cannot account for most of the authority actually claimed by at least decent states.

But there is something peculiar, indeed unattractive, about this underlying assumption about the *point* of inquiry into political obligation. It implies that it is somehow an important part of the political philosopher's brief to make good on the claims asserted by states. Some have seemed to say as much: "The aim of political philosophy is to discover the grounds on which the state claims to exercise authority over its members."[12] This statement could be read as suggesting that political philosophy is itself a failure to the extent that it fails to "discover" grounds that legitimate the authority claimed by the state. But why saddle political philosophy with this conservative aim? For example, why should it be, as one prominent theorist of political obligation has recently written, "clearly desirable to develop a theory of obligation consistent with the beliefs of liberal citizens"?[13] (Here, "liberal citizens" is code for people generally disposed to recognize and comply with authority in basically decent, nontyrannical regimes.) To my mind, it would be "clearly desirable" only if we *already* have some reason to think that the relevant beliefs and attitudes are themselves sound. But surely that is precisely what we need to know and cannot simply assume.

It is a mistake, then, to assess the adequacy of our theoretical conclusions about political authority against the presumed validity of widely accepted beliefs about political obligation, rejecting as a failure any that do not correspond to the conventional wisdom. We should instead embark on

[11] Klosko (1992), p. 5.
[12] Weldon (1947), p. 1.
[13] Klosko (2005), p. 13.

a more detached inquiry into the questions of what it might mean to say that authority is legitimate, and of when, exactly, authority may be legitimately or illegitimately exercised. If it turns out that the states' claims to legitimate authority are less extensive than they claim, this need not be a sign of failure; if, for example, we were able to pin down with precision when authority is legitimately and illegitimately exercised, this might be a sign of progress, even if our conclusions require that conventional assumptions be substantially revised.

Obviously these remarks are directed primarily against traditional theories of political obligation, but they also help us to perceive limitations in philosophical anarchism, notwithstanding the cogency of its critical arguments. Parasitic as it is on the conservative ambitions of theories of political obligation, philosophical anarchism tends to assume that, with the failure of the traditional arguments for political obligations, there is little further to be said than that the authority claimed by existing states is largely illegitimate. But in themselves such sweeping generalities are not terribly informative and this, I think, is why philosophical anarchism is a rather unsatisfying position. While leading philosophical anarchists announce the likely "illegitimacy" of state authority as a major finding, they have not generally found it necessary to provide much clarification of the concepts either of legitimacy or of authority. Nor, for that reason, have they devoted very much attention to specific questions about when, exactly, the authority of the state might be legitimate rather than illegitimate. For they assume (I think prematurely) that the failure of the traditional theories of political obligation settles these questions and obviates further inquiry.

This has also led them to ignore the question of why, how, and indeed whether the "legitimacy" of authority *matters*. John Simmons, the leading contemporary philosophical anarchist, insists that judgments about the legitimacy of states are independent of judgments about their justification in terms of the possible ideals (justice, the common good) they might realize.[14] His point is that even if a state (say) met ideal criteria of justice and so in this sense satisfied relevant canons of *justification*, it would still not follow that it has a legitimate claim to the obedience of its citizens.

---

[14] Simmons (2001), pp. 122–57.

After all, the fact that certain firms, corporations, churches and other organizations satisfy certain ideal desiderata of justice does not show that they have the right to force people to participate in their activities. Simmons admits the possibility that agents have some sort of "natural duty" to support just (or otherwise admirable) institutions in such cases. But, for reasons noted earlier, this is not by itself a sufficient warrant for a state's or an organization's claim to impose whatever obligations *it* chooses on citizens. It also cannot explain the special allegiance states claim from their own citizens, as opposed to agents generally.

These points are surely sound, but merely drawing this distinction does not establish how much weight judgments about legitimacy (as opposed to justification) ought to carry. Esthetic criteria for judging states are also independent of standards of justice, but it would be strange to complain about a state that was in all relevant respects ideally just, that it was nevertheless not particularly beautiful. One might reasonably respond, "So what? We were talking about a *state*, not a purported artwork." That is not to say that judgments about legitimacy are as plainly irrelevant to the assessment of political institutions as esthetic criteria. But it is to say that if legitimacy and justification in terms of ideals like justice *are* (as Simmons has it) separate "dimensions of institutional evaluation," we need to be given some account of their relative importance and salience. The significance of "legitimate authority" is not self-explanatory. It is not clear that either philosophical anarchists or their opponents have provided an adequate account of these matters, and it seems likely that this failure reflects the unpropitious terms on which they have chosen to conduct their debate.

A fresh start

We need, therefore, to approach the question from a fresh perspective, one that fixates less on the Arthurian quest for a theory of political obligation, and yields a more detached, discriminating account of authority and its possible legitimacy. The most promising gesture in this direction has been pioneered in recent years by Joseph Raz, and I conclude this chapter by outlining his proposal.[15]

---

[15] Raz (1986), chs. 2–4.

Raz's analysis starts from the assumption that, if it is to be properly understood, authority must be explained in relation to agents' "practical reasons," their reasons for acting in one way rather than another. Practical reasoning in this sense is a familiar phenomenon. The pouring rain supplies a reason to bring an umbrella, flashes of lightning a reason for golfers to seek shelter immediately, someone's supreme achievements a reason to praise them, and so on. As we noted in chapters 1 and 3, we normally assume that part of what it means to be a rational agent is to recognize and respond properly to reasons of this kind. In the sorts of cases just mentioned, acting rationally in this sense is a simple matter: there is little mystery about the irrationality of golfers who continue to swing their metal clubs about amidst a lightning storm. But since our reasons for action often conflict – I both have reasons to have a second helping (the cake is delicious) and reasons to refrain (I am trying to lose weight) – exactly what choices are rational or irrational is often more complex and controversial.

One such source of controversy, of course, is the claim that recognizing moral properties (something's being right, wrong, just, obligatory) provides agents with reasons for acting one way rather than another. Philosophers disagree about whether moral properties do provide such reasons, and, if they do, about how they do so, and about their weight relative to other reasons (prudence, self-interest). We touched on these matters earlier in this book (chapter 1) when we considered Plato's efforts to explain the rationality of recognizing and conforming to the requirements of some conception of justice. But authority presents its own special problems in this regard.

As we noted earlier, authorities purport to give agents reasons for acting in the ways they command, and also to *change* those reasons in a particular way. In itself, the capacity to give and change agents' reasons is unmysterious. It happens all the time: when I threaten you, advise you, provide you with incentives, make a compelling argument before you, I introduce new, or make you newly aware of hitherto unrecognized, reasons bearing on your decisions about what to do. But in none of these cases is the preemptive quality of authoritative directives present. In warning, threatening, or offering you incentives for acting in a certain way, I add new considerations for you to take into account in your decision-making. Nevertheless, the eventual decision is still in some sense yours, even if the warnings, threats, or incentives are so overwhelming as to make certain choices irresistible. Authorities, however, do not merely add new or overwhelming reasons to the list of factors for you to weigh up. They claim the right to preempt your judgments entirely. One's personal judgments are not merely *complicated* by authoritative directives, but in a puzzling way actually *excluded*. Authorities simply expect us to recognize their say-so as a reason for action, regardless of our own views about what it is appropriate for us to do.

This generates two questions. First, how can there be such reasons, and what is their characteristic structure? Second, under what conditions (if any) ought free and autonomous agents to recognize as legitimate an authority's right to preempt their own judgments? The limitations of traditional theories of political obligation and the views of their philosophical anarchist critics stem from their misguided effort to address the latter question without first providing an adequate answer to the first. Raz's analysis attempts to correct this lacuna.

Authority and practical reason

To develop Raz's proposal, it will be helpful to focus on an example. In most modern states, driving is intensively regulated by public authorities. Traffic lights, for example, are essentially robotic authorities, issuing authoritative instructions in the form of color-coded signals. Signposts announcing speed limits are similarly like frozen commands, endlessly repeating their instructions to all who pass them by.

But, apart from the reasons these instructions purport to give us for driving in particular ways and at particular speeds, a variety of familiar considerations would do so in any case. For example, we all have an interest in efficient mobility, and this provides reasons in favor of driving fast. The fact that driving is, for many, an inherently enjoyable, challenging, and potentially exhilarating activity also tends to provide agents with reasons for driving relatively fast. But driving is also dangerous, and its various risks (e.g. the possibility of mechanical failure, the presence of hazardous climatic and road conditions, and the possibility of collision with other vehicles) provide reasons for precautions of various sorts (insuring proper maintenance, driving more cautiously in bad weather or in heavy traffic). Driving also has unwelcome environmental effects – noise, pollution – and this gives agents reasons to drive and maintain their vehicles in ways that minimize such adverse effects. Whether or not they are regulated by traffic signals and other authoritative regulations, responsible drivers ought anyway to recognize and respond appropriately to these various familiar reasons.

According to Raz, the key to understanding the practice of authority is to understand properly the relation between the reasons for action that authorities purport to give their subjects and the more basic reasons that should already guide responsible agents' decisions about how to act. One side of this story is by now familiar: authority is preemptive. I may have my own views, based on my own judgment of the relevant considerations, about how fast it is safe to drive on a particular road, or how best to negotiate particular intersections, but a red light or a posted speed limit is supposed to render these personal judgments irrelevant. Even though the road is deserted, so that under other circumstances I would proceed across an intersection without stopping, authorities still expect me to obey the red light.

But, as Raz points out, preemption is only part of the story. For, in designing the highway code and programming the traffic signals in particular ways, it is not as if transport authorities are entirely indifferent to the considerations that responsible drivers would have to weigh up for themselves anyway. Speed limits are determined by judgments about safety and fuel economy (which relate to the considerations of efficient mobility we mentioned above); traffic signals are programmed to allow drivers to coordinate their movements at large intersections efficiently and safely; the same is true of rules requiring agents to take tests certifying their ability to drive safely or the roadworthiness of their cars. In all of this, the public authorities seem to be weighing up the very same set of considerations that ought to govern responsible drivers' decisions in any case.[16]

According to Raz, then, authorities do not merely claim the right to preempt our judgments. They also replace them with judgments based on the very same considerations that should guide agents' practical reasoning anyway. This feature is particularly clear in the case of traffic regulation. But it seems characteristic of practices of authority more

---

[16] Raz calls this the "dependence thesis." See Raz (1986), pp. 42–53.

generally and, for Raz, serves to demarcate them from other modes of control or influence.

For example, both muggers and authorities attempt to control others' conduct by altering their reasons for acting in particular ways, but we can now see more sharply exactly where these modes of influence differ. Earlier we noted that muggers manipulate our decisions by introducing overwhelming coercive threats, while authorities claim to supply reasons for action that cannot be reduced to such threats. But we can now see another difference: muggers take a strikingly different view of their victims than do authorities of their subjects, at least if Raz's account is on target. For muggers do not usually care about the considerations that bear upon their victims' efforts to live responsibly, that is, to respond properly to the various reasons, prudential, moral, and affective, that ought to guide their daily decisions about how to behave. The mugger simply wants to manipulate her victims into compliance with her plans. Authorities have plans, too, and their instructions declare wishes ("We want you to drive no faster than 70 miles an hour"). But if Raz's analysis is correct, those wishes are typically linked to, and reflect a concern for, the considerations that already bear upon subjects' rational choices in a way that is rarely if ever true of the wishes of a mugger. When this is not the case, we will be reluctant to count the relevant agent as having, or claiming, any sort of authority.[17]

It is important to stress that so far nothing has been said about how to assess the legitimacy of authority. To this point, we have been concerned only to draw attention to the characteristic structure of the reasons for action given by authorities and of their relation to other reasons bearing on agents' choices. The analysis enables us to perceive more clearly exactly how authorities characteristically operate and how their claim to intervene in agents' practical choices is structured. Whether (and when) these claims are legitimate is an independent question, and we shall shortly explore Raz's suggested way of answering it.

---

[17] Of course, that is not to deny that, like muggers, states often manipulate agents' conduct by exercising power. States do not *only* claim authority; they also wield power. But it is important to distinguish those cases in which a state exercises naked force from those in which it acts as an authority.

Before we do so, however, another important clarification deserves stress. According to Raz, authorities replace our reasons for *acting* one way rather than another. But this does not entail that subjects must renounce personal *beliefs* about how the authority ought to have decided the matter. We are merely asked to comply, to let the authority's command determine our action. But we are still free to *believe* that it is safe (say) to exceed the posted speed limit on a particular road. Authorities merely expect us to conform our actions to their wishes; but they need not also expect that we change our beliefs about the correctness of their directives. This is a crucial point, because it captures something important about our characteristic relation to authorities, and qualifies the sense in which submission to authority problematically involves a "surrender of judgment," at least to some extent.

For, on the one hand, we often find ourselves in a position of disagreeing, morally or otherwise, with a particular authoritative directive, yet at the same time recognizing an obligation to comply nonetheless. Raz's account helps us to understand exactly how this is possible and what is going on in such familiar situations. And on the other hand, these considerations make submission to authority seem less sinister and totalitarian than it might at first appear. It is true that such submission involves allowing alien judgments to dictate some of our actions; but this need not entail that our very capacity for autonomous judgment on the merits must merge completely with that of institutional authority. Within the areas in which they have jurisdiction, authorities claim the right to sever the link between our judgments and our actions. But they do not thereby eliminate the very possibility of autonomous judgment on the part of their subjects, nor need they pretend that their subjects will always personally agree with their decisions and directives.

Legitimate authority

Raz proposes that we assess the legitimacy of authority by means of a test that he calls the "Normal Justification Thesis": authorities are legitimate insofar as agents who submit to them more successfully conform their actions to the reasons that apply to them than they would if they did not follow their directives.[18] So, in the case of traffic regulation, we are

[18] Raz (1986), pp. 53–7.

to ask whether drivers are more likely to drive in the ways rationally required by considerations of efficiency, safety, etc., if they submit to the direction of traffic lights, speed limits, and so forth, than if they each weighed these considerations up for themselves. Imagine a complex, busy, intersection: would drivers' efforts to drive with due concern for efficient mobility and those of safety likely be enhanced or hindered by a system of traffic lights? It is difficult to believe that they could do better without the aid of traffic lights, a conclusion that might be quickly confirmed by observing what happens at busy intersections when the electricity powering the traffic lights cuts off. In this case, then, it seems likely that submission to authority meets Raz's normal justification criterion.

Raz distinguishes five general ways to satisfy the Normal Justification Thesis. I quote his words:

1) The authority is wiser and therefore better able to establish how the individual should act.

2) It has a steadier will less likely to be tainted by bias, weakness or impetuosity, less likely to be diverted from right reason by temptations or pressures.

3) Direct individual action in an attempt to follow right reason is likely to be self-defeating. Individuals should follow an indirect strategy, guiding their action by one standard ... [an authority's instructions] ... in order better to conform to another.

4) Deciding for oneself what to do causes anxiety [or] exhaustion, or involves costs in time or resources the avoidance of which by following authority does not have significant drawbacks ...

5) The authority is in a better position to achieve (if its legitimacy is acknowledged) what the individual has reason to but is in no position to achieve.[19]

The requirements of social coordination are prominent on this list and their importance in Raz's account deserves stress. In chapter 4, we discussed cases in which agents recognize a responsibility to cooperate in promoting some desirable outcome (we focused on relieving global poverty), but face problems in coordinating their collective efforts towards

[19] Raz (1986), p. 75.

such ends. These cases lend themselves to analysis in terms of Raz's theory of authority. The severe needs of the globally deprived supply the affluent with reasons to provide assistance. But the affluent may be in a stronger position to respond properly to those reasons when they submit to authoritative rules to coordinate their efforts. Raz's account implies that insofar as submission to such rules enables a more effective and appropriate response than would be possible through spontaneous and uncoordinated action, we ought to regard it as submission to a legitimate authority.

Conclusion

One obvious problem with Raz's test of legitimacy is that it requires agents to compare the likely results of their submission to an authority with some alternative situation. But this immediately invites the question: *Compared to what?* For example, if the alternative is a Hobbesian state of nature, then it turns out that almost any state capable of maintaining basic social order, regardless of any other shortcomings, wields legitimate authority. But if the relevant comparison is with *any imaginable* alternative, it may be very difficult to show that existing schemes of authority are ever legitimate. Whenever we can imagine a scheme that would coordinate agents' responses to sound reasons more effectively than is now the case, we shall be tempted to conclude that the current arrangement is illegitimate. This may lead us to worry that Raz's test of legitimacy is indeterminate.

This point raises a serious issue, but there are at least some reasons to suppose that it exposes a strength rather than a weakness of Raz's account. Our earlier criticisms of traditional theories of political obligation led us to doubt that when we inquire into the legitimacy of a state's authority we are asking a simple question to which we should expect a simple yes-or-no answer. Notwithstanding its critical power, philosophical anarchism seemed thin and ultimately uninformative precisely because it expects and settles for one of these answers, in this case a flat "No." But why should authority not be "legitimate to various degrees regarding different people"? As Raz points out, "We are used to thinking in such terms concerning tourists and temporary residents." Why not apply "the same reasoning to all"?[20]

With this in mind, the Normal Justification Thesis seems attractive precisely because it allows a more flexible and discriminating approach to the various questions we might raise about the legitimacy of authority. We can, for example, isolate particular areas of public regulation and use Raz's test to answer carefully formulated questions about the legitimacy of authority in these specific contexts. This is what we did when we discussed the regulation of complex and busy intersections by traffic signals. We did not encounter any significant problems of indeterminacy there. Of course, reaching a conclusion about the legitimacy of traffic rules does not permit a general verdict on the legitimacy of all the forms of authority claimed by modern states. But again this is a problem only if we assume that it is possible or desirable to reach a simple guilty/ not guilty verdict across the board. Once we abandon that assumption as unrealistic, Raz's more piecemeal alternative promises more discriminating answers to questions about when particular authorities are legitimate and when not, for whom, under what conditions, and over which areas of conduct.

It may also lead us to understand better what sort of value legitimacy might be, an issue that we criticized philosophical anarchists for failing to clarify. We noted at the start of the chapter that legitimate authority seems not to be a political ideal of the same order as justice or the common good. That is presumably why it makes sense to take pride in fighting or sacrificing oneself for the realization of social justice, but eccentric to view oneself as a *crusader for legitimacy*. In the light of Raz's analysis, it seems better to say that political legitimacy is not an independent political or social ideal, but a possible virtue of the relation between rulers and ruled.

On Raz's account, this virtue is displayed to the extent that authorities assist agents in their efforts to live rationally and responsibly, in accordance with the reasons that ought to guide their actions. These reasons may sometimes be derived from considerations of justice or from other moral ideals, but they may also reflect reasons grounded in prudence or

---

[20] Raz (1986), p. 104.

self-interest (think about the way in which judgments about safety were in play in our discussion of driving, for example). The practice of authority therefore ranges widely across the full gamut of possible reasons for action, and is not exclusively concerned with those deriving from justice and other ethical or social ideals. To this extent, Raz's argument vindicates the philosophical anarchists' claim that judgments about political legitimacy and about the justification of political institutions in terms of moral ideals are distinct.

On the other hand, ideals of justice plausibly form a major source of reasons for political action of various sorts. Moreover, as our discussions in previous chapters have emphasized, principles of justice seem often to require or protect just those forms of social coordination that are integral to the practice of political authority. For these reasons, it will often be impossible to dissociate our concrete judgments about the legitimacy of particular institutional authorities from judgments about how they might ideally realize justice. So while justice and legitimacy are analytically distinct values, in many if not most concrete political contexts they must also surely be inextricably linked.

8   Liberty

We have already felt the force of claims about liberty and freedom (terms I will use interchangeably) at various points in our discussion so far. In chapter 4, we saw how Rousseauan and Rawlsian contractualists seek to justify political arrangements by asking whether agents motivated to maintain their autonomy would freely accept them under appropriate conditions. The possible impact of various forms of economic regulation on personal freedom was a persistent theme in chapters 5 and 6, and in the previous chapter we worried about the compatibility of freedom and authority. But these issues have come up occasionally and unsystematically, much as they do in ordinary political debate. Can we move beyond these rather informal claims about freedom and develop more precise and systematic accounts of the various different forms of human liberty and of their political implications?

For good or ill, recent philosophical efforts in this direction have been profoundly shaped by Isaiah Berlin's seminal essay *Two Concepts of Liberty*, originally his inaugural lecture as Chichele Professor of Social and Political Theory at the University of Oxford.[1] When Berlin delivered it in 1958, the world was divided into two ideologically opposed blocs — the liberal democratic West and the communist East (from which Berlin himself was an émigré). His lecture was an effort to understand how, despite their bitter enmity, both sides of this Cold War division could nonetheless claim to be crusading for liberty.

Berlin's explanation hinged on a distinction between two rather different understandings of political liberty that emerged from the European Enlightenment. The first, a "negative" concept of liberty, to be found predominantly in English writers (e.g. Hobbes, Bentham, and Mill),

---

[1] Berlin (1969).

takes freedom to be a function of the degree to which agents are inter-fered with, or obstructed. The second, a "positive" concept of liberty, to be found especially in the writings of Rousseau, Kant, and Hegel, interprets freedom in contrasting terms, as a matter of autonomy and self-determination. This distinction, or variants on it, had been long recognized before Berlin's essay. Berlin's particular contribution was to chart the diverging historical careers of these two concepts over the course of the nineteenth and early twentieth centuries, and to explain how they eventually came to be at loggerheads, with the positive concept evolving into a rationale for very illiberal forms of totalitarianism, and the negative concept underwriting the more benign institutions of liberal democracy.

Berlin's readers have generally been more interested in the theoretical distinction between the two concepts of liberty than in his historical argu-ment about the evolution of two traditions of thinking about freedom. And perhaps because Berlin intended his lecture primarily as an essay in intellectual history, he left the underlying distinction itself tantalizingly vague. As a result, Berlin's typology has generated an extraordinarily extensive critical discussion among commentators who take a variety of competing views: some believe they hold the key to understanding the distinction; others deny that there is such a distinction and claim that there really is only one basic concept of liberty; some claim that Berlin's way of drawing the distinction is too crude and needs to be replaced with more discriminating ones; still others accept the distinction but maintain that there are other concepts of liberty that it cannot capture.

The resulting debate has become bewilderingly complex and is, I believe, rife with confusion. Whether it has shed much light on the issues is arguable. My aim in this chapter is simply to guide readers through this thicket and ward off some common confusions. My hope is that they can emerge better placed to appreciate the various substantive issues raised by efforts to promote ideals of a free society.

Positive and negative freedom

Whatever infelicities plague his discussion, and whether or not it captures exactly what Berlin intended to convey, there really is a basic conceptual divide between "negative" and "positive" ways of thinking about freedom.

Unfortunately, as we shall see, this division is easily obscured by careless thinking, so it requires a certain effort to keep it clearly in view. The basic distinction, I submit, is this:

Negative liberty: On a negative construal, freedom consists fundamentally in the *absence* of something else — forms of constraint, interference, and impediments to possible action. I am therefore free, under this analysis, to the extent that opportunities for action are available rather than foreclosed by constraints and obstacles. For example, the liberty of a man manacled to a wall in a secure prison cell is in this sense severely curtailed. In contrast, whether or not they choose to leave, persons not prevented from leaving a similar-sized room enjoy greater freedom. The point is that this option remains *available* to them insofar as certain obstacles (locked doors, chains, handcuffs, gags) are absent.

Positive liberty: On a positive construal, freedom consists fundamentally in the *presence* of something quite specific — namely a certain sort of self-direction, independence, or autonomy. Agents who are brainwashed, enslaved, under the sway of addiction or overwhelming emotional impulse, or subject to manipulation lack freedom in this sense. They are not masters of themselves: their actions are dictated by some alien force, that is, something, whether inside or outside, that is not *them*. When, in the previous chapter, we worried about reconciling the practice of authority with the freedom of its subjects, it was liberty in this positive sense that was at issue. The relevant threat to individual freedom is difficult to analyze in terms of negative liberty. The worry was not that authorities may use their power to limit our options and thus reduce our negative liberty to an unacceptable degree, although that, of course, is a serious concern in its own right. The worry rather concerned the way in which authorities preempt our own judgments about how we are to act, and thereby impose upon us the direction of alien rule. This suggestion that someone other than ourselves has a right to determine our actions raises a question about positive, not negative, liberty, at least as I propose to construe the distinction.

An ideological distinction?

The first important point to make about this distinction is that there is no immediate reason to suppose that these two concepts of liberty are

politically partisan or necessarily affiliated with rival ideological traditions such as liberalism, socialism, or totalitarianism. They simply pick
out two differing senses in which we might say of persons that they are
(relatively) free or unfree. No important political questions are obviously
settled by accepting the distinction or by opting for one of the two concepts over the other. Nor are we necessarily forced to choose between
them. Indeed, as the remarks about authority above suggest, we probably
need to recognize both in order to do justice to the full range of ways
in which freedom may matter in political contexts.

This point runs against the grain of conventional wisdom, which often
assumes that these two concepts are ideological rivals or are otherwise
mutually opposed, so that we must at some point declare our allegiance
to one rather than the other. Berlin's original discussion has caused
confusion on this point because his historical story about the respective
development of liberal democratic and totalitarian understandings of
freedom tempted his more careless readers to suppose that he thought
the two concepts, and the political theories they imply, must always be
at theoretical loggerheads. Thus many interpret Berlin as arguing that
negative liberty is essentially a "liberal" concept of freedom and positive
liberty is essentially a "nonliberal" and perhaps "totalitarian" one. But
this interpretation strikes me as too simple, and may seriously misrepresent
both Berlin's own view and the nuances of our ways of thinking and
talking about political freedom.

True, Berlin did speak of his distinction as picking out "two profoundly
divergent and irreconcilable attitudes to the ends of life."[2] And he certainly
did argue that, as a matter of historical record, the positive concept
of liberty has proven more open to political abuse by the harbingers of
modern totalitarianism. Undeniably also, Berlin saw this abuse as originating in a conceptual feature of positive liberty, its association of liberty
with the presence of control, self-determination, and self-discipline.[3] Berlin
suggested that this allowed the protagonists of positive freedom to confuse
liberty with the exercise of political control, and to indulge Rousseau's
notorious dictum that citizens must sometimes be "forced to be free."

[2] Berlin (1969), p. 166.
[3] Berlin (1969), pp. 132–4.

As these ideas were recruited to various collective liberation movements (especially nationalist self-determination, democratic self-government) during the nineteenth century, the cause of positive liberty paradoxically evolved into a source of oppression, or so Berlin argued. The leaders of the relevant groups began to regard the exertion of certain forms of collective control and discipline as integral to the realization of the (positive) freedom of groups, nations, associations, majorities, etc. And again, as a matter of history, Berlin argued that those who construed political liberty primarily in negative terms had proved themselves less prone to any of these proto-totalitarian impulses. Indeed, as Berlin also documented, they often spoke out against them.

But despite all this, I find no suggestion in Berlin's essay that the evolution of theories of positive liberty into doctrines purporting to justify oppressive collective control and discipline was inevitable or necessary. This was, for Berlin, a contingent historical development, and he was careful to acknowledge that many political philosophers − notably Kant − deployed positive concepts of liberty in ways that need not lead to, and indeed would preclude, the confusion of liberty with oppressive collective control.[4] He also noted that concepts of negative liberty are in principle open to dangerous misinterpretation. Finally, he explicitly insisted that "it is often necessary to strike a compromise between" the two concepts because they both represent "ultimate values" with "an equal right to be classed among the deepest interests of mankind."[5]

This more subtle and flexible understanding strikes me as closer to Berlin's actual views. But whatever Berlin himself meant to say, this seems to me the correct position to adopt in any case. We should not assume at the outset that negative and positive liberty necessarily represent politically antagonistic camps or affiliate respectively with liberal and nonliberal worldviews.

Two families of ideas

This leads us to a second important clarification of the distinction. If these two senses of freedom are "concepts," they are concepts of a very

---

[4] Berlin (1969), pp. 136−9.
[5] Berlin (1969), p. 166.

open-ended kind, in each case susceptible of a very wide range of possible political interpretations. Any connotations of definiteness evoked by the word "concept" would here be quite misleading. It is better to think of these two senses of freedom as picking out two broad ways of thinking about freedom, each of which may be developed in quite different ways for a variety of political purposes despite an underlying family resemblance.

For example, when we think of political freedom in terms of negative liberty, we immediately face a number of interpretative questions. These surface because the sorts of obstacles that might limit agents' possible actions are many and varied: some obstacles make actions strictly impossible, while others make them merely more difficult; some obstacles are the result of intentional action by other agents, while others are not; some obstacles may be more readily removed by public action, while others may be more recalcitrant; some obstacles may be completely external to the agent, while others may be partly or fully internal to the agent. (Does agoraphobia — the fear of open spaces — reduce an agent's negative liberty? Not clear.) They may or may not interfere in activities to which agents do, or should, attach importance; some obstacles result from the activities of private citizens, while some are imposed by the state; and it may or may not be possible to remove some obstacles without imposing new and perhaps greater constraints on others.

People may disagree about which of these various kinds of impediments to freedom of action are of more urgent political significance and about whether they necessarily limit political liberty at all.[6] They may also disagree about what general goals ought to guide us in seeking an appropriate division of liberty so understood. Thus some might argue that the goal ought to be the overall "maximization" of negative liberty. Others might argue that the state ought to be responsible only for guaranteeing to all individuals certain basic personal liberties, regardless of whether this would maximize overall negative freedom, whatever that might mean.

On all of these points, then, there is plenty of room for argument within a general framework of negative liberty. So, by the time we have settled — like Rawls — on an enumerated list of basic liberties that states are responsible for securing, we will presumably have gone far down the

---

[6] Carter (1999) is the best recent effort to grapple with these complexities.

road of facing and resolving some of these issues. Rawls's list of basic liberties and opportunities fits very well with the notion of negative liberty, for it is natural to think of these liberties in terms of the state's responsibility to prevent specific forms of interference in individuals' possible choices and activities. The list effectively defines a range of protected activities – voicing opinions, participating in religious practices, forming associations of the like-minded, and participating in democratic politics – that are in specified ways not to be interfered with either by the state itself or by other citizens. Whether or not citizens actually make use of these opportunities, the state is to insure that they remain available. But again, Rawls's account is but *one* view of which negative liberties are of most urgent political significance. Others, also concerned about an appropriate division of negative liberty, may disagree with Rawls's judgments about which freedoms are most fundamental.

To illustrate, we noted in earlier chapters that libertarians think that the freedom to own property is more fundamental than those liberties Rawls recognized. In their view, the state has overriding responsibilities to refrain from interfering with, and to prevent others from interfering with, the activities of holding, inheriting, enjoying, buying, selling, and investing personal property. But quite apart from Rawls's alternative view, there are good reasons to question this libertarian claim even while maintaining a focus on negative liberty. It is important to remember, for example, that the enforcement of property rights has implications for the negative liberty, not only of property-owners, but also of nonowners. Thus in the United Kingdom the rights of landowners are qualified by legal duties to maintain an extensive network of public rights of way (footpaths, bridleways), along which citizens are free to walk. Farmers who erect fences and other enclosures on their land are expected to maintain stiles and gates to allow members of the public to travel along these rights of way unhindered. These paths total over 117,000 miles in length (almost half the distance to the moon), and so they afford citizens a great deal of freedom to move about the countryside on foot.

In the United States, by contrast, there is no such extensive system of public rights of way, and typically landowners have few legal duties to permit members of the public to cross their land. In the absence of systematic provision of public rights of way, the fences and barriers that private owners erect to deter trespassers significantly limit citizens' freedom of movement. Hiking is thus usually possible and worthwhile only on publicly owned reservations like state forests and national parks. While in the United Kingdom one can almost always devise a cross-country route between any two towns without having to walk along regular roads, this option is rarely available in the United States. If one tries it, one is apt to be sued, threatened at gunpoint, snared on barbed wire, or simply defeated by walls, gates, security fences, and the other barriers property-owners put up to keep the rest of us out.

Clearly, then, the enforcement of private-property rights can restrict as well as expand agents' negative liberty. So we cannot simply presume that a concern for negative liberty naturally favors the cause of private property, as libertarians often contend. Of course, this hardly establishes that the libertarian conclusion about the primacy of property-based freedoms is wrong. But it does mean that we cannot decide these questions about the relative importance of the different negative freedoms individuals might enjoy just by appealing to the concept of negative liberty itself. Which particular scheme of negative liberties makes the best political sense must be determined by independent considerations (e.g. whether they promote justice, equality, personal well-being, order, efficiency, security, and so on). The concept of negative liberty is thus not politically self-interpreting: the exact political ramifications of a concern for negative freedom will differ depending on the other considerations we think bear upon its application to public life.

The modalities of positive freedom

The same is true of the positive concept of liberty. The question of what, exactly, must be *present* in order for an agent to be deemed "positively (un)free" raises as many complex questions as does that of what counts as an obstacle to one's negative freedom.

Some of these questions shade into the vexed matter of the compatibility of free will and causal determination. Many, like Kant, have worried that our ordinary notions of moral responsibility, of praise and blame, are threatened by the thesis of universal causal determinism. If human actions are no less causally determined than the behavior of thunderstorms and computers, it is unclear that it makes any more sense to praise and blame them for their actions than it does to praise a tornado for missing our home, or to blame a computer for losing our data as a result of a bug in its system. Driven by this anxiety, Kant's entire ethical theory is essentially a morality of positive freedom. It seeks to cultivate a conception of human beings as autonomous, self-determining agents, fully responsible for their own choices. That is why a stringent prohibition on coercion and personal manipulation lies at the heart of Kant's political ethics.[7] For Kant and his many followers, when we manipulate, coerce, and exploit others merely as "means" to our own ends, we treat them as if they were little more than objects to be shoved about and bent to our will. In treating others in this way, we fail to respect their own capacity for self-direction and threaten an aspect of their (positive) freedom.

As I have suggested, Kant himself was much concerned with the metaphysical implications of this doctrine, and in particular with the question of the compatibility of this positive notion of freedom as self-direction or autonomy with the thesis of determinism, which he also accepted. The question here is how *self*-determination is even possible, given our difficulties seeing anything but causes and effects in the world we observe, a world that also includes us. The more we explain our behavior in terms of heteronomous causes and effects, whether they be genetic, chemical, electrical, cellular, or neuronal, the more our conventional notions of autonomous agency seem to slip out of view. (It is worth noting here that negative liberty raises few such metaphysical difficulties. As Hobbes noted, even inanimate objects can be more or less negatively free: he gave the comparison of a body of water that is constrained to flow down a channel and water that is by contrast free to "spread" unhindered "into a larger space."[8])

One set of issues raised by notions of positive freedom, then, concerns their metaphysical preconditions. As with the questions we encountered in connection with the classification of relevant "obstacles" to negative liberty, people may disagree about whether these metaphysical complications must be explained in order for the concept of positive liberty to make sense. And those who think that this is necessary may well disagree among themselves about the correct explanation. But still others will

---

[7] Kant (1993), pp. 35–45.
[8] Hobbes (1994), p. 136.

think that the metaphysical aspects of the doctrine of positive freedom are of less interest and significance. They will agree with Kant that respecting agents' autonomy is of fundamental importance, but suspect that the really crucial conditions for autonomy are social, political, and psychological, rather than metaphysical.

For example, a condition of slavery — hardly a metaphysical state — surely precludes the relevant sort of self-determination. Slaves lack the right to control their actions: their bodies, energies, and personal assets are at the disposal of their masters. They are, by definition, not masters of themselves and so not in any plausible sense positively free. It is uncontroversial, then, that the abolition of slavery is a necessary condition for securing the positive liberty of all members of society.

But few would want to claim that the abolition of slavery is a *sufficient* condition for all possible forms of self-determination or autonomy. What exactly it means to be an autonomous person is a complex question. Depending on how one conceives autonomy, ideals of personal self-determination may be more or less demanding. At their most demanding, ideals of autonomy become equivalent to perfectionist doctrines of self-realization. Some theorists of positive liberty have openly embraced just this conclusion. T. H. Green, for example, argued that "real freedom consists in the whole man having found his object" or to "have realized his ideal of himself."[9] One of Berlin's major concerns about positive liberty was that, when it is equated with perfectionist ideals in this fashion, it can become (and historically has sometimes become) an excuse for oppressive forms of paternalism. When this happens, considerations of positive and negative liberty are likely to come into conflict.

But it is important to acknowledge that these strongly perfectionist accounts of positive liberty represent only one possible species of the genus. Other theorists of positive liberty may favor more relaxed accounts of autonomy that do not invite Berlin's criticism. Perhaps to be accounted positively free it is enough simply to have a psychological constitution in which certain impulses, addictions, neuroses, or delusions play little or no role. Or, moving from the psychological to the social arena, perhaps it is enough that agents are not systematically subject to certain easily preventable forms of coercion and manipulation by others.

[9] Quoted in Skinner (2001), pp. 240–1.

And even those who interpret positive liberty in a more demanding perfectionist fashion need not hold the state responsible for realizing the relevant ideals directly. To take just one example, Mill favored a perfectionist ideal of autonomous self-development, what he called simply "individuality."[10] Admittedly, Mill did not generally use the terms "freedom" or "liberty" to describe this ideal of self-fashioning autonomy. He preferred to restrict those terms exclusively to claims about negative liberty. Whatever his own nomenclature, however, nothing stops *us* from viewing his ideal of an autonomous life as a conception of positive liberty. It surely is, and a rich and ambitious one at that. But as we noted in chapters 2 and 3, Mill expressly rejected the idea that the state ought to promote this ideal of positive liberty paternalistically. Such efforts, he thought, would invariably be self-defeating. In his view, individuals are more likely to realize the ideal of autonomous self-development if they enjoy a high degree of (negative) freedom to pursue their own good in their own way unhindered by paternalistic interference.

There is no automatic inference, then, from the claim that X is a condition for agents' positive liberty to the claim that the state should be responsible for guaranteeing X. Indeed, as Mill's argument illustrates, it may turn out that rights to noninterference (enumerated negative liberties of the sort protected by Rawls's first principle of justice) are justified for the sake of ideals of positive liberty. Here, then, is a political argument in which conceptions of both positive and negative liberty play complementary, rather than antagonistic, roles.

So, as with the negative concept of liberty, there is no single, canonical theory of positive liberty and its political implications. Rather, there several variants on the general theme, each of which raises different issues and will seem more or less plausible depending on the larger political goals we have in mind.

Degrees of freedom and free persons

Sometimes we speak of freedom as if agents can be more and less free, and at other times we talk as if there is a categorical distinction between

---

[10] Mill (1972), pp. 124ff.

being free and being unfree. A third important clarification of the distinction between positive and negative liberty, still not sufficiently appreciated, is that it is not neutral between these two ordinary language usages.

While the notion of a categorical partition between freedom and unfreedom fits naturally with the concept of positive freedom, it is much harder to accommodate within a framework of negative liberty. This is because negative freedom is an inherently scalar property, admitting of degrees. Agents are more or less (negatively) free depending on the configuration, number, and surmountability of the obstacles they face. It is hard to imagine human activity occurring without any obstacles at all, or conscious life in which literally *no* opportunities for action are left open. So as long as we are talking about the (negative) freedom of human agents, we are unlikely ever to be wholly without some measure of negative liberty or negatively free *simpliciter*.

Of course, once we have, like Rawls, enumerated a list of basic liberties and opportunities that states are responsible for guaranteeing to their citizens, we can speak of categorical violations of individuals' rights not to be interfered with in the specified ways. Thus, on a Rawlsian view, a state that prevents citizens from publishing material critical of the government violates their right to express their political opinions unhindered. Clearly, such violations are not a matter of degree. One's right to speak unimpeded is not more or less violated: either it is violated or it is not. But here it is the presence of rules defining *entitlements* or *rights* to specific forms of noninterference, not the concept of negative liberty by itself, that allows us to talk this way. And anyway, such violations, indefensible though they may be, do not necessarily render anyone absolutely "unfree" in a negative sense. Certainly, my options may be drastically reduced if the state carts me off to prison for my political opinions. But even shackled to the walls of my cell I may not be prevented (say) from rattling my chains or swearing at my captors. Insofar as these options remain available, I still enjoy a measure of negative freedom, albeit trivial, pointless, and far less than anyone would normally desire.

For these reasons, I think it is misleading to speak, as many philosophers (including Berlin) have done, of *violations* of negative liberty *per se*. Negative liberty may be reduced, curtailed, and sometimes expanded, but strictly speaking it cannot itself be violated or infringed (insofar as the word "infringement" implies a categorical breach rather than a diminution).

Those who speak of violations or of categorical "infringements" of negative liberty, then, are either confused or using a shorthand for claims about enumerated rights and entitlements. We can be negatively free only to greater or lesser degrees. We are never simply negatively free rather than unfree.

Contrast this now with positive concepts of liberty. We have seen that theorists of positive liberty can and do disagree over what exactly must be present for an agent to be genuinely autonomous or self-determining. But, on any of these positive accounts, freedom becomes a *condition* under which pertinent criteria are satisfied. If agents are to be judged positively free, these qualifications (whatever they are) must be met. Analyses of freedom along these lines mesh far better with the notion of a categorical partition between agents who are free and those who are unfree. For if the criteria for autonomy are satisfied in the case of some agent, then we will say that she is in a condition of (positive) liberty; if they are not, we will want to say that she is not in that condition and so categorically unfree. Thus slaves, subject to the will of their masters, lack a necessary condition for autonomy. For that reason it makes sense for us to describe them as unfree in a categorical sense.

Something similar seems true of agents subject to manipulation or coercion. The mugger who coerces me into handing over my wallet subjects me to her will through threats of force. One reason why we resent such coercion and often view it as degrading or an assault on our freedom is that, in suffering such subjection, we are revealed to be under alien control. Unlike slavery, such coercion renders us temporarily rather than permanently unfree. But as long as we are suffering such coercion, we are, like slaves, unable to view ourselves as fully self-determining beings. For the moment, we find ourselves in a condition of unfreedom, and it is in the light of a tacit positive account of liberty that we recognize this. Mere reductions of negative liberty need not effect categorical changes in status of this kind. This suggests that we cannot fully explain the resentment to which coercion and similar phenomena give rise from the point of view of negative liberty alone; we must also understand its impact in terms of some suitably interpreted account of positive liberty.

This is an important and often overlooked point. Coercion and other forms of personal manipulation temporarily alter my status as a free, self-determining agent by subjecting me to an alien will, *and* place obstacles in the path of my possible choices. They carry implications, then, for their victims' liberty both positive and negative. Although these are often mixed up in the complex reality of actual human encounters, a complete account of the ways in which coercion and similar phenomena may affect individual liberty must therefore attend to both concepts.

These reflections reveal as misleading the pervasive tendency to define negative liberty as the "absence of coercion." We may be troubled by coercion either because it reduces my options or because it involves subjection to an alien will (or both). But only if we object to coercion on the former grounds are we appealing to the authentic negative concept of liberty. If we complain about coercion as an assault on agents' autonomy and self-determination, we are actually appealing to a positive concept of liberty. When they are motivated by this worry, demands for the "absence of coercion" assume that what really matters is the *presence* of (some sort of) autonomy, despite appearances to the contrary. Defining negative liberty as the "absence of coercion" fudges these important differences of emphasis.

Republican liberty: a third concept?

Inspired especially by the pioneering historical scholarship of Quentin Skinner,[11] several contemporary philosophers have attempted to rehabilitate an account of political liberty characteristic of the tradition of classical republican thought. This tradition has roots that stretch back far into classical antiquity, and is especially associated with the political theory of the Roman republic. But it was also influential in early modern Europe, thanks to a revival during the Renaissance. Its central feature is a determined opposition to discretionary exercises of power, and the concomitant claim that a "people" can enjoy true political liberty only to the extent that it has at its disposal the means to prevent arbitrary "domination" at the hands of its rulers. To combat this, classical republicans characteristically recommend an active and politically engaged citizenry, the cultivation of civic virtues, a culture of civility and mutual trust, and various institutions of public accountability. For republicans, these measures and institutions are partly constitutive of political liberty.

[11] Skinner (1998).

This republican account of liberty pre-dates the negative concept of freedom. Indeed, as Skinner has shown, the concept of negative liberty was developed by Hobbes as an alternative and intentionally anti-republican account of political liberty. As we have noted before, Hobbes defended the modern state's claim to wield unlimited authority over its citizens. He thus defended exactly the kind of arbitrary, discretionary authority that republicans regard as anathema to authentic political liberty. But, against the republicans, Hobbes maintained that subjects of an absolute and arbitrary sovereign can nonetheless enjoy liberty. By interpreting political liberty as negative freedom, Hobbes was able to argue that citizens will always be free to the extent that the sovereign leaves their actions unobstructed. As our earlier discussion of degrees of freedom suggests, this move is philosophically powerful (as well as cheeky) because, from the point of view of negative liberty, individuals can never be wholly deprived of their freedom, but can at worst only have it drastically reduced. If Hobbes's argument works, then, the republican suggestion that citizens are rendered categorically unfree or are enslaved by the mere existence of political rulers wielding arbitrary authority over them is exposed as muddled. Thus Hobbes famously ridiculed the claim that citizens of popular republics like Lucca and Venice are necessarily freer than subjects of the despotic sultanate of Constantinople.[12]

But republican critics of Hobbes, like his contemporary James Harrington, insisted that the citizens of Lucca are free in a way that subjects of the sultan are not. This is because, as Skinner has it,

> Your freedom in Constantinople, however great in extent, will remain wholly dependent on the sultan's goodwill ... You will find yourself constrained in what you can say and do by the reflection that, as Harrington puts it, even the greatest Bashaw in Constantinople is merely a tenant of his head, liable to lose it as soon as he speaks or acts in such a way as to cause the sultan offence. The very fact that the law and the will of the sultan are one and the same has the effect of limiting your liberty.[13]

So even if the sultan is a benevolent and liberal-minded ruler, leaving to his subjects wide areas of negative freedom, republicans will still deny

---

[12] Hobbes (1994), p. 140.
[13] Skinner (1998), p. 86.

that his citizens are authentically free. They are not really free because these negative liberties are not provided at their own hands; they are rather conditional benefits enjoyed at the pleasure of an agency beyond their control. His subjects therefore remain in a state of dependence akin to slavery, and are therefore fundamentally unfree.

This republican contention that, to be free, agents or peoples must enjoy independence from arbitrary domination of others, regardless of the extent of their negative liberty, looks like a straightforward appeal to a conception of positive liberty. The claim is presumably that a certain quality of autonomy or independence must be present in order for us to judge someone or some group free.

However, some contemporary exponents of republicanism deny that their concept of liberty is a species of positive freedom. Thus Philip Pettit insists that republican liberty is fundamentally negative in that it calls for the "absence of mastery" or "nondomination" by others, not, as in true positive accounts, for the *presence* of mastery by the self.[14] Skinner, too, has sometimes suggested that republican liberty requires the "absence of dependence" and so involves a largely negative rather than positive concept of freedom.[15] Indeed, some suggest that republican liberty is an intermediate hybrid sufficiently different from both positive and negative liberty as to constitute a third concept in its own right.

But these suggestions are unconvincing; we need not look beyond the distinction between negative and positive liberty in order to capture the republican analysis and I see no reason to deny that republican liberty is a form of positive freedom. I take it that, for republicans, what is objectionable about dependence, domination, and mastery by others is that they preclude those forms of independence and self-determination that must be present for agents to be free in the relevant sense. But again, this is a straightforward positive concept of liberty. Of course, we can, like Pettit, turn this around and make it *look* like a negative concept by saying that for republicans freedom consists in the absence of dependence, domination, or mastery. But this looks like sleight of hand. Since presence and absence are opposites, it is always possible in this way to reformulate claims about a presence in terms of an absence and vice versa. The absence

[14] Pettit (1999), pp. 21–31.
[15] But Skinner, at least, notes some doubts about this. See Skinner (2001), p. 255, n. 90.

of obstacles, for example, implies the presence of opportunities. The presence of slavery can be redescribed as the absence of self-mastery. And, as we noticed earlier, the presence of autonomy requires the absence of coercion.

But we should not allow the possibility of such inverted formulations to confuse us about whether the republican view is oriented essentially around a positive or negative concept of liberty. What republicans fundamentally care about is the presence of a certain kind of political independence, and about the satisfaction of criteria necessary to securing an agent's or "people's" status as (categorically) free. To suggest that republicans are interested "merely" in the absence of domination, mastery, and dependence, as if this doesn't automatically, and indeed more importantly, assume that true freedom requires the presence of independence and autonomy, is to appeal to a distinction without a difference. This remains a positive concept of liberty, even if it can be reexpressed in negative terms.

It is true, of course, that republican freedom does not involve a strongly *perfectionist* interpretation of positive liberty, under which groups or individuals are free only when they achieve full personal or collective self-realization. But, as we noted earlier, there is a whole family of positive conceptions, of which perfectionist self-realization views form but one subset. Republicans interpret political autonomy in very different terms, but that does not mean that their position falls outside the orbit of positive freedom.

It is also true that republicans have often called for certain negative freedoms for the sake of securing positive ideals of political independence. But again this illustrates the ways in which the two concepts can often play complementary roles within political argument. It is not a sign that we must devise a third distinct concept of liberty in order to make sense of the republican position. Skinner's work has greatly enriched our understanding of the possible ways to value and interpret political liberty, but fortunately not in a way that requires further complication of our basic repertoire of liberty concepts.

The free society

I have argued here for a more flexible account of the distinction between positive and negative liberty than most today accept. Against the thrust of prevailing orthodoxy, I have denied that these are necessarily opposed concepts. Rather, I have insisted that there may be as much disagreement *within* each of these two ways of conceiving freedom as between them. And I have suggested that we may need both concepts in order to appreciate fully all the ways in which liberty might matter in public life, and that, in the context of many political arguments, the two concepts may complement rather than exclude each other.

If my analysis is on target, less depends on the decision to work with one of the two concepts itself than on the various substantive concerns that lead us to believe that different forms of human freedom have urgent political significance in particular circumstances. This is surely as it should be: our concerns about freedom are not simple, but complex and varied. Nor does freedom, however it is understood, define the ultimate ends of all political activity; at best our views about freedom form one cluster of important values among several others (justice, security, equality, the common good). While some forms of freedom may matter for their own sake, others may do so only because they secure other goals, and even those that do matter for their own sake may sometimes be outweighed by yet more important values.

Still, the distinction between positive and negative liberty can help us to clarify exactly how various possible ideals of a free society are structured and might be defended. The range of such ideals is very wide indeed, and any comprehensive account of these matters would require several volumes of detailed argument. The following brief discussion is therefore at best a beginning rather than an ending.

The priority of liberty

In chapter 6 we noted Rawls's view that his first principle of justice, protecting certain equal basic liberties, is "lexically prior" to his second principle, which concerns the distribution of economic advantages. As Rawls recognized, this is an interpretation of the proviso, today often identified as quintessentially "liberal," that "liberty can only be restricted for the sake of liberty itself."[16] This proviso is best understood as a claim

---

[16] Rawls (1999a), p. 214.

about burdens of proof. Any argument that purports to justify infringements of some citizens' liberties can on this view succeed only if it
establishes that the infringements are necessary to preserve equal liberties
for all. Under this proviso, arguments that would restrict liberty for
the sake of other goals (e.g. improving overall welfare, national glory,
the common good, or victory in war) cannot qualify as sound justifications for the contemplated restrictions on people's freedom. I will call
this proviso the "priority of liberty" principle or sometimes simply the
"priority principle".

Exactly what this principle means will depend on how we interpret the
forms of liberty we primarily want to protect and, as we have noted, this
is a point on which different theorists disagree. For example, to Rawls,
taxation of wealth does not count as an infringement of a basic liberty in
the first place, because the right to accumulate private wealth unimpeded
is not included on his list of guaranteed basic liberties. So, on Rawls's
view, the "priority of liberty" principle will not automatically prohibit
taxation to pay for projects other than the preservation of liberty. But
of course libertarians disagree, because for them the right to accumulate private wealth unimpeded *is* the most basic form of freedom worth
protecting. As libertarians interpret it, then, the priority principle implies
that violations of private-property rights are justified only when necessary
to enforce and guarantee everyone's rights to his or her property.

One might debate these competing interpretations of the priority
principle in terms either of negative *or* of positive liberty. For example,
if the former, our decision to endorse or reject the libertarian interpretation will turn on the question of whether restrictions on the right to
accumulate private wealth objectionably narrow the options available to
people, that is reduce their negative freedom. If the latter, it will hinge
on our assessment of whether the suggested restrictions are objectionably
coercive, so that their imposition threatens the status of property-holders
as autonomous, self-determining agents. On either argument, however, the
case for a specifically libertarian interpretation of the priority principle
seems weak.

We have already hinted at some of the difficulties facing the effort
to defend libertarian conclusions on the former grounds, by reference to
negative liberty. As our discussion of public rights of way suggested, while
enforcing property rights may increase property-owners' negative liberty,

it may also reduce people's other options. For example, it may restrict their freedom of movement or, by imposing legal barriers to certain forms of redistribution, limit the opportunities of disadvantaged groups to use the law or other political means to obtain for themselves a larger, and perhaps fairer, share of the national wealth than they currently enjoy. It is at least arguable that lifting these and other obstacles is a more urgent concern for a free society than removing *any* that curtail the negative freedoms specifically enjoyed by property-owners.

But efforts to defend a libertarian priority principle in terms of positive liberty are equally problematic. Arguments along these lines typically display a strongly Kantian character. Kantians insist that disrespecting agents' autonomy and independence, and exploiting people as mere "means" to others' ends, are among *the* most basic ways to abuse people. They conclude that there should be an extremely strong presumption against any such coercion. Kant argued that this presumption against coercive intervention in others' choices is so strong that it prohibits *all* coercion except that which is itself essential to preserving agents' general immunity from coercion, and hence their status as autonomous agents. This is, of course, simply a formulation of the "priority of liberty" principle in terms of positive liberty.

By leaning on this Kantian interpretation of the priority principle, libertarians often argue that, unless strictly necessary to protect citizens from coercive force, fraud, and theft, any further restrictions on the freedom to dispose of one's personal property as one wishes must themselves be prohibited. In this account, respecting autonomy (positive freedom) and respect for private-property rights become equivalent; property rights may be violated only in order to protect the overall system of private property-rights on which our autonomy allegedly depends. This line of thought leads many libertarians to interpret personal autonomy in terms of "self-ownership." As we noted in chapter 6, the idea that people own themselves seems attractive precisely because it prohibits exploitation by others and gives agents the final say over how their distinctive bundle of personal assets, talents, and resources are to be used. Its appeal thus derives from concerns about agents' positive freedom, their capacity to conduct their lives on their own, autonomous terms.

But this move from a Kantian interpretation of the priority principle to libertarian conclusions about the special importance of property-based freedoms is questionable. To see why, notice that the whole apparatus of Rawlsian contractualism is itself little more than an application of this same Kantian interpretation of the "priority of liberty" principle. We saw in chapter 4 that the foundations for this kind of contractualism were first clearly laid by Rousseau, even before Kant. Its leading idea is that, to be legitimate, political arrangements must establish that those who submit to them can remain as "free as before" in the sense of being in a position to "obey only themselves" − that is, to remain positively free. It follows that any legitimate forms of coercion that survive this test, however it is exactly formulated, are ones that leave room for agents' autonomy. Since, as Rousseau, Kant, and Rawls would all agree, the exercise of political power is inherently coercive, the question on which the legitimacy of any proposed political arrangement ultimately hangs, in their view, is whether the required forms of coercion can or cannot be reconciled with agents' autonomy.

Viewed from this angle, the whole contractualist endeavor rests upon this interpretation of the "priority of liberty" principle, for it presupposes that coercion (i.e. limits on positive freedom) can be justified only if they are themselves essential to guarantee agents, personal autonomy (i.e. only for the sake of positive liberty). But we already know from discussion in earlier chapters that there are reasonable ways to conceive this contractualist test of legitimacy − Rawls's, for example! − under which libertarian conclusions about the priority of property-based freedoms do not follow. So long as these alternative views are available and stand unrefuted, there is no obvious reason to think that Kantian interpretations of the "priority of liberty" principle point uniquely in the direction of libertarianism.

Nor do bare appeals to metaphors of self-ownership suffice to vindicate the libertarian view. As noted above, there is disagreement among proponents of positive concepts of liberty over how best to interpret the kind of freedom that is at stake, and here is one of the places at which such disagreement occurs. Self-ownership represents one possible interpretation of personal autonomy, but it is not clear that it is an adequate one, and certainly many have rejected it. For example, it is at the very least inconvenient for libertarians that Kant himself emphatically rejected the idea that autonomous agents own themselves. Echoing Kant's concerns, some contemporary philosophers have doubted whether any adequate or appropriately "liberal" interpretation of personal autonomy can rest content with the assumption that agents are any sort of property, even their own.[17] And even if there is something to be said for the idea that people own *themselves*, there remains the further issue of whether that automatically establishes that they have an equally strong claim to control all the external profits they garner from economic exchange.[18]

The Harm Principle

So far we have given the priority principle itself the benefit of the doubt: the disagreements we have just looked at arise among those who, while accepting that principle, differ over its proper interpretation. But is the principle itself sound? I noted earlier that many today regard it as a quintessentially liberal principle, but it is worth noting that many liberals have not accepted it. One such was John Stuart Mill, who defended a significantly weaker principle, the so-called "Harm Principle":

> That principle is, that the sole end for which mankind are warranted, individually or collectively in interfering with the liberty of action of any of their number, is self-protection. That the only purpose for which power can rightfully be exercised over any member of a civilized community, against his will, is to prevent harm to others. His own good, either physical or moral, is not a sufficient warrant.[19]

Like the priority principle, Mill's Harm Principle allocates burdens of proof. It asserts that any adequate justification for reducing someone's liberty must show that the interference is necessary to prevent harm to others. Mill clearly understood this principle in terms of negative liberty. At stake, for him, are the possible ways in which the state and the law might limit agents' opportunities for action. The Harm Principle insists that these restrictions are justified only if they prevent harm to others.

It is important to notice that, under Mill's principle, harm to others is a necessary, but not sufficient, condition for justified interference in personal liberty. The Harm Principle does not require that we restrict agents' liberty *whenever* this will prevent harms to others. Rather,

[17] Johnston (1994), ch. 2; Bird (1999), ch. 6; Freeman (2001).
[18] For an excellent discussion, see Kymlicka (2002), pp. 110–21.
[19] Mill (1972), p. 78.

it asserts that only under this condition are we allowed to *consider* doing so. But even if this condition is met, independent reasons against interfering in agents' liberty may in many cases remain.

The Harm Principle is much weaker than the priority principle. Unlike the latter, Mill's argument allows us to restrict liberty for the sake of considerations other than those of liberty. For example, any restrictions on the liberty of some that are necessary to avert certain economic harms suffered by others are may be presumed to be justifiable under Mill's principle. Suppose that redistributive taxation to alleviate the harm of global poverty reduces the negative liberty of affluent property-owners. Even so, the Harm Principle generates no objection. For here we are proposing to do exactly what that principle allows (though, again, not necessarily what it requires). We are contemplating restrictions on the liberty of some in order to prevent harm to others.

The only absolute prohibition imposed by the Harm Principle concerns limitations on individuals' liberty contemplated for their own good. Mill's principle categorically rules out paternalistic interference of this sort. So, it permits us to interfere in agents' liberty to drink *and drive*, because drunk drivers may cause serious harm to other drivers and to pedestrians. But alcohol use in itself is not subject to similar regulation under the Harm Principle. As long as drinkers harm only *themselves*, no case for restriction can be mounted within the terms of Mill's principle.

Mill's argument therefore provides one basis on which to challenge the priority of liberty principle. On Mill's view, the most urgent concern in a free society is protecting individuals' right to pursue their own good in their own way. This requires, most crucially, that we resist the temptation to indulge in paternalistic legislation that restricts their liberty for (what *we* see as) their own good. But that is not the same as requiring that liberty be restricted only for the sake of liberty: restrictions on liberty to protect the good of others are perfectly legitimate under Mill's proposal. If we are satisfied with Mill's position, then, we may see no need to endorse the stronger "priority of liberty" principle.[20]

But of course, Mill's antipaternalist vision is itself open to challenge from still other angles. For example, in chapter 2 we encountered the

---

[20] For a critique of Rawls on the priority of liberty from this standpoint, see Hart (1975), and Rawls's response in Rawls (1993), lec. VIII.

Platonic argument that leaving people free to "pursue their own good in their own way" is likely only to sabotage their well-being. On any such view, Mill's absolute prohibition on paternalistic practices will seem irrational. One might think that any argument for paternalism along these lines must *ipso facto* be motivated by considerations beyond those of freedom. That is certainly true of Plato's arguments and of those who follow his classic criticisms of a permissive society. On this sort of argument, liberals who accept either the priority principle or the Harm Principle simply *overvalue* freedom – they give it too much weight relative to other important goals, especially that of promoting individual well-being.[21]

But it is also possible to imagine arguments for certain forms of paternalism, or at least against the Harm Principle, that are themselves motivated by concerns about freedom. We have noted, for example, that many have cashed out positive conceptions of liberty in terms of perfectionist ideals of autonomy. Indeed, we saw that Mill himself justified his position for the sake of just such an ideal of positive liberty. According to this view, the best sort of life consists in a pitilessly honest, open-minded, self-critical pursuit of one's own good. But this ideal, and the acquisition of the various skills and traits needed to realize it, are complex accomplishments, and agents may need help in attaining them. Paternalistic intervention to assist agents in realizing their autonomy might therefore be required. Indeed, paternalistic legislation prohibiting, for example, addictive substances (whose use plausibly sabotages personal autonomy) is often urged on just such autonomy-based grounds.

However, despite his endorsement of this ideal of personal autonomy, Mill's principle disallows restrictions of someone's negative liberties contemplated on these grounds. This would be a direct form of paternalism that the Harm Principle absolutely forbids: there must be a showing of harm to others for such restrictions to be justified under that principle.

This underlines the paradoxical quality of Mill's position. His argument is that a wide latitude for free experiments in living is justified for the sake of promoting ideals of personal autonomy, but that we must never restrict individuals' negative liberties in order to assist them directly

---

[21] See Schwartz (2004); Lane (2000).

in realizing that ideal in their own lives. Mill himself resolved this paradox by appealing to the empirical speculation that *direct* efforts to promote personal autonomy by outside coercion are systematically self-defeating. He maintained that, as a matter of fact, we shall better promote agents' autonomy by resisting the temptation to do so by direct paternalist means. But that empirical claim is certainly open to question. If we doubt it, Mill's case for a distinctively liberal vision of a free society must strike us as incomplete, and the paradox that lies at its heart unresolved.

Conclusion

Modern liberalism is often identified with the claim that liberty is in some sense the master political value, entitled to take precedence over all other values. We have seen, however, that not only is the precise meaning of such a precept open to very different interpretations, with quite divergent political implications, but that not all liberals have accepted it. Moreover, on any of these alternatives, there remain further questions about whether liberty in the relevant senses really is as important as liberals believe, or whether, even if it is, this tells for rather than against characteristically liberal recommendations about how political power may legitimately be used.

While I hope that the discussion in this chapter has cleared away some of the confusions about freedom and liberty that have plagued recent discussions, I also hope that it has highlighted the unsettled and open-ended character of familiar liberal assumptions about the free society. They cannot simply be taken for granted, in the manner of much contemporary "liberal theory." Unless these assumptions about freedom, and the difficulties they present, are "fully, frequently, and fearlessly discussed," they can be offered only as "dead dogma, not living truth."[22]

---

[22] Mill (1972), p. 103.

9   Democratic rule

Democracy is today a central part of the self-image of Western nation-states. This is no disinterested self-description. It is also a *cherished* self-image. Hence the celebratory, even self-congratulatory, tenor of much contemporary discourse about democracy: it is, our leaders tell us, a noble yet realistic political ideal, worth fighting and perhaps dying for. And they continually remind us how fortunate we are to live in societies committed to realizing it, and in large measure (allegedly) succeeding in doing so. The endless incantation of this view may lead us to take it too much for granted. This chapter asks whether there is anything to be said for it.

What is democracy?

"Democracy" is an adjective (sometimes an adverb) masquerading as a noun. Literally, it means "rule of or by the people." But this concept does not really designate some simple nameable object like a stone or a cat, still less any sort of natural kind. Rather, it refers to a possible and variable property of a particular social practice, the practice of "ruling," or (more broadly) that of "collective decision-making." The focal usages of the concept of democracy are therefore adjectival or adverbial qualifications of such practices, as in "This decision was reached democratically"; "The legislative process in Pacifica is very undemocratic"; "Democratic procedures promote freedom."

Of course, we do often speak of certain regimes or states as "democracies" *tout court*. But we should be careful not to take such classifications too literally; they are usually best understood as shorthand for more variegated underlying claims about different regimes' decision-making mechanisms. Perhaps, for certain (let's face it, often propagandist) purposes, it makes sense to distinguish democracies categorically from nondemocratic regimes and associations (tyrannies, authoritarian dictatorships, corporations), but even so such distinctions tend to beg some important questions. For example, this opposition might lead us to think that tyranny and democracy are mutually exclusive. But many have worried, from Aristotle to Mill and Tocqueville, that tyranny can take democratic forms, a possibility that an exclusive dichotomy between democracy and tyranny will require us to discount. Similarly, is there any reason to assume, *a priori*, that democratic decisions could not exemplify "authoritarianism" (whatever that is), or that dictatorships could not arise democratically, or even sustain themselves through democratic means?

The complexity of democratic forms

So even if excluding certain regimes as "nondemocracies" is appropriate for some legitimate purpose, the remaining ones are not helpfully understood as democracies *simpliciter*, but rather as democratic in various ways and to different degrees. These ways and degrees are far more complex than one might initially think. Jack Lively notes that "rule by the people" might mean at least:

1. That all [should] govern, in the sense that all should be involved in legislating, in deciding on general policy, in applying laws and in governmental administration.
2. That all [should] be personally involved in crucial decision-making, that is to say in deciding general laws and matters of general policy.
3. That rulers [should] be accountable to the ruled; they should, in other words, be obliged to justify their actions to the ruled and be removable by the ruled.
4. That rulers [should] be accountable to the representatives of the ruled.
5. That rulers [should] be chosen by the ruled.
6. That rulers [should] be chosen by representatives of the ruled.[1]

This helpful list is already complicated enough, but several of Lively's provisions themselves invite further complication. For example, provisions 1 and 2 speak of (personal) "involvement" in decision-making processes. But what sorts of "involvement" might democratic procedures require?

---

[1] Lively (1975), p. 30.

The obvious possibility is participation in elections, and especially voting, but it is worth noting that the association of democracy and election is relatively recent: from antiquity until roughly the eighteenth century, political theorists more often associated voting and election with elitist forms of rule — like oligarchy or aristocracy. In contrast, democratic rule was associated with the selection of public officials by lot ("sortition"), the mechanism by which today we select jurors.[2] From this classical point of view, what we now often identify as a form of democratic rule is better described as a kind of elective aristocracy, in which political elites, organized as political parties, compete for votes in regularly held elections. There is therefore scope for debate about how democratic competitive party politics really is.

This distinction between election and sortition is also relevant to the notions of choice and representation mentioned in Lively's provisos 4, 5, and 6. For sortition is one way of choosing rulers, and it is certainly arguable that the random selection of leaders by lot would, over the long term, secure a fairer representation of social interests than majoritarian elections. Why should we not pick democratic representatives in this way? This is a good question.

On the other hand, as Lively's provisions 1–4 imply, the selection of rulers is not the only issue that needs to be considered. There is also the question of how far policies and decisions reflect the beliefs or preferences of the ruled. If one thought that the main point of democratic participation was not to pick rulers but to translate citizens' various opinions about public policy into an overall judgment that can be ascribed to everyone (the "will of the people"), one might think that voting, understood as a way of expressing preferences for different policies, is better suited to democratic purposes than sortition. Referenda on particular issues, for example, and direct ballot initiatives as practiced in some American states, plausibly exemplify democratic rule in this sense. Similarly, the rather elusive notion of "public opinion" plays an important role in modern democratic politics, and one standard way of accessing information about it is through "opinion polls," participation in which resembles voting in elections. Against this, however, one might argue that efforts to divine "public opinion" using

---

[2] See Manin (1997).

deliberative "focus groups" rather than through aggregate polling data involve important concessions to sortition.

But even if we set aside sortition and stick simply with voting and election, further complications arise. Are voting procedures more or less democratic to the extent that they approximate unanimity, majority rule, or plurality rule? Which system of election is more democratic: first-past-the-post or proportional representation? There is also the question of whether the right to vote (or indeed to participate in other ways) is actually *exercised* by large numbers of people. One could hold, for example, that procedures are democratic mainly to the extent that the ruled enjoy formal rights to participate, whether or not they choose to exercise them.

Against this, though, it may seem odd to claim that a polity in which only a small minority of citizens choose to exercise their formal right to vote is fully democratic. Historically, many proponents of democratic rule have urged that formal rights to participate are necessary but not sufficient for genuine rule by the people to be realized. They argue that popular self-government in this sense requires the active and widespread participation of citizens: insofar as citizens become politically disengaged and apathetic, democratic rule becomes corrupted and eventually moribund.[3] This notion that democratic participation should be thought of as a civic duty rather than a right has, however, been contested by some modern theorists of democracy who claim that a degree of apathy and political disengagement may actually be functionally necessary for stable democratic rule.[4]

Finally, there are complications about the *levels* of decision-making at which one might think democratic participation is appropriate. Modern political thought, for example, has sometimes distinguished between the state and the government. This distinction tends to become elusive on close inspection, but the general idea is clear enough. The "government" here refers to the particular groups of people who actually occupy positions of official responsibility at particular times, and who therefore operate the organs of political control (presidents, members of parliaments or cabinets, ministers of this or that department of state, and so on) on a day-to-day basis. The "state," on the other hand, refers to the more basic and enduring

---

[3] Rousseau (1987), p. 198; Mill (1972), p. 207.

[4] See Pateman (1970), ch. 1.

legal framework within which these officials work and that circumscribes their powers, especially the constitutional rules that define sovereignty, empower legislative bodies, and authorize the various branches of government to perform various general functions.

Either or both of these loci of political power could be organized democratically. In chapter 4, we saw that Rousseau argued that, to be legitimate, forms of political rule must be subject to a General Will that can be articulated directly only by a popular sovereign. So for Rousseau the _state_ must be organized democratically: sovereignty can on this view be exercised legitimately only by the full assembly of citizens. Curiously, however, Rousseau rejected the idea that the _government_ ought to be democratically organized, apparently on the grounds that the majority of a population is unlikely to be sufficiently virtuous to be entrusted with the day-to-day execution of the General Will.[5]

In contrast, it can be argued that the institutions of modern representative democracy exemplify something like the reverse combination. That is, what is most obviously democratic in "liberal democracies" is the selection of governments or "administrations" to occupy positions of official responsibility for defined periods of time. The deeper constitutional framework that defines these official responsibilities, their scope and limits, and indeed the rules of democratic elections themselves, is less obviously subject to democratic control, certainly on any regular basis. The tenuously democratic nature of this constitutional background is nowhere more evident than in the practice of judicial constitutional review, which in many societies (notably the United States) gives a tiny minority of specially trained legal experts the right to override legislation supported by democratically elected governments.

Democratic ideals

The modalities of democratic rule are thus extremely complex. Recognizing this complexity already inflicts some damage on the conventional wisdom about democracy with which we began. When our leaders tout the virtues of Western democratic institutions, they frequently speak of democracy

[5] Rousseau (1987), pp. 179–80.

as if it were a single, simple ideal. This view implies that there is a simple scale of democracy, such that we can always compare how near or far particular regimes are to realizing "the" ideal of democratic rule. It is often combined with a unilinear theory of political development, according to which the trajectory of political societies from barbarism to maturity is a story of progressive approximation toward truly democratic institutions.

But our discussion so far tends to undermine the assumption on which all these views rest — that democracy is a unique, simple ideal. In chapter 3, we questioned whether human well-being is reducible to some single, common measure of utility. We saw there that, insofar as well-being comes in many, incommensurable forms, the utilitarian effort to "maximize human well-being" seems incoherent. Acknowledging that there are many different and sometimes inconsistent ways for political rule to be democratic encourages a similar conclusion in the context of democracy. It is not clear that "promoting democracy" *as such* is a meaningful political project. There are only various, and possibly conflicting, *sorts* of democratic arrangements to be promoted for various, and similarly conflicting, *sorts* of reasons.

Given this, it comes as no surprise that the range of social ideals that are often mobilized to justify democratic arrangements is extremely wide. Below I distinguish and assess five major strands of argument for democratic rule of various sorts. This list is neither exhaustive nor comprehensive, but it is a start, and, I hope, conveys the complex relations between the various different ideals at stake in democratic political forms. The first three lines of argument recommend democratic arrangements in terms of certain ideals that they allegedly promote; these I will call the *positive arguments*. The last two do so on the grounds that democratic procedures stave off certain evils or abuses; I call these *defensive arguments*.

The positive arguments

A.   Common-good justifications

The first of the positive arguments recommends democratic decision-making because it helps society to recognize and pursue its own common good. This argument has many possible forms, but the most basic version runs as follows. Promoting the common good requires rule in the interests of the ruled, but we cannot trust exclusive subgroups of citizens to supply reliable and impartial information about the true interests of the ruled. They are likely to be unduly partial to their narrow sectional interests. By comparison, a fully inclusive democratic consultation of all citizens seems more likely to identify the common good accurately and impartially. Democratic procedures are therefore our best hope for promoting a sound understanding of the public interest and for pursuing it intelligently together.

B.   The argument from self-government

This second argument defends democratic procedures on the grounds that they promote the independent value of collective self-determination or political autonomy. Behind this argument are the suggestions that a society is not free unless it follows its own will, and that "its own will" must mean the will of the people who comprise it. Since only democratic procedures can identify the popular will, they are necessary, and perhaps sufficient, conditions for realizing the value of political freedom or self-government, or so the argument maintains.

This argument assumes that political autonomy in this sense is inherently valuable. Although it therefore readily implies that self-government is a good, perhaps an aspect of citizens' common good, it is important not to confuse it with the common-good justification for democracy. In contrast to the latter, the argument from self-government need not contend that democratic rule is valuable because it enables citizens to identify, appreciate, and therefore effectively pursue their shared interests. Rather, it claims that democratic decision-making is valuable simply because, in realizing collective self-government, it directly realizes something of value, whether or not citizens consciously understand that this is the case, and whether or not it helps citizens to appreciate properly their other common interests.

C.   The argument from egalitarian justice

This argument asserts that democratic procedures are required in order to achieve an equitable division of political power. Assuming that justice requires that citizens be treated as equals, it seems natural to conclude that everyone subject to political rule is entitled, as a matter of justice, to an equal say in political decision-making. Political arrangements that deny anyone subject to coercive power an equal voice in determining how that power is to be used must, this argument contends, be fundamentally unjust. Since only democratic arrangements include everyone on suitably egalitarian terms, nondemocratic arrangements must on this view be systematically unjust.

The defensive arguments

D.   The conflict-resolution argument

Any stable society needs some mechanism for resolving conflicts among its members and between groups with opposed interests. This argument contends that democratic arrangements represent the most propitious basis for the peaceful resolution of these potentially destabilizing conflicts. Even if one were pessimistic about the capacity of democratic decision-making to identify the common good, realize ideals of collective self-government, or satisfy the requirements of justice in the distribution of political power, one could still find redeeming merit in this putative ability to manage and settle social conflict. The value of democracy, on this account, lies in its ability to avert the dangers of social instability, disorder, violence, and – at the limit – civil war.

This argument sometimes takes a purely pragmatic form. For example, some claim that the virtues of democratic arrangements consist in the following features. Under democratic decision-making procedures everyone is invited to participate in a recursive process: (a) over which no one group has exclusive control; (b) with systematically uncertain outcomes; and (c) whose results on particular occasions are always revisable and so never final. These features foster a disposition on the part of conflicting social constituencies to bargain and compromise with each other.[6] Moreover, the fact that democratic outcomes are always revisable gives those groups that lose out on particular occasions hope that their view might prevail another day. In this way, even losers come to have a stake in collaborating with, rather than subverting, the rules of the democratic game. In contrast,

---

[6] For a sophisticated version of this view, see Przworski (1991), ch. 1.

less inclusive decision-making procedures systematically alienate the excluded groups, for by hypothesis they lack the ability to influence political outcomes and therefore any stake in the official process by which decisions are reached. This threatens order and social peace; democratic inclusion is hence an advisable preventive.

But this argument is also often formulated in terms of the desiderata of political legitimacy, and in this guise it presents a more moralized cast.[7] In chapter 4, we saw that contractualists often argue that legitimate institutions, laws, and policies must show themselves to be acceptable to all those subject to them. Clearly, democratic procedures cannot guarantee that this standard of legitimacy is always met. However, many argue that the conditions of democratic discussion force citizens to take it seriously and therefore promote political legitimacy in this sense. In a democracy, for example, citizens hoping to advance a certain policy or proposal must often persuade at least a plurality, and if possible a majority, of their fellows to go along with it. In seeking to do so, they must address each other as equals, each entitled to his or her own opinions and judgments, for this notion of civic equality is part and parcel of democratic political culture. Citizens are thereby forced to couch their arguments in terms that people with diverse beliefs could all find acceptable. In this way, the discipline of democratic compromise and debate increases the chances that political outcomes will be justifiably viewed by citizens as legitimate. This in turn facilitates peace and political stability even in the face of deep moral, religious, and political disagreement, or so the argument goes.

E.   Safeguarding liberty against power

This is perhaps the simplest and most familiar argument of all. It rests on the assumption that, given the frailties of human nature, unchecked power is always an invitation to abuse and oppression. As Lord Acton famously put it, "Power tends to corrupt and absolute power corrupts absolutely." The argument is that democracy is best defended as a response to this problem. Democratic accountability is valuable, on this view, because it provides

[7] See Gutmann and Thompson (1999); Cohen (1989).

an essential means for the subordinated to check the machinations of the powerful.

Insofar as it appeals to a notion of (collective) political freedom, this line of reasoning resembles the argument from self-government. It certainly seems natural to say that when a people is deprived of ways to replace their masters, call them to account, or overrule their mandates, it is in an important sense *unfree*. As we saw in chapter 8, classical republicans have often described this condition as a form of political enslavement. They therefore insist that political freedom requires the vigilant monitoring of rulers by the ruled. But the notion of political freedom involved in this republican argument is weaker than that to which the argument from self-government appeals. The latter argument interprets political freedom in terms of the ambitious ideal of a society identifying and following its own "collective will." But the republican argument need not rest on anything so caffeinated. It involves the less demanding notion of citizens collectively defending their (individual) liberties against the predations of political elites through mechanisms of democratic accountability.

Before raising some questions about each of these arguments, it is important to note that their very diversity reinforces our earlier conclusions about the complexity of democratic forms. It is surely misleading to suggest that the five arguments represent complementary and mutually support-ive elements of a simple case "for democracy." Even a cursory inspection suggests that they do not all point toward democratic arrangements of the same sort. It is far more likely that each supports quite different, perhaps incongruous, visions of an appropriately democratic order.

The common-good justification

Plato's *Republic* provides the classic statement of the most important objection to this first argument. Plato's objection grants that political rule should be guided by the interests of the ruled, but questions the claim that the common good (in this sense) is likely to be effectively appreciated and pursued through democratic means. As we saw in chapter 2, Plato believed that properly understanding the common good is an extremely complex and challenging task: for example, it requires knowledge of the conditions of human well-being. It also depends on informed insight into the complicated interplay between social forms and entrenched moral beliefs on the one hand, and the psychological dispositions of character that they tend to promote on the other. Only those with the necessary wisdom, experience, and training are likely to be up to these challenges. Untutored democratic publics are very unlikely to be so equipped, or so Plato maintained. That is why we do not have passengers on aeroplanes vote on how they are to be flown, or patients vote on the medical treatments each should receive.

This objection is often dismissed for seeming to turn on Plato's easily ridiculed claim that only philosophers are competent to rule. But this overlooks the burden of proof in the argument. The common-good justification contends that democratic arrangements (of some sort) are valuable because they entrust political power to those individuals most likely to reach sound judgments about the common good. The onus is on the proponent of this argument to convince us that this surmise is reasonable, for it is just this point that Plato contested. Insisting that Plato was wrong to assume that only philosophers are qualified to rule is beside the point. Plato's proposal about philosopher-rulers was his suggested cure for the (alleged) ills of democratic rule, but rejecting this cure as mistaken does nothing to undermine Plato's initial diagnosis. The central doubt remains: are democratic publics competent to appreciate and intelligently pursue their shared interests?

An example may dramatize the question. Today, the manipulation of interest rates has become a major tool of economic policy. But in many states – including the United States and the United Kingdom – interest rates are determined by a largely unaccountable elite of economists working in central banks (the Federal Reserve, the Bank of England). Whatever we think about Plato's philosopher-rulers, it seems quite plausible that trained economists are more likely to control the money supply skillfully than are members of the public who lack any understanding of economics. This is presumably why we do not hold democratic referenda to determine interest rates. But if we reject democratic rule here, on the grounds that the relevant issues are better left to informed experts, are there any areas of policy-making in which the presumption tilts in favor of democratic judgment? That is the question that proponents of the common-good justification must answer.

One might resist Plato's argument for seeming to assume, without justification, that members of the general public are simply too dim to contribute constructively to public decision-making. This certainly looks like a rather hasty (as well as patronizing) assumption. Doubtless the public is, as a matter of fact, often *uninformed* about complex questions of public policy, like the control of the money supply. However, one might respond that, rather than abandoning democracy in favor of unaccountable techno-cratic rule, a more appropriate remedy would be to educate democratic citizens better than we currently do.

But this tempting move underestimates the issues raised by Plato's objection. For one thing, educating *everyone* to grasp the complexities of (say) monetary policy would be extremely costly, and one might wonder whether it is a rational investment of social resources, if we already have a pool of competent economists sufficient to provide the required expertise. This point only gains in force when we try to imagine educating everyone to become experts on *all* areas of social policy (foreign affairs, health-and-safety policy, legal reform, fiscal policy, social-welfare policy, the provision of health care and benefits, the regulation of trade and industry, or military affairs).

For another, Plato's argument, at least its most striking and challenging kernel, does not really rest on the crude assumption that ordinary people are naturally stupid. The *Republic* actually defends the more subtle position that democratically ordered institutions themselves *cause* certain sorts of irrationality and stupidity. Plato's objection is that, whatever the *natural* distribution of intelligence among members of a population, democratic arrangements *artificially* corrupt citizens' capacity to identify their common interests intelligently. Seeking the common good through democratic means is, he feared, a self-defeating enterprise.

Plato's reasons for drawing this pessimistic conclusion were complex, but the essence of his worry was this. As we noted in chapter 2, he thought that democratic political culture tends to erode those abilities and dispositions necessary to a sound and rational appreciation of the human good. It does so (he thought) because democratic notions of equality tend to imply that, as long as individuals respect others' rights to pursue their own good in their own way, we ought to give their own opinions about their best interests the benefit of the doubt. But this, Plato feared, simply floods society with an indiscriminate array of opinions about the good life, some sound, many not, without supplying agents with any rational principle on which to choose intelligently between them. Under these conditions, individuals are left to live their own lives in their own way, but (in effect) deprived of the ability to certify that their own way *really is* in their best interests.

Plato accepted that some individuals in democratic societies will reach defensible and well-grounded views about their own and others' real interests. But his point was that, under democratic conditions, citizens lack any reliable way to distinguish these better views from the many other, quite indefensible views also likely to emerge. Meanwhile, democratic procedures give both sets of views the same chance to influence public decisions. It is as if we were to check into a hospital in which there are as many medical opinions as there are patients, each claiming equal rights to influence decisions about how particular diseases are to be treated. Some of the opinions may in fact be correct, but under these conditions how is anyone supposed to distinguish sound medical opinion from quackery? A disposition to defer to the majority opinion in such circumstances will seem sensible only to those who have already lost their grip on such a distinction. Moreover, majority rule will predictably result in many very irrational medical decisions. Who would agree to be admitted to a hospital on these terms?

This Platonic characterization of democratic political culture and its irrationality is obviously controversial. Against it one might cite Mill's memorable argument (in *On Liberty*) that free and open discussion among individuals with diverse views about the good life is a necessary condition for intellectual progress. According to Mill, our ability to distinguish truth from error precisely *requires* the sort of democratic marketplace of ideas of which Platonists are suspicious. On the other hand, it is rather telling that Mill's endorsement of this general view did not prevent him from insisting that democratic decision-making is acceptable only if those with university degrees (Mill: the "mentally superior") are given as many as seven votes for every one vote cast by others.[8]

Furthermore, the modern empirical research bearing on this issue makes rather grim reading for democrats, consistently finding democratic citizens to be ill-informed and worryingly prone to inconsistency in political judgment. In 1957 Anthony Downs made the striking (and rather Platonic)

---

[8] I am grateful to an anonymous reviewer for clarification of Mill's position.

suggestion that we should not be surprised at this: democratic citizens, he argued, may often be *rationally* ignorant. His thought was that, given the infinitesimally small likelihood of any one citizen's vote making a significant difference to the outcome of elections, the expected benefits of voting cannot make it rational for citizens to expend much effort in acquiring reliable political knowledge, and may indeed make voting itself irrational.[9]

Finally, we might note that, under our own procedures of representative democracy, public policies are rarely if ever directly formulated and discussed in detail by ordinary members of the public. Rather, they are formulated from above by members of educated, professionalized elites (economists, experts in foreign affairs, "think tanks," etc.), and later integrated into political parties' election platforms. The general public is consulted only at the very end of the process, when parties compete for votes in general elections, and is given little or no power to alter the menu of alternatives on offer. The fact that few question the elitism of this practice may betray a tacit acknowledgment of the force of Plato's general critique.[10]

The argument from self-government

As we saw earlier, this argument centers on the ideal of a society identifying and then following the "will of its people." This raises the obvious question of whether any sense can really be attached to the notion of a "collective will." No doubt individuals are autonomous agents with their own wills, but can this be true of collectivities? And even if it can be, is it the case that democratic procedures can tell us what the popular will is?

One powerful reason to think that it is not the case derives from an observation first made by Rousseau's contemporary, the French philosopher and mathematician Condorcet. He noticed the following problem. Suppose

---

[9] Downs (1957); see also Hardin (1993).

[10] These facts also make it implausible to suggest, as some claim, that under representative democracy the people choose the general *goals* that ought to guide public policy, and then elites of technocrats and civil servants identify appropriate means to their realization. Surely the elites determine the goals, too.

that there are three individuals, *A*, *B*, and *C*, with the following three preferences (the character " $>$ " means "are preferred over"):

A: *socialists* $>$ *conservatives* $>$ *liberals*
B: *conservatives* $>$ *liberals* $>$ *socialists*
C: *liberals* $>$ *socialists* $>$ *conservatives*

In this case, majorities (i.e. two out of the three individuals) prefer the socialists to the conservatives, the conservatives over the liberals, and the liberals to the socialists. What, then, is the majority will? It looks like *socialists* $>$ *conservatives* $>$ *liberals* $>$ *socialists*. But what could that mean? Here the socialists are preferred to both the conservatives and the liberals, but both of the latter are preferred to the socialists! This seems logically impossible, a *nonpreference*. Such "cyclical" or "intransitive" preferences are without meaning. In this case, then, no meaningful "will" can be attributed to a democratic majority.

In a seminal monograph first published in 1951, the economist Kenneth Arrow proved a famous theorem generalizing Condorcet's finding. Arrow's Theorem showed that there is no way to aggregate individuals' separate preferences over three or more alternatives into a transitive collective preference that does not violate various absolutely obvious democratic requirements. Specifically, it proved that the only aggregation rules capable of yielding logically coherent collective preferences involve either deferring to the judgment of a dictator or unacceptably narrowing in advance the range of preferences citizens are permitted to express.[11]

This is a disturbing result, one that puts the argument from self-government firmly on the defensive. Arrow's work inspired the development of a whole academic field, known as social-choice theory, devoted to examining and deepening the sort of analysis he pioneered. Subsequent writings in this field have unfortunately only confirmed and expanded Arrow's pessimistic conclusions about the intelligibility of a popular will. Despite the ingenuity of various attempts to salvage our intuitions about the "will of the people" in the face of the Arrow-Condorcet argument, none is entirely without difficulties. The findings of social-choice theorists

---

[11] Arrow (1963).

therefore pose a serious challenge to the argument from self-government, and indeed to the very concept of democratic self-government.[12]

It is important to stress, however, that social-choice theory need not rule out all conceptions of, or arguments for, democracy. For example, many social-choice theorists retreat to the conception of democracy proposed by the twentieth-century Austrian economist Joseph Schumpeter.[13] Schumpeter rejected the notion of a popular will as a utopian fiction (for reasons independent of Arrow's result), but held that democracy could still be meaningfully understood as a process by which oligarchically organized elites (political parties) compete for votes in just the way that corporations compete for consumers of their products and services. On this view, elections are like ruled—governed games with winners and losers; but they do not and cannot communicate information about a popular will, except perhaps in a purely metaphorical sense. But since it dispenses with claims about a popular will, this way of understanding democratic rule clearly cannot rescue the argument from self-government. It seems to have a greater affinity with the defensive arguments, and especially the conflict-resolution arguments, considered below.

But even if we were able to make sense of the notion of a popular democratic will, the argument from self-government would still face another kind of objection. The argument assumes that there is something inherently valuable about a group of people knowing their democratic will and pursuing it. But this assumption faces serious pressure from two different directions.

From one side, there are obvious doubts about the relative importance of the "will of the people" and the will of the individuals to be ruled by it. Some would suggest that, compared to the value of individual autonomy, collective autonomy has little inherent ethical importance. It is all too easy to imagine cases in which the popular will (somehow determined) poses a threat to the autonomy of particular individuals. It is such cases that inspire familiar liberal worries about the "tyranny of the majority" over the individual; the standard response is to define certain constitutional rights protecting individual freedoms with which democratic majorities

---

[12] For further analysis, see Bird (2000).
[13] Schumpeter (1956); Riker (1988).

cannot tamper. But this significantly qualifies the scope of discretion left to the democratic will, supposing it to be identifiable; and as we noted earlier, such rights are often actually enforced through rather undemocratic judicial means.

One might still suggest that this area of discretion is wide enough to permit significant and valuable forms of democratic self-rule. But here the claim that collective autonomy in this sense is inherently valuable faces pressure from another direction. We suggested earlier that the argument from self-government regards the realization of rule in accordance with the will of the people as valuable independently of whether it actually promotes citizens' shared interests, or whether it helps citizens correctly to appreciate their common good. But is this assumption plausible? Imagine a democratically organized people that autonomously chooses unwise policies. By following the "will of the people," they ruin the economy, condemn many in their society to poverty, ill-health, and insecurity, and bring about the decay of their major cultural and educational institutions. Should citizens of this society cheer themselves with the thought that "at least we did it to ourselves"? If this seems hollow consolation, it may indicate that collective self-rule is not really inherently valuable in the way the argument from self-government claims.

It seems likely, then, that our beliefs about the value of democratic self-government are conditional on its consistency with individual autonomy and with the effective pursuit of society's common interests. But we have also seen that democratic arrangements do not necessarily secure either of these seemingly more important goals, and may actually threaten them. So whether there is anything left over in the ideal of collective self-government that specifically supports democratic arrangements remains open to debate.

The argument from egalitarian justice

The main difficulty facing this argument comes to light once we distinguish between what are often termed "substantive" and "formal" conceptions of equality and justice. According to this familiar distinction, which is another of those that turns out to be harder to draw when one looks closely, it is one thing (say) to enjoy *formally* equal rights to participate in decision-making, but another to actually receive the *substantive* treatment appropriate to one's standing as a civic equal. For example, members of minority groups might enjoy a formally equal right to participate in democratic elections under the principle of "one person, one vote." But clearly this is not sufficient to prevent winning majorities from denying to members of the minority groups whatever civil liberties and economic opportunities are necessary for them to enjoy genuine *substantive* equality. Guaranteeing substantive equality thus seems to require principled limits on the scope of democratic procedures. So, even if we accept egalitarian conceptions of justice, it is unlikely that they provide unqualified support for formally egalitarian democratic arrangements.

In reply one might still insist that, even if not *sufficient*, equal inclusion in decision-making is *necessary* to meet the requirements of egalitarian justice. The problem here, though, is that the relevant notion of equal inclusion is hopelessly ambiguous and admits of an indeterminate range of interpretations, from the unduly weak to the implausibly strong. At the weak end of the spectrum we have: one (adult) person, (at least) one vote. (Even Mill accepted this principle.) Other (increasingly strong) interpretations include: one adult, (no more than) one vote; one adult, (no more than) one vote plus a meaningful range of options over which to choose; one adult, (no more than) one vote plus an equal right to run for office; equal liability to be called up by lot to hold office; an equal right to veto (legislation? constitutional provisions?); equal consideration (or representation?) of individuals' interests (by whom?)... Here again we must face up to the sheer diversity and complexity of possible democratic arrangements. Is it clear that any of these forms of "equal inclusion" is strictly necessary for true civic equality, and that if some are, they demand procedures that we would on reflection want to call democratic?[14]

The conflict-resolution argument

One might think that this penultimate argument does not really raise any philosophical issues because it hinges on simple empirical judgments about the preconditions for political stability. If true, this is bad news for the argument, for, given the enormous number of very undemocratic regimes

---

[14] For a fuller discussion of political equality, see Beitz (1989).

that have stably persisted for long historical periods, it is surely impossible to believe on purely empirical grounds that democratic arrangements are in any sense necessary or even advisable for political stability.

But we cannot dismiss the argument so easily, for it is a mistake to assume that in the present context questions about political stability raise only empirical issues of this simple kind. This assumption wrongly overlooks the important issue of how we should *conceptualize* political stability for various purposes (including that of measuring it empirically), a matter that raises questions that are largely philosophical in nature. For example: Is a society appropriately "stable" if its formal legal structure remains invincibly resilient despite widespread and violent disruption of citizens' personal lives? What if the regular, uniform functioning of a society's institutional routines is based on fear or bought at the price of brutal indoctrination and psychological repression? These questions indicate that political stability comes in different shapes and sizes, and that not all kinds of stability are equally worth wanting. A more charitable way to interpret the conflict-resolution argument, then, is to see it as making a claim about the capacity of democratic procedures to obviate unacceptably repressive ways of maintaining political stability.

It is natural, for example, to interpret the "legitimacy" version of the argument along these lines. That version, remember, emphasizes the capacity for democratic deliberation to yield outcomes that citizens could, and should, regard as at least "legitimate" despite any conscientious doubts they might have about them. Animating these legitimacy arguments is the hope that citizens with opposing views on divisive questions can nonetheless find a reasonable basis on which to "agree to disagree," and thereby reconcile themselves to political outcomes otherwise distasteful to them. One can construe the more pragmatic version of the argument in a similar way: what makes democracy valuable, on this account, is its tendency to foster dispositions of compromise and a willingness to play by certain recognized rules, even if the resulting outcomes run counter to the preferences of some of the parties involved.

Interpreted this way, then, neither argument is claiming crudely that democratic arrangements are a unique or important precondition for any sort of political stability whatever. Both are, rather, concerned to avert those forms of political stability based on fear, repression, manipulation, violence, indoctrination, and strife. Instead, they seek political arrangements that achieve political stability through (to resurrect an archaic term) voluntary "complaisance" on the part of citizens.[15] Complaisance of the relevant kind promotes a form peaceful social cooperation based on mutual compromise, accommodation, respect, and tolerance. In this way, democratic procedures secure political stability and resolve conflicts without sacrificing civility and a sense of concern for others or imposing undue psychological burdens on citizens.

But even if we accept that complaisant stability of this kind is valuable, and perhaps somehow more "legitimate" than alternative varieties, one can still question whether democratic procedures are the best way to promote it. As before, empirical doubts remain: Is it clear, for example, that democratic discussion and procedures tend to promote complaisance in practice? Or do they more often sabotage the required attitudes by exacerbating and polarizing political disagreement?

But there is a more fundamental philosophical objection to this proposal. The question of what ideally complaisant citizens ought to recognize as a decent or "legitimate" compromise is one that, in principle, can be answered independently of any actual democratic process. For example, we know that appropriately complaisant citizens should not simply impose their preferred policies on other citizens with conscientious objections; rather, they should be willing to make concessions and reach an accommodation that even the objectors could regard as legitimate or at least reasonable. Suppose, however, that a particular policy to which significant social groups reasonably object is nonetheless supported by an overwhelming majority. Is there reason to believe that democratic arrangements will encourage members of that majority to seek accommodations with the objecting minorities? Is it not the case that democratic procedures in such a situation will simply invite majorities to press home their advantage and uncompromisingly impose their will on the minority? Here, democratic procedures seem unlikely to foster appropriately complaisant dispositions. As Thomas Christiano has noted, it might be better in such cases to refer the matter to some impartial outside arbitrator capable of dispassionately identifying an appropriately legitimate or reasonable compromise on which all citizens could agree.[16] This, after all, is how we promote complaisance

---

[15] See Hobbes (1994), p. 95.
[16] Christiano (1996), pp. 51ff.

in the context of legal disputes; and legal decisions are rarely reached in democratic ways. It is not clear that democratic procedures always compare favorably to such nondemocratic ways of achieving complaisance.

Safeguarding liberty against power

It is difficult to quarrel with the general proposition on which this final argument is based – that unchecked political power is a threat to those subject to it. Still, this proposition is as much a challenge to democratic rule as a defense of it. After all, democratic procedures necessarily empower particular majorities and coalitions. There is no immediate reason to assume that these groups are any less likely to abuse this power than the narrower, more exclusive groups empowered under less democratic procedures. We have already noted the familiar worry that the will of the democratic majority may often act in a "tyrannical" fashion, suppressing the freedoms of the minority.

This argument, then, points not exclusively towards democracy, but rather towards a mixed form of rule, in which political power is dispersed among various different agencies, some democratic, some not, that can check and balance each other. This notion of a "mixed" constitution, denying exclusive power to any social group, is an ancient one, going back at least to Aristotle, and, as noted above, it powerfully shaped the modern republican tradition. But insofar as a successfully "mixed" republican constitution has some democratic elements, it must, by hypothesis, include much that is nondemocratic, and perhaps antidemocratic. This is one reason why the founders of the American republic were often at pains to deny that they were proposing any sort of democracy.

At best, then, this general argument generates an extremely qualified defense of democracy. On the one hand, it abandons the idea that democracy is a necessary means for the realization of strong positive ideals (justice, the common good, the popular will), arguing instead that such value as democratic procedures possess consists in their capacity to check the abuse of power. On the other, it does not give democratic procedures any presumption over the (unmixed) alternatives, assuming instead that, in principle, democracy is no better or worse than any other simple form of rule. This is hardly a ringing endorsement of democratic practices.

Conclusions

Although we have found serious limitations in all five arguments we have considered, we should remember that the arguments we have looked at do not form an exhaustive list. Moreover, perhaps advocates of democratic rule can circumvent the most serious difficulties confronting their view by combining elements from the five arguments discussed separately here. Still, enough has been said to expose the conventional wisdom about democracy in the liberal West as deeply complacent. While our discussion has not shown that the widespread contemporary support for democratic ideals is ultimately misplaced, it should dent our confidence in them. The rationale for democratic rule is a far more complicated matter than our leaders generally acknowledge; indeed, the very identification of different political forms as "democratic" or "undemocratic" is fraught with usually unrecognized complexity. If we are honest, then, our concepts of democracy are ambiguous and unsettled, and our sense of its value haunted by long-standing yet still unstayed doubts. These received views certainly do not form simple intuitions that we can conveniently take for granted as fixed points in an appropriately critical reflection about politics.

10 War

Admittedly, there is something futile, even ridiculous, about philosophers stepping forward to offer dispassionate critical judgments about the topic of war. For one thing, war is waged today by the colossus of the modern state, bristling with weapons and armaments, some of which now possess apocalyptic power. Philosophical analysis and argument can seem an absurdly mismatched David when pitted against this monstrous Goliath. For another, war is often waged under conditions of extreme stress. As such, it is both cause and symptom of some of the darkest human impulses – fear, violence, hatred, suspicion, and the desires to inflict harm, to humiliate, to terrorize, to destroy, or to avenge. These potent human motivations have little place in, and are, alas, rarely influenced by, intellectual reflection of any kind.

But to picture war as simply a mindless orgy of violence would also be misleading. Wars are fought for reasons, sometimes even for the sake of moral ideals, and not usually waged on impulse alone. They are often initiated as a result of cool strategic calculation on the part of statespeople who claim, quite conscientiously and dispassionately, to be duty bound to pursue the national interest. War is also an *institution* as much as a collective manifestation of personal aggression. Soldiers often recognize and abide by written and unwritten conventions and codes of conduct. War is conducted by complex organizations – the armed forces – structured by elaborate rules of authority and deference, and characterized by a very distinctive professional ethos. For that reason among others, it is also a venue for the cultivation of certain virtues – those of courage, honor, selfless devotion to a cause, loyalty, among others. War as we know it would be unthinkable without these elements of structure, ethos, and organization.

Indeed, it is precisely because war presents itself as in these ways a rationally organized practice that it often seems especially horrifying. One thinks, for example, of the famous "Christmas Truce" that occurred sporadically but spontaneously in December 1914 along various stretches of the Western Front early in World War I. For a brief period, soldiers from both sides stepped out of their roles and trenches to fraternize with their opponents. They sang carols, drank beer, and (reportedly) even played soccer in the "no man's land" between the lines. Many cite this as an inspiring story of hope and common humanity amidst the bleak reality of war. To my mind, however, the haunting image of these men saluting and bowing to each other before returning to the trenches, like players in a game, to continue the organized killing attests to a more depressing truth about the power of institutional expectations to overwhelm sane and decent human relations.

In any case, at least in principle, the institutionalized and organized nature of war makes it available for philosophical assessment. As with any other human institution, we can ask when (if ever) it might be justified, how it should be regulated, and whether (and how) it might be eliminated. This chapter considers some of these questions, although we shall be able only to scratch the surface of an inexhaustible topic.

Three views

That war is an evil is not in dispute; the interesting question is what follows from this. Three broad lines of response have developed. The first claims that, while war is presumptively bad, it may nevertheless be justified in certain circumstances. On this view, not all wars are unjust, and it falls to philosophers to explain the conditions under which fighting a war might be just rather than unjust. Those who take this view defend the theory of "just war."

The second response is a pacifist one. It claims that the evils of warfare are so grave as to be beyond any possible justification. The use of violence even to promote justice is, on this view, always a losing gambit. Thus many in the pacifist tradition argue, like Gandhi and Martin Luther King, that legitimate political action must be nonviolent. While they agree with the just-war tradition that war is open to moral assessment, then, pacifists doubt that resorting to arms is just or justified under any conditions.

The third response claims that, if war is an evil, it is an evil like disease and natural disaster, not subject to moral assessment as just or unjust. On this view, often termed "realist," the division of the world into separate, mutually suspicious powers, restrained by no authority beyond their own conceptions of their "national interest," makes war as inevitable as the tectonic friction that causes earthquakes. The international arena is thus essentially anarchic and perhaps amoral, and it is futile to criticize wars by reference to systematically irrelevant criteria of justice.

We encountered a version of this realist view in chapter 4, in our discussion of Hobbes's state of nature. We saw there that Hobbes's individuals retain a right to decide for themselves how best to preserve themselves against attack. They therefore possess the "blameless liberty" to launch violent preemptive attacks on those they fear might be a threat. The fact that everyone knows that they are in this way vulnerable to the suspicions of others makes war endemic in the state of nature. For, as Hobbes put it, "as the nature of foul weather lieth not in a shower or two of rain, but in an inclination thereto of many days together: so the nature of war consisteth not in actual fighting, but in the known disposition thereto during all the time there is no assurance to the contrary."[1] Hobbes draws the realist conclusion in the following passage:

> To this war of every man against every man, this also is consequent;
> that nothing can be Unjust. The notions of Right and Wrong, Justice and
> Injustice, have there no place. Where there is no common Power, there
> is no Law; where no Law, no Injustice. Force and Fraud are in war the two
> Cardinal virtues.[2]

It is a short step to the depiction of the international arena, or of civil wars resulting from the collapse of organized government, in similarly amoral terms.

I will discuss each of these three views in turn.

War and justice

As we have seen throughout our discussions in this book, rules and principles of justice are centrally concerned with the recognition of boundaries and responsibilities. Thus such rules may often mark off spheres of personal responsibility and forbid meddling by outsiders as unjust.

[1] Hobbes (1994), p. 76.
[2] Hobbes (1994), p. 78.

But they may also draw the boundaries so as to license specified forms of interference with others. This will be the case, for example, when they permit defined agencies to (say) tax property-holders in order to compel them to make fair contributions to the provision of some valuable public service, or to search someone's home as part of a criminal investigation. In such cases, justice makes it someone's business to interfere in ways otherwise denied to others.

But how might justice understood in this way bear upon the regulation of war? War involves the organized use of violence by some group of people against others they designate as enemies. This cultivation of *enmity* is, I think, the defining feature of war-making, and we can normally assume that violent aggression against others is by itself sufficient to create enmity in the relevant sense. For it is surely uncontroversial that such violence will normally be unwelcome, resented, and resisted by its victims. That is why belligerence is frequently self-fulfilling, breeding enmity in those with whom an aggressor chooses to pick a fight. Michael Walzer captures this nicely when he refers to the "morally coercive" character of aggression. It involves, Walzer tells us, more than the effort to manipulate behavior through threats in the manner of a mugging. It represents a moral challenge to its victims' independence and drags them into the violent effort to vindicate their rights against that challenge.[3]

The self-fulfilling quality of belligerence also accounts for the appeal, to some, of that form of Christian pacifism that demands love for one's enemy and that one "turn the other cheek." For one can see this as a psychological tactic intended to frustrate an aggressor's intentions to incite conflict. It is, in its own way, an act of defiance – a refusal to accept an aggressor's terms. Unfortunately, however, whatever its psychological satisfactions, such defiance may also fail to frustrate an aggressor's hopes of seizing one's land, possessions, and people.

The just-war criteria

In any case, given what we earlier said about justice, to ask whether war can be just is presumably to ask two questions: (a) Under what conditions is it

---

[3] Walzer (1977), p. 53.

ever someone's place to declare others as *enemies* and to organize violent attacks against them? (b) How are "enemies" to be properly identified and how is it appropriate to treat them in the course of fighting them? The theory of the "just war" has always distinguished these questions, referring to (a) as "*jus ad bellum*," the matter of what justifies a resort to war in the first place, and to (b) as "*jus in bello*," the issue of *how* and *against whom* violence may permissibly be directed.

The traditional "just-war" answers to these questions are easily summarized:

Jus ad bellum:

1. *Formal and legitimate declaration:* Wars must be openly declared by legitimate and recognized political authorities; thus "wars" supposedly declared by private individuals or organizations are unjust. On this view, Osama Bin Laden's 1996 "Fatwa" declaring "War against the Americans Occupying the Land of the Two Holy Places" is already excluded as unjust. For neither Bin Laden, nor his Al Qaeda organization, is a recognized public authority with the requisite standing to make a valid declaration under this provision.
2. *Just cause:* Wars must be a response to some already unjust aggression or to grave injustices inflicted upon innocents. Just-wars are therefore always defensive wars: imperialist aggression, religious crusades, commercial wars, and preventive wars are all ruled out as unjust.
3. *Right intention:* Wars must not be fought with ulterior motives. Legitimate belligerents must be motivated by a sincere and unsullied intention to respond appropriately to the just cause, whatever it is.
4. *Proportionality 1:* The value of a belligerent's intended aim must outweigh the likely costs of fighting a war to achieve it and there must be a "reasonable prospect of success."
5. *Last resort:* Other nonviolent means of attaining a war's aim must have been fairly tried and exhausted.

Jus in bello:

1. *Proportionality 2:* Soldiers must not use excessive force, given their immediate military objectives.
2. *Noncombatant immunity:* Civilians must not be deliberately targeted or harmed. Only soldiers are legitimate objects of attack.

This list of desiderata is intricate and raises many complex issues. I will focus here only on two questions about it: First, what is the relation between the *ad bellum* and *in bello* criteria? And second, how should the crucial "just-cause" criterion be interpreted?

Before I do this, however, I note a more general issue that the very complexity of these criteria raises. Presumably the purpose of enumerating criteria for a just war is to remove confusion or disagreement about whether particular wars are just or unjust. We saw in our discussion of Rawls's notion of "reflective equilibrium" in chapter 4, for example, that an important role for "theories" of justice is to refine equivocal general convictions into sharper criteria yielding clear critical judgments about just and unjust arrangements. Such an enterprise fails to the extent that people who accept the proposed criteria nevertheless quite defensibly reach opposed conclusions when they apply them in similar cases. If the point of "theory" is to help us discriminate, the tendency of a theory to remain equivocal counts against it.

A serious worry about the just-war formula is that its complexity guarantees that it fails in precisely this way. With so many criteria to satisfy, open to so many possible interpretations, it seems inevitable that just-war theorists will reasonably reach divergent conclusions about the same cases. To take a recent example, many just-war theorists, including those speaking officially for the Catholic Church, opposed the recent US invasion of Iraq on just-war grounds. But others used the same criteria to argue that the liberation of Iraq was a just war. One such was Jean Bethke Elshtain, an avid defender of just-war thinking. Noting that "other just war thinkers may well disagree with my analysis," Elshtain modestly conceded that "the just war tradition does *not* provide a handy, stipulative tick-list. It rarely yields a unanimous knock-down argument. Rather, it is a way of analyzing and arguing based on the assertion that a resort to war justified solely on an appeal to national interest will not pass ethical muster."[4]

This strikes me as a poor defense of the just-war theory. The theory is of significant value only if it helps us to vindicate judgments about war that are not already largely uncontested, like the claim that naked appeals to national interest are insufficient to justify war. No doubt, asking of

---

[4] Elshtain (2004), p. 2.

any theory that it achieve "knock-down unanimity" is to ask too much, but surely we need something more than just a bland concession that those who accept the same theory may reasonably reach quite opposed conclusions when they apply it in specific cases. Such academic courtesies seem especially misplaced when, as here, lives are at stake. Given the magnitude of the sacrifices we are potentially asking troops and others to bear, it seems only fair to demand that just-war criteria yield pretty unequivocal conclusions. Would it seem adequate to console someone who has just lost a loved one in combat by saying, "*Arguably* he died in a just cause"? Perhaps, if we are being honest, that is all we can ever say, but the just-war theory holds out the promise of our being able to say more. If that is an empty promise the theory fails.

In bello and *ad bellum*

Just-war theorists usually insist on the independence of the *in bello* and *ad bellum* requirements. This independence reflects an implicit division of responsibilities between civilian officials and members of the armed forces: the former, but not the latter, are responsible for satisfying the *ad bellum* provisions. But both are responsible for seeing to it that the *in bello* standards are met. On this view, soldiers cannot be responsible for violations of *jus ad bellum*; but both soldiers and officials can be war criminals in respect of *jus in bello*.

Insisting on the independence of these sets of criteria carries two significant consequences. First, it implies that even in a war that is not justified by the *ad bellum* requirements, soldiers remain responsible for fighting with restraint and regard for innocent life. This is important because it prevents soldiers even in spectacularly unjust military campaigns, like Nazi troops and officers, from citing this as mitigating their responsibility for any atrocities they commit in the course of fighting.

Second, the independence of *jus in bello* and *jus ad bellum* renders the just-war theory strongly anti-utilitarian. In particular, it rules out the view that Michael Walzer helpfully refers to as the "sliding scale."[5] According to this utilitarian view, the *in bello* requirements weaken in proportion to the

---

[5] Walzer (1977), pp. 228ff.

justice of the cause for which we fight. Proponents of the sliding-scale view might argue, for example, that in a war of overwhelming righteousness there is a stronger justification for relaxing (say) noncombatant immunity than would apply in a war whose aim was of less urgent significance. The ends, in other words, justify the means.

True to the traditional just-war position, Walzer rejects the sliding-scale argument, insisting that certain means are to be ruled out regardless of the value of our military goals. On this view, exposing millions of innocent civilians to the risk of nuclear incineration through the Cold War policy of "nuclear deterrence" could not be justified even if the defeat of Soviet communism was an overwhelmingly just cause. Still, Walzer admits one important exception, arguing that, in genuine cases of "supreme emergency," states may suspend the *in bello* criteria. On this basis, Walzer entertains the conclusion that the British bombing of German civilian targets in World War II was justified, at least up to 1942, when a plausible "supreme emergency" existed. But the subsequent continuation of these raids after this "emergency" had passed, culminating in the terror bombings of Hamburg, Dresden, and Berlin towards the end of the war, represented a lapse into utilitarian calculations that the just-war theory forbids.[6] Still, because this judgment invokes the independent *in bello* requirements, this lapse does not cast doubt on the justice of the Allied cause from the point of view of *jus ad bellum*.[7]

Just cause

We have already noted that, as usually interpreted, the just-cause proviso requires that just wars be defensive responses to illegitimate aggression. But what counts as such aggression? One standard answer is enshrined in current international law. Thus Article 2(4) of the UN Charter: "All Members shall refrain in their international relations from the threat or use of force against the territorial integrity or political sovereignty of any state." On this view, what Walzer calls the "crime of aggression" consists in assaults on the territory or sovereignty of a state.

---

[6] Walzer (1977), pp. 255–63.

[7] For a criticism of the claim that *ad bellum* and *in bello* requirements can and should be kept apart, see McMahan (2004).

Walzer's metaphor of criminality is important, for it underlines an implicit assumption in the traditional account of just cause. Aggression is understood, not merely as an assault on the particular states attacked, but as a challenge to a broader norm of international order, according to which all states deserve equal respect as independent sovereign powers. As Vattel, the great eighteenth-century theorist of international law, has it:

> A dwarf is as much a man as a giant: a small Republic is no less a sovereign state than the most powerful kingdom.
>
> By a necessary consequence of that equality, whatever is lawful for one nation, is equally lawful for any other, and whatever is unjustifiable in the one, is equally so in the other.
>
> A nation then is mistress of her own actions ... If she makes an ill use of her liberty, she is guilty of a breach of duty; but other nations are bound to acquiesce in her conduct, since they have no right to dictate to her.
>
> Since nations are *free, independent, and equal* — and since each possesses *the right of judging*, according to the dictates of her conscience, what conduct she is to pursue in order to fulfil her duties; the effect of the whole is, to produce, at least externally and in the eyes of mankind, a perfect equality of rights between nations, in the administration of their affairs and the pursuit of their pretensions, without regard to the intrinsic justice of their conduct, of which others have no right to form a definitive judgment; so that whatever may be done by any one nation, may be done by any other.[8]

So, for Vattel, states cannot forcibly intervene in each other's affairs "without violating the liberty of some particular state and destroying the foundations of their natural society."[9]

Walzer's understanding of the "crime of aggression" moves in close orbit around this statist conception of global politics. There already exists, he and others maintain, a discernible vision of justice ordering the community of nations, assigning responsibility for the internal affairs of nations to the separate states that govern them, and imposing on them a corresponding duty of mutual forbearance. On this view, aggressive transgressions of these responsibility-defining boundaries provide just cause for war.

---

[8] Vattel (1844), pp. lxiii.
[9] Vattel (1844), pp. lxiii.

The obvious problem with this position is that it gives too much latitude to states to abuse their own citizens. If Vattel's statism does describe a certain vision of justice, it seems a very imperfect exemplar, as Walzer himself concedes. In a puzzling passage, Walzer writes: "The boundaries that exist [between states] at any moment in time are likely to be arbitrary, poorly drawn, the products of ancient wars. The mapmakers are likely to have been ignorant, drunken or corrupt. Nevertheless, these lines establish a habitable world. Within that world, men and women (let us assume) are safe from attack; once the lines are crossed, safety is gone."[10] But *can* we assume that such lines establish a "habitable world"? Habitable for whom? What about those persecuted by their own state for their religious beliefs, ethnically cleansed by their compatriots, or shot by the tyrants that rule them?

Such considerations encourage modifications so as to permit, over statist objections, "humanitarian intervention" to rescue individuals from gross abuses ("crimes against humanity" – torture, enslavement, "disappearance," genocide, etc.) at the hands of their own rulers. Darrel Moellendorf, for example, proposes a "cosmopolitan" account of just cause, according to which "just cause for the use of military force exists if and only if the intervention is directed toward advancing justice in the basic structure of the state or the international effects of its domestic policy." This cosmopolitan interpretation of the just-cause provision requires us to consider "whether the justified claims of persons are met before one accepts that sovereignty provides a shield against the use of military force."[11] According to Moellendorf, this corrects the fundamental weakness in the statist account.

Elshtain's arguments for the justice of the 2003 American-led invasion of Iraq turn on a similar appeal. Since the theory of just war pre-dates the entrenchment of modern state sovereignty from the mid-seventeenth century up to the present, Elshtain argues that just cause need not be interpreted in exclusively statist terms. Citing the authority of St Thomas Aquinas, she claims that a well-established track record of abusing its own citizens renders a state liable to military attack in defense of the victims

[10] Walzer (1997), p. 57.

[11] Moellendorf (2002), pp. 159–60.

or as "punishment" for its misdeeds; since the Iraqi regime had such a record, just cause for war existed whether or not it posed any immediate or direct threat to the sovereignty of the United States.[12]

Such views invite the rejoinder that they are too permissive of military intervention. They establish, it seems, a presumption in favor of violent intervention whenever there is serious injustice in the relations between citizens and their states. But, since the violation of human rights by governments, even on a large scale, is unfortunately quite common, this position would seem to commit us to large-scale belligerence in defense of human rights around the world; more so if we follow Elshtain's suggestion that not only efforts to avert ongoing abuse but also the need to punish *past* abuses constitute just cause for war.

In response Moellendorf rightly reminds us that there are other *ad bellum* conditions that must be satisfied in order for a war to be permissible, according to the just-war theory. If it is merely a necessary but not a sufficient condition for the justice of a war, the presence of a just cause does not automatically commit us to launching a military strike. For example, there must also be a reasonable prospect of success, and we must have exhausted all nonviolent alternatives.

But this response underestimates the special importance of the just-cause condition. I earlier suggested that the defining feature of war-making is the cultivation of *enmity*. Here it is relevant to recall Hobbes's claim that war refers not merely to belligerent acts, or to the actual initiation of hostilities, but more basically to a possible state or disposition of two or more parties *vis à vis* each other. Thus Hobbes denied that a state of war requires actual fighting; it requires merely a "tract of time, wherein the will to contend by battle is sufficiently known."[13] The great seventeenth-century jurist Hugo Grotius opened his seminal *De Jure Belli ac Pacis* with a closely related observation. Having quoted (approvingly) Cicero's definition of war as "a contention by force," Grotius noted the etymological origins of our concept of war in words signifying multitude, diversity, disunity, and discord.[14] Enmity is an extreme manifestation of such disunity and division; it involves the open recognition of implacable causes of contention between

[12] Elshtain (2004), p. 3.
[13] Hobbes (1994), p. 76.
[14] Grotius (1901), p. 18.

separate individuals and groups, and precludes their peaceable unification under agreed terms.

These considerations reveal a difficulty with Moellendorf's reply that just cause is a necessary but not sufficient condition for a resort to arms, for it seems to overlook the symbolic significance of an open acknowledgment of just cause. Even in the absence of actual fighting such an acknowledgment nonetheless nurses enmity and the disposition to "contend by force." It implies that, but for contingent considerations having to do with the likelihood of success, last resort, and judgments about proportionality, when states are judged to have unjustly abused their own citizens a violent military response is in principle justified.

But encouraging states to draw this conclusion seems an uncertain recipe for peace. It is difficult not to have some sympathy for Vattel's worry that allowing nations a presumptive right to intervene by force in other states' internal affairs "opens the door to all the ravages of enthusiasm and fanaticism, and furnishes ambition with numberless pretexts."[15] Under this dispensation, when states are accused of maltreating their own citizens they have good reason to fear that these criticisms express hostile intentions, whether or not military action is actually unleashed. Insofar as this heightens a sense of enmity and therefore insecurity, this approach seems only likely to encourage belligerence and to sabotage peace. The statist alternative has significant costs, too, but its proponents can argue that its redeeming virtue is an accepted norm of mutual forbearance around which states can unite in pursuit of peace, notwithstanding their other differences.

One might respond that justice is more important than peace. But that is exactly what is in dispute. For example, pacifists, to whose views we turn next, think that the evident evil of war requires that peace be preserved at all costs, even if this means tolerating some injustice. To them, war remains the greater evil. They may be wrong, but flat assertions that justice trumps peace simply beg that question.

The claims of peace

Many assume that just-war theory and pacifism are mutually exclusive. But here some care is needed. In particular we need to notice that pacifists could

---

[15] Vattel (1844), p. 137.

be opposed to just-war theory in at least two ways. They might hold, on independent grounds, that war is always unacceptable and then argue that, since it regards war as sometimes acceptable, the just-war framework must be incorrect. If, for example, Gandhi and King were right to insist that violence is never an acceptable means of pursuing political ends, then clearly just-war theory goes wrong at the outset in assuming that it can be. Clearly, this radical version of pacifism represents a direct challenge to just-war theorists.

On the other hand, pacifists might accept the just-war criteria but deny that any actual wars could possibly satisfy them. Taking their cue from those proponents of the just-war theory who have admitted that the number of truly just wars must be vanishingly small, "just-war pacifists" could regard the *in bello* and *ad bellum* criteria as useful reminders that the notion of a "just war" is a utopian fiction.

It is not hard to see how they might make this argument. They might agree, for example, that justice in war requires that a belligerent declare war for the sake of a just cause and without any ulterior motives at all, but argue (surely plausibly) that motives of the requisite purity are hardly ever displayed by states in the world that we know. Alternatively, they might suggest that the judgments about proportionality required by both the *in bello* and *ad bellum* criteria presuppose a degree of foresight and precision that is unattainable in the context of international conflict, and especially in the heat of battle. Rather than rejecting the theory of just war, then, pacifists who argue along these lines actually lean on it to make their case against the resort to military force.

Pacifism is often correctly associated with a commitment to nonviolence, but here too we must be careful to avoid two possible misunderstandings. First, a commitment to nonviolence is not necessarily the same as a renunciation of all forms of force as means to achieve political ends, or even of all expressions of enmity. In a memorable passage from his *Letter from Birmingham Jail*, for example, the pacifist Martin Luther King made this point clear:

> Non-violent direct action seeks to create such a crisis and foster such
> a tension that a community which has constantly refused to negotiate
> is forced to confront the issue. It seeks so to dramatize the issue that it
> can no longer be ignored ... just as Socrates felt that it was necessary to

create a tension in the mind so that individuals could rise from the bondage of myths and half-truths to the unfettered realm of creative analysis and objective appraisal, so must we see the need for non-violent gadflies to create the kind of tension in society that will help men rise from the dark depths of prejudice and racism to the majestic heights of understanding and brotherhood. The purpose of our direct action program is to create a situation so crisis-packed that it will inevitably open the door to negotiation ... We know through painful experience that freedom is never voluntarily given by the oppressor: it must be demanded by the oppressed.[16]

Quite clearly these are fighting words, but they are also an admonition to fight an enemy through nonviolent means. This is not a paradoxical idea: talk of the "pen" being "mightier than the sword," or of "battles" of ideas and for "hearts and minds," need not be empty rhetoric.

Second, at least some pacifists have distinguished between the lawless violence of war, which they regard as absolutely wrong, and the "force of the magistrate," the acceptable legal use of violence to punish wrongdoers and maintain social order. This is the position taken, for example, by Quaker pacifists. It allowed William Penn, who attempted to govern Pennsylvania on Quaker principles in the seventeenth century, to reconcile his pacifism with the view that government nonetheless has a right to "terrify evildoers" through the use of violent punishment.[17] On this view, it is the cultivation of violent enmity that marks the special evil of war. But from the fact that violence is often an expression of enmity it does not follow that all forms of violence express enmity. For Penn and other Christian pacifists, penal violence channeled and restrained through legal means need not be motivated by enmity. It may rather reflect an impartial desire to see justice done, and may even reflect love and benevolence towards those sanctioned, as in the case of parents disciplining recalcitrant children.

Killing in self-defense

In any case, pacifist views draw their strength from conventional beliefs about the wrongness of violence and especially that of killing innocents.

[16] King (1989), pp. 59–60.
[17] Penn (1682).

It is precisely because war inevitably involves both of these that pacifists deny that war is ever justifiable. Against the thrust of the *in bello* provisions, many pacifists are even inclined to resist the conventional assumption that *soldiers* engaged in combat forfeit the right not to be killed. After all, they argue, soldiers are rarely themselves directly responsible for any wrongful aggression in which they are engaged — they are often innocent pawns in campaigns planned and authorized by their superiors, both officers and politicians. This presumption of innocence will seem particularly strong when soldiers are conscripts, but often remains plausible even when they have volunteered for military service. Soldiers may volunteer only because they cannot find other forms of employment, and few ever do so on the understanding that they may ignore orders whenever they personally disapprove of the wars they are later asked to fight.

Pacifist doubts about killing innocents in war come under the greatest pressure in the context of self-defense. Most believe that they have a right to use violence to repel physical assault, and *in extremis* a right to kill in self-defense or in the defense of others. The most natural way to defend war against pacifist objections is to extrapolate from these relatively uncontentious individual rights to the right of states to kill in defense of its citizens. Both Hobbes and Walzer, despite their many other differences, use this form of argument to defend the resort to war.

Whether pacifist views falter in the face of such arguments depends on how wide the right to kill in self-defense really is. For Hobbes, it is of course as wide as one can imagine, since on his view it entails not only the right to use violence to repel an attack but also the right to decide who might be a threat in the first place. On his account, individuals in a state of nature, and by extension states in the international arena, reserve the right to destroy, even preemptively, whomever they judge to be a threat to their safety. We will consider Hobbes's views in our later discussion of realism. However, we can set it aside here because both pacifists and just-war theorists like Walzer will agree in rejecting Hobbes's hair-trigger interpretation of the right of self-defense. The challenge posed by pacifism to just-war theorists is thus to provide a principled basis for rejecting Hobbes's extremely permissive view while still leaving enough room for justified killing of even innocent soldiers in a just war.

A standard way of meeting this challenge is to appeal to cases in which pacifists would on reflection have to admit that individuals reserve the right to use violence against innocents in self-defense. Moellendorf offers two such examples on behalf of the just-war theory:

> Case 1: In the middle of the night a hatchet bearing sleepwalker attacks my housemate. I do not know that the attacker is sleepwalking, but I can repel the attack only by killing her. Case 2: A group of armed thugs has already attacked my neighbour once. I see them coming for a second attack. I do not know that one member of the group has been urging restraint. I can prevent the imminent attack only by firing on the group, which will probably kill all of them. Does the innocence of the person in each case prohibit that person being killed?[18]

Moellendorf claims not, and concludes on the strength of these examples that "the activity of unjustly attacking defeats the presumption of the wrongness of killing innocents."

Against this, some pacifists concede that the use of violent force against attackers in situations like those Moellendorf describes is permissible but deny that this carries over into the relevant case of *states* killing innocents in wars. This was the position taken by C. E. M. Joad in a pacifist tract (still worth reading) written between the two World Wars. Denying that "the use of force is always and necessarily wrong," Joad continued:

> I should find no difficulty ... answering the historic question put by military personages on tribunals to those who appeared before them pleading conscientious objection to military service in the last war: "What would you do if you saw a German coming at your wife, mother, daughter, sister, cousin, aunt, or what-not, with intent to rape her?" My answer is that I should quite certainly try to stop him with whatever means were at my disposal, and with whatever means were at my disposal I should, in similar circumstances, try to defend myself. What I should not do, is to regard the aggression of the hypothetical German as a ground for proceeding to drop bombs on *his* wife, mother, daughter, sister, cousin, aunt, or what-not.[19]

Moellendorf would respond that Joad misses the point because there is no disagreement about the targeting of civilians in bombing campaigns. This, he might remind us, is ruled out anyway by the *in bello* criteria.

---

[18] Moellendorf (2002), pp. 152–3.
[19] Joad (1939), p. 59.

The purpose of Moellendorf's two cases is then not to justify killings of this sort, but rather to make room for the defensive killing of (even innocent) combatants engaged in aggressive military campaigns.

This is a fair point, but pacifists might in turn respond that until weaponry has become far more discriminating than it actually is, or until wars are fought with androids without relatives and dependants who will be crushed or ruined by their loss, as a practical matter war still involves unacceptable collateral damage to innocents. Just-war theorists will be unimpressed by this reply, since, on their view, as long as it is *unintended*, and every effort made to avoid it, such damage is not necessarily unjust or impermissible.

Against this, however, pacifists can argue that while such philosophical niceties about intention seem plausible when reflecting on war from a distance, they are disloyal to the lived experience of warfare. When our missiles miss their intended military targets and instead destroy (say) a school and its pupils, the relatives of the victims will surely be quite reasonably disgusted with official statements to the effect that "we didn't mean it." For the parents, the more immediate point will be that, had "we" not chosen war, their children would still be alive. Nor is the unintended nature of the damage likely to assuage significantly any (quite under-standable) feelings of guilt afflicting the soldier who wrongly calibrated the missile's targeting mechanism that day.

Killing combatants

Even if we are not convinced by these counter-arguments about noncombat-ants, several other features of Moellendorf's examples raise doubts about whether they can even justify the killing of *combatants* on the terms just-war theorists usually defend it. In particular, those examples *stipulate* that killing specific attackers is the only available means to save specific victims. They also assume that we already know exactly who is attacking whom. Moreover, in both cases the attack is imminent and demands immediate preventive action. But examples with these features expose as many questions about the just-war position as they remove.

For one thing, even if we concede — with Joad — that when there *really is* no alternative to killing specific attackers to save their victims, individuals and perhaps states retain the right to kill, this arguably leaves us well short of the right to go to war against an enemy that just-war theorists usually defend. The right of a state to shoot down a military aircraft that is about to bomb a civilian neighborhood is one thing. But a formal declaration of war, and initiation of hostilities, against a state whose forces (say) merely violate the territorial integrity of a state but do not immediately, or to anyone's knowledge, threaten innocent life, are others. (Perhaps the forces are marching through uninhabited lands, actually welcomed by the indigenous population though not by their government, or crossing into foreign airspace on a surveillance mission.)

And what of cases in which "just" war is contemplated after, and as a response to, some already consummated outrage such as an assassination, an invasion, a terrorist attack, or a massacre? In such instances we cannot plausibly maintain that attacks on combatants are necessary to prevent the relevant outrages because, by hypothesis, it is already too late to prevent them. Perhaps we are worried about similar outrages in the future. But generic anxiety of this sort is quite different from the immediate and unambiguous encounters with specific attackers and specific victims presumed in Moellendorf's discussion. It is not obvious, then, that his examples license the resort to war in such cases, though not all just-war theorists will be content with that conclusion.

Another problem is that in Moellendorf's examples it is not so much the *injustice* of the attack as its overwhelming *imminence* that triggers the resort to preventive force. After all, if we knew that someone was planning a similarly unjust attack to take place next week we would not normally think that killing him is the appropriate, or even a permissible, response. In such a case, calling the police and having the would-be attacker arrested while finding the intended victims a place of safety seems nearer the mark.

This suggests that our reactions to Moellendorf's discussion may be controlled, not by considerations of justice, but by our natural tendency to identify strongly with the psychological stress experienced by individuals intimately confronting violent attack. We realize that they may not have time to consider their options carefully and their responses may therefore be largely reflexive and instinctive. But pacifists might admit that, under such conditions of extreme necessity, agents have an excuse for killing, but nevertheless insist that this is not sufficient to establish that such killings are positively justified or no longer "presumptively wrong," as Moellendorf claims. There is an important difference between having an excuse for doing something that we recognize as unjust or otherwise wrong and claiming — as just-war theorists do about killing innocent combatants in a just war — that it is actually the *right thing to do*. Pacifists might also point out here that, while soldiers in combat will often face imminent threats of the sort Moellendorf describes, the civilian leaders who authorize and declare the wars that put them in such dangerous situations rarely do so under conditions of similar necessity. While soldiers may have an excuse for wrongdoing, then, the official authors of war may not. (We shall return to this issue of excuse in our later discussion of realism.)

Finally, is Moellendorf's principle compatible with the *in bello* requirement that only combatants may legitimately be killed? Moellendorf says that the "activity of unjustly attacking" justifies the killing of the attackers, but often members of the civilian command (civil servants in the ministry of defense, say) are themselves implicated in this activity. *Jus in bello* confers immunity upon them, but the thrust of Moellendorf's argument points in a different direction. If we can most effectively halt imminent military aggression by killing civilian leaders rather than soldiers on the ground, his principle presumably recommends that course. Indeed, since they are more directly responsible, it seems only fair that they, rather than the (often innocent) soldiers they order around, ought to bear the costs of unjust aggression.

These considerations suggest that defending the just-war position against pacifist objections is a more complex task than we may at first suppose. Whether just-war conclusions are completely congruent with conventional moral assumptions about the wrongness of killing innocents is unclear. On the other hand, many will think it unrealistic to suppose that our judgments about war can ever be fully and neatly reconciled with even fairly uncontroversial moral principles. To them, insisting on keeping our moral hands squeaky clean[20] makes little sense when we think of those cowering in London Underground stations while the Luftwaffe bombs their homes, or of thousands of Muscovites fleeing in panic upon hearing that the *Wehrmacht* is within 50 miles of the city. We turn now to consider this sort of view, which holds that war is in some sense a special case, not fully capturable within the framework of conventional moral assessment.

---

[20] See on this point Walzer (1973).

Realism

Those, like just-war theorists and pacifists, committed to the moral criticism of war (and of international institutions more generally), often regard the refutation of Hobbesian realism as a high priority.[21] It is easy to understand this impulse. Realists often seem to assert that international politics is necessarily an amoral struggle for power unrestrained by ethical principles. But, if true, this makes the moral criticism of war as pointless as the moral criticism of the natural selection of species. ("Use of venom by predators is wrong!")

If realists really claim that the global order is an ethical vacuum, in which moral assessments of states' actions are systematically unavailable or beside the point, their view becomes difficult to distinguish from a broader skepticism about moral judgment in general. Accordingly, its critics often contend that realism is defensible only by sacrificing the assumption that individual conduct is itself subject to moral restraints.[22] Since few realists have been so radical as to abandon the conventional belief that individuals' choices are open to moral assessment, this line of criticism reveals a serious tension in their position. If states are engaged in an amoral struggle for power, why suppose that it is any different for individuals generally? This suggests that crude realist doctrines of this sort either are confused or merely reiterate a more generic moral skepticism with very controversial implications far beyond the international case. Given these difficulties, this rudimentary realist claim seems unworthy of serious attention.

But there is a more interesting and subtle version of the realist view. Proponents of this alternative interpretation do not claim that moral judgment is *impossible* in the international arena; nor do they draw from realist premises the conclusion that we must simply resign ourselves to the inevitability of war. Rather, they have used the realist view as a springboard for an unsentimental critical analysis of the institutions of war making. One thinker who developed this line of argument with particular clarity

---

[21] Thus Walzer (1977), ch. 1; Holmes (1989), chs. 2–3; Beitz (1999), part 1; Moellendorf (2002), pp. 143–8.

[22] This is the essence of Beitz's critique. See Beitz (1999), pp. 14, 15–17, 34.

was the American pragmatist John Dewey. Dewey's endorsement of a version of realism is clear from the following passage:

> Lamentations as to the gulf which divides the working ethical principles of nations from those animating decent individuals are copious. But they express the pious rather than the efficacious wish of those who indulge in them. They overlook the central fact that morals are relative to organization. Individuals ... can be [moral] ... because they are partakers in modes of associated life which confer powers and impose responsibilities upon them. States are nonmoral in their activities just because of the absence of an inclusive society which defines and establishes rights. Hence they are left to their own devices, secret and violent if need is deemed imminent, in judging and asserting their rights and obligations ... The nations exist with respect to one another in what the older writers called a state of nature, not in a social or political state.[23]

The problem to which Dewey draws attention in this passage is not the complete absence of ethical criteria by which to judge states' actions. The problem is rather that of making such norms *effective*, such that states are prepared to recognize their direction as authoritative over their own judgments about their national interests. Dewey continued:

> If only there were a general recognition of the dependence of moral control upon social order, all of the sentiment and well-wishing opinion that is now dissipated would be centered. It would aim at the establishment of a definitely organized federation of nations not merely in order that certain moral obligations might be effectively enforced but in order that a variety of obligations might come into existence ... Warlikeness is not of itself the cause of war; a clash of interests due to the absence of organization is its cause. A supernational organization which oversees, obviates and adjusts these clashes ... possible only with the coincident outlawing of war itself, will focus moral energies now scattered and make operative moral ideas now futile.[24]

In a similar vein, Rousseau used a recognizably Hobbesian realism to mount a powerful critique of Hobbes's own argument that accepting the authority of sovereign states is sufficient to end the state of nature struggle.

---

[23] Dewey (1939), pp. 508–9.
[24] Dewey (1939), pp. 510–11.

He argued that Hobbes's conclusions create a "manifest contradiction": "As individuals we live in a civil state and are subject to laws, but as nations each enjoys the liberty of nature." The resulting predicament "is worse than if these distinctions were unknown. For living simultaneously in the social order and in the state of nature, we are subjected to the evils of both without gaining the security of either." In this way, Rousseau pessimistically concluded that "the vain name of justice serves only to safeguard violence."[25]

The "war system"

While still essentially realist, this position is more complex than the crude doctrine that international power politics is simply an ethical vacuum. For it assumes that distinctive (and dangerous) configurations of power tend to promote and to be sustained by distinctive (and dangerous) ethical beliefs. Dewey's depiction of the international world of states as a "war system" nicely captures this point:

> It is inevitable that disputes, controversies, conflicts of interest and opinion shall arise between nations as between persons. Now to settle disputes . . . the experiences and wisdom of the world have found two methods and only two. One is the way of the law and courts; the other is the way of violence and lawlessness. In private controversies the former way is now established. In disputes among nations the way of violence is equally established. The word "established" is used advisedly . . . the world lives today under a war system; a system entrenched in politics, in diplomacy, in international law and in every court that sits under existing international law. The proposition, then, is not the moral proposition to abolish wars. It is the much more fundamental proposition to abolish the war system as an authorized and legally sanctioned institution. The first idea is either utopian at present or merely sentiment. This other proposition, to abolish the war system as an authorized, established institution, sanctioned by law, contemplated by law, is practical . . . Recourse to violence is not only *a* legitimate method for settling international disputes at present; under certain circumstances it is the only legitimate method, the ultimate reason of state.[26]

---

[25] Rousseau (1990), p. 186.
[26] Dewey (1939), pp. 514–15.

Here Dewey echoes Rousseau's dark thought that the most dangerous features of the current global order actually reflect ethical understandings that are "established" or "reigning" within it. The "war system" is pathological, on this view, not because it is an ethical vacuum, but precisely because the ethics regulating it are unduly permissive of dangerous conduct on the part of states.

One might think that this view is incompatible with Hobbes's realist claim that in a state of nature "nothing can be unjust" and that "notions of right and wrong, justice and injustice have there no place". Clearly, the two views are incompatible if Hobbes is understood as suggesting that there are no ethical assumptions *at all* governing a state of nature. But there is another possible interpretation of Hobbes that corresponds to the more subtle version of realism that Dewey seems to have had in mind.

Suppose we understand Hobbes as arguing that the special conditions of the state of nature *excuse* conduct that is nonetheless without justification and perhaps indeed immoral. On this view, the extenuating circumstances of the state of nature diminish responsibility for morally questionable actions. This interpretation is supported by Hobbes's own talk of individuals' "blameless liberty" to defend themselves as they choose in a state of nature. Whether or not they are justified in choosing to defend themselves (say) by preemptively attacking a perceived threat, individuals must be excused from blame for such judgments as long as they remain in a state of nature.

But what is the basis for this supposed excuse? As we saw in chapter 4, Hobbes's answer was that under the anarchical conditions of a state of nature, individuals will contrive a self-fulfilling mutual suspicion and mistrust. Under these conditions, individuals will be driven to assume that they (like everyone else) reserve the right to protect themselves as they choose. Overwhelmed by fear and mutual suspicion, individuals in the state of nature will find this habit difficult to kick, like an addictive drug. In this way, the duress of fear and insecurity induces a kind of collective addiction to violence as a way of dealing with perceived threats and to concomitant beliefs about agents' right to use it. While such beliefs do not amount to, and indeed preclude, a systematic consensus about what is justified or unjustified as just and unjust, they nonetheless have ethical content. The multipurpose excuse of self-preservation effectively institutes an ethical permission, of uncertain limit, for the resort to violence. Applied to the international case, this view implies that a similar addiction to the logic of excuse is likely to develop among self-protecting states interacting under global anarchy.

The resulting possibility that states are addicted to a "war system," and habitually view violence as a legitimate means of conflict resolution, is a powerful and disturbing one. According to this Deweyan/Hobbesian hypothesis, it is in the nature of this addiction that states presume themselves and their peers to have a systematic excuse ("*raison d'état*") for conduct they might nonetheless acknowledge as morally questionable or as without justification. On this basis, pleas of necessity, self-defense, national interest, and the like in due course come to be accepted as legitimate excuses for wrongdoing.

Unfortunately there is considerable plausibility to this gloomy hypothesis about the addictive, even obsessive, quality of states' interest in violence as a mode of conflict resolution. One writer refers memorably to the "monstrous dissipation of resources in the search for military security."[27] Particularly striking is the famously self-defeating phenomenon of arms races, of which the nuclear proliferation during the Cold War is the most spectacular recent example. In a recent discussion lamenting the reluctance of the Cold War protagonists to renounce their ridiculously superabundant stockpiles of nuclear weapons, former US Secretary of Defense Robert S. MacNamara wryly observes:

> Although any proposed reduction [in nuclear arsenals] is welcome,
> it is doubtful that survivors — if there were any — of an exchange of
> 3,200 warheads (the U.S. and Russian numbers projected for 2012), with a
> destructive power approximately 65,000 times that of the Hiroshima bomb,
> could detect a difference between the effects of such an exchange and one
> that would result from the launch of the current U.S. and Russian forces
> totaling about 12,000 warheads.[28]

Writing before the outbreak of World War II, and before public knowledge of nuclear weapons, Joad wrote:

> Give a schoolboy an airgun and he may shoot a few sparrows or break a
> window . . . give him a revolver and he becomes a public danger. One does

27 Stone (1984), p. 157.
28 MacNamara (2005), p. 34.

not, after all, present one's children with dangerous toys, until they are old enough to play with them without harming themselves ... Yet these are precisely the gifts with which science has dowered modern man, with the result that he is in measurable distance of destroying himself through his inability to devise the political machinery which is necessary to canalize and direct for the public safety the powers with which science has invested him. Unless he can devise this machinery before it is too late, our civilization will follow its predecessors to destruction, and man himself may be superseded and sent to join the Mesozoic reptiles upon the evolutionary scrap-heap of life's discarded experiments.[29]

The important point Joad makes here is that the technological enhancement of the means of violence is a necessary but not sufficient condition for war to become an unacceptable menace. The sufficient conditions include institutions disposed to deploy and use lethal weapons, and the political environment likely to foster this disposition. It is just such an environment that Dewey and other realist critics intend to pick out when they speak of a "war system" that renders futile "serious efforts at disarmament."

Arguments along these lines do not so much condemn war on moral grounds as regard it as a symptom of pathological irrationality. Thus one contemporary pacifist writes:

A man overeats, smokes heavily, drinks too much, and gets no exercise. He learns that he has high blood pressure and a weak heart. He decides to switch to filters, drink a little less, skip seconds on desserts, and walk a few blocks now and then. Is that not a step in the right direction? Certainly. But it probably will not save him. What he needs is a change in his whole way of life. We, too, can go on fueling the furnace of war and take our chances on being able to control the heat. But let us not deceive ourselves that this is likely to save us either. The whole history of civilization shows that we have never been able to resist heaping more fuel onto the fire. Or to avoid burning ourselves periodically with increasing severity. Less of what we have been doing wrong is not good enough. We must stop doing it.[30]

This argument is better understood as criticizing potentially catastrophic *imprudence* rather than censuring any sort of *immorality* or *injustice*. Indeed,

---

[29] Joad (1939), pp. 159–60.
[30] Holmes (1989), p. 11.

as we have seen, such arguments can be viewed as condemning an irrationality itself bred by certain moral beliefs. These are the ideas that underpin what Charles Beitz calls the "morality of states," the Vattelian view that states are sovereign over their own affairs, equally entitled to respect as autonomous defenders of their national honor. It turns out, then, that a consistent realism need not preclude a criticism of war, and may in fact be compatible with a broadly pacifist orientation that seeks, with Dewey, somehow to outlaw the institutions of war-making.

Conclusions

This pessimistic diagnosis of the irrationality of a morality of states has not gone unchallenged. There is a rival view, according to which a world of independent nation-states need not degenerate into the jealous suspicion of a Hobbesian state of nature. It turns out, proponents of this view suggest, that the best means for states to maintain order and prosperity at home tend also, at least in the long run, to deprive international conflict of the oxygen it needs to ignite. This more optimistic line of thinking can also be discerned in Hobbes. He sometimes suggested that, by promoting industry and economic development within their own borders, states may eventually attain a kind of self-sufficiency, unavailable to *individuals* interacting in a state of nature, that renders war among nations pointless and unnecessary.[31]

This thought was modified and articulated more fully by Kant in *Perpetual Peace* and several other important essays.[32] Writing at the end of the eighteenth century, Kant foresaw that prosperity and commerce might also foster international economic interdependence and in turn engender collaboration and consensus among nations committed to broadly liberal democratic ideals of equal opportunity and individual freedom. Although the expansion of global commerce would itself exacerbate conflict in the short run, the long-term prognosis, Kant claimed, was hopeful. Eventually, a core of prosperous liberal democratic states could settle the terms of a *"foedus pacificum"* (a "league of peace") that would obviate war among them.

---

[31] Hobbes (1998), p. 150.
[32] Kant (1991), pp. 41–54, 93–131.

A "perpetual peace" then becomes possible through gradual expansions of such a league until its membership encompasses the entire globe. A currently fashionable variant of this more optimistic vision is defended by proponents of the so-called "liberal democratic peace theory," which asserts that liberal democracies do not, and predictably will not, go to war with each other. In many ways Rawls's *Law of Peoples*, discussed briefly in chapter 6, represents a synthesis of these views, for it is at once heavily indebted to Kant's vision of perpetual peace and openly reliant on assumptions drawn from the liberal democratic peace theory.[33]

In the light of recent world history, the prescience of Kant's view is striking. But while some developments — the foundation of the United Nations and the entrenchment of an increasingly rich body of international law, for example — seem to vindicate his predictions, the overall record is too mixed to allow us to embrace his optimism with wholehearted confidence. To take just one example from the other side of the ledger, we might remember that during World War II large-scale terror bombing was not only practiced by nasty Axis powers but also enthusiastically pioneered by the Allies in Tokyo, Hiroshima, Nagasaki, Cologne, Dresden, Hamburg, and Berlin among others. The targeting of civilians in such campaigns was not dictated by ideology. Rather, it reflected the massive mobilization of the economic infrastructure characteristic of modern warfare. Under these circumstances of "total war," traditional *in bello* distinctions between combatants and noncombatants tend to blur. Smashing the morale of the civilians who work on the assembly lines making armaments or sewing military uniforms comes to seem as legitimate a tactic as cutting an army's supply lines on the field of battle.

The liberal democratic states, too, bear much of the responsibility for further blurring these distinctions by aggressively researching and then threatening to use "weapons of mass destruction," a term whose recent mindless repetition in the media should not be allowed to obscure its actual, quite outrageous, meaning. These developments can only have encouraged the idea that terrorizing civilians is a legitimate means for promoting political ends. These considerations naturally lead one to suspect that, in their current desperation to contain nuclear proliferation,

---

[33] Rawls (1999b), pp. 46–54.

and to win their self-declared "war on terror," the liberal democracies, and the community of nations more generally, are struggling to control Frankenstein monsters partly of their own creation.

Can states succeed in these endeavors? Or are they, like relapsing addicts, fated to repeat the mistakes of the past despite their best intentions, and perhaps with ever greater destructive force? Unfortunately these are open questions. It is still too early to say whether the tendency of modern statism is to eliminate or to exacerbate the problem of war.

11 Living with difference

The phenomena of human difference and disagreement have set the agenda for this book, and for political philosophy as a whole, from the beginning. As authors from Plato to Rawls illustrate, many political philosophers have sought to overcome the conflicts and disagreements that mark ordinary politics by postulating and delineating comprehensive political ideals (of justice, the common good, human flourishing, the "free society") by which to judge existing institutions. But while this sort of speculation may be illuminating in many ways, it can also foster an overly simplistic attitude to political disagreement. From the vantage point of such high ideals, the persistence of conflicts between those of fundamentally opposed religious and ethical persuasions may seem trivial and uninteresting, little more than a symptom of the current imperfection of political reality, or of errors destined to pass away once the "truth" is gradually understood and realized.

But surely indulging this thought is both naïvely optimistic and a serious evasion of the complex realities of political conflict. People differ, sometimes very widely, in their beliefs, their modes of conduct, their religious or cultural sensibilities and their identities. We cannot normally expect people to change these often deeply ingrained traits at the drop of a hat, just because we think we have strong philosophical arguments in favor of ways of life, beliefs, and practices they reject. Doing so is often resented and resisted, and a cause of enmity, violence, and war. Some accommodation of difference and disagreement is thus usually a precondition for peaceful cohabitation. And apart from these more pragmatic considerations, many will anyway repudiate the spirit of Bossuet's declaration that "I have the right to persecute you because I am right and you are wrong." They will say that Bossuet's attitude to persecution is wrong on principle even if his religious beliefs are indeed true.

The question of how political institutions and citizens ought properly to negotiate their various differences and disagreements is therefore a topic in its own right. What principles ought to govern our encounters with those whose conduct and beliefs we conscientiously reject? This chapter considers this question.

Why can't we all just get along?

Today the issues surrounding this question are often swept under the rug with nice-sounding pronouncements that "everyone is equally entitled to their own opinions," that we should learn to "live and let live," that anyone's "perspective" is as worthy of respect as everyone else's, that it is bad to be "judgmental," etc. But these assertions are even more naïve than those views, just rejected, that dismiss disagreement as a mere symptom of the failure to recognize the "truth" of certain grand ideals.

Even if we are talking simply about personal beliefs, rather than about people's actions and conduct, claims to the effect that everyone is equally entitled to his or her own opinions, that we should refrain from judging them, or that individuals' views are equally worthy of respect, are unsustainable. Presumably, one is entitled to one's opinions to the extent that one has adequate grounds for accepting them. If so, then saying that all are equally entitled to their opinions implies that all have equally good grounds for the beliefs they proclaim. But this cannot be right; there is just too much stupidity and claptrap for it to be remotely plausible.

Furthermore, one belief excludes another: one cannot, for example, simultaneously profess atheism and Christianity. Believing that there are good reasons to deny the existence of God commits me to suspecting that Christians make some sort of mistake — that what they take to be adequate grounds for belief in God actually are not. And if a self-proclaimed atheist genuinely thinks that her grounds for her beliefs are *no worse than* those of Christians, then she really has no business professing atheism rather than Christianity. She ought to conclude that the question is open and suspend judgment. Even then, she implies that Christians are making a mistake, for (as Christians) they can hardly regard the existence of God as an entirely open question.

These considerations led Hobbes to notice that merely *expressing* one's disagreement with others is potentially offensive. For, in rejecting beliefs they accept, it is difficult, perhaps impossible, to avoid "tacitly accusing" them of "error" and hence of being "fools."[1] As long as people take their beliefs seriously, then, and as long as those beliefs are mutually contra- dictory (as they very often are), we have no choice but to recognize and deal appropriately with the standing potential for offence. Empty slogans about people being equally entitled to their own views simply overlook these inconvenient facts of life.[2]

But they become even less helpful when we consider, not just people's beliefs, but the various actions and practices that they may justify. Some religious traditions require animal sacrifice, encourage polygamy, employ narcotic substances in their rites, incite various forms of violence, and call for other practices to which many of us object. Others denounce homo- sexuality, abortion, unbelief, the use of alcohol, Sunday trading, and the teaching of Darwinian evolution in schools, and urge their legal restriction. Many, regardless of their religious beliefs, are offended by pornography, obscenity, and public nudity, believe that the recreational use of drugs should be criminalized, or denounce immigrants who refuse to assimilate to the dominant national culture. Still others reject these views. Some deny that it is the business of the state to enforce essentially religious ideals or to prohibit activities on purely religious grounds. Others believe that we ought to extend the legal privilege of marriage to same-sex couples, or see nothing wrong with drinking, shopping on Sundays, letting women terminate their unwanted pregnancies, consuming pornography, recreational drug use, and so on.

The important point underlying all of this is that people's ethical beliefs are action-guiding. Disagreements in ethical beliefs inevitably foster conflicts over the forms of conduct they inspire and purport to justify. There is rarely any way for public policy to remain entirely neutral in these

---

[1] Hobbes (1998), pp. 26–7.

[2] Perhaps there is something to the view that people are worthy of respect in virtue of the *sincerity* of their commitment to their convictions, regardless of their validity. But there is nearly as much insincerity in the world as there is folly, and so even this view implies that we should withhold respect from those whose beliefs strike us an insincerely professed (e.g. those "spin doctors" paid to defend in public what they [must!] secretly acknowledge as indefensible, or those who adopt certain beliefs just to fit in, or to appear fashionable). And anyway, who wants to be respected as a sincere fool?

disputes, as the case of abortion vividly illustrates. None of the possible ways in which the state might regulate reproductive rights is entirely satisfactory to adherents of all the dominant ethical and religious positions on the subject. The effects of doing nothing are often just as objectionable to some as doing something is to others. What goes for abortion goes for almost all controversial areas of public policy.

For all of these reasons, we cannot expect people to "get along" automatically. Developing acceptable principles of accommodation to negotiate our differences requires that we look beyond well-intentioned but vapid injunctions about everyone's being entitled to his or her own opinions.

Two angles: tolerance and respect

Broadly speaking, we might consider such principles of accommodation from two slightly different, though not necessarily exclusive, angles. On the one hand, one might approach the question from the point of view of those who have (or think they have) reasons to disapprove of others because of the particular ethical or religious beliefs they already accept. Traditional theories of toleration, as they developed within the Western Christian tradition, typically addressed agents in this sort of situation. Historically, Christianity has often been an intolerant religion, both in its practice and in its theory. Its adherents have sometimes recommended the burning of unbelievers and apostates, have brutally suppressed unorthodox ("heretical") interpretations of its own theology, and have strongly objected to, and sought to prohibit, a variety of forms of conduct as immoral (e.g. masturbation, homosexuality, alcohol use, usury).

Within Christendom, then, advocates of religious toleration had to offer reasons why, despite their principled objections to heresy, apostasy, sin, etc., Christians ought nonetheless to put up with them on certain terms. Importantly, these arguments did not require that their addressees reconsider or drop their objections to the beliefs and practices in question. Rather, they asserted that, even if they were entirely right to condemn the relevant beliefs and practices, there are overriding reasons to refrain from suppressing them.

This, indeed, is the characteristic feature of all arguments for *tolerance*. Our concept of toleration presupposes disesteem of that which is to be tolerated. One does not "tolerate" something that attracts one's approval;

one tolerates that which one has reason to dislike. This has led some to claim that toleration is paradoxical: why should one value something (tolerance) that leaves in place what one recognizes as bad?

In any case, debates over toleration typically proceed from the assumption that certain groups already possess principled reasons for objecting to the beliefs or conduct of others. The issue is whether these objections warrant action to suppress the behavior and beliefs in question, or whether there are yet stronger reasons to forbear. While it has often been debated in the context of the attitudes Christians ought to take to nonbelievers, apostates, heretics, and sinners, in principle this question arises whenever adherents of particular religious, ethical, or ideological views confront others of whom they must disapprove.

On the other hand, we might approach the issue of mutual accommodation from a different angle. For we might start with the presumption that it is actually desirable, or perhaps required by justice, to encourage, acknowledge, and embrace certain forms of diversity.

Suppose, for example, that we agreed with Isaiah Berlin that the valid ideals and values for whose sake we might act do not form a unified, systematic structure, but are rather irreducibly diverse and often mutually conflicting.[3] This sort of "pluralism" (as it is usually called) is not relativism. Relativists deny that we can ever definitively show that any values or ideals are sound (they assert in contrast that they are only ever sound relative to some partial social or personal point of view). Against this, pluralists grant that there are rationally defensible distinctions to be drawn between sound and unsound claims about goods, values, and ethical ideals. But they deny that they are all mutually reconcilable or that they can all be reduced to or ranked against a simple, monistic, standard of value. These goods are incommensurable in the sense discussed in chapter 3. So, for pluralists, while we must sometimes choose between options that are verifiably good rather than bad, at least sometimes we must face "tragic choices," that is, choices between exclusive options both of which are justifiable in terms of sound values. According to pluralism, then, there is no single way to realize the good, but an array of diverse and often conflicting ways to pursue many valid goods.

---

[3] See Berlin (1969), pp. 167–72; Galston (2002).

If we are pluralists of this kind, we are very likely to reject the imposition of monistic uniformity in favor of the presumption that individuals and groups ought to be given a certain latitude to live in their own way. For, on the pluralist view, imposing uniformity almost certainly involves suppressing some valid goods. It also looks like a threat to freedom. If pluralism is true, and people and societies are left to develop unhindered, they will predictably contrive a wide array of different religious creeds, ethical beliefs, and forms of life. For pluralists, this diversity has positive value as an expression of the free play of human activity. Viewed in this light, efforts to standardize the terms on which individuals and societies seek the good undermine an important aspect of human freedom.

Whereas principles of toleration involve the management of disapproval, approaching the issue of mutual accommodation from this different angle implies that it is important to cherish diversity and difference. If we thought, for example, that justice requires respect for people's freedom, we might well conclude, on the basis of the remarks in the previous paragraph, that justice requires that diversity actually be welcomed, rather than merely put up with. Contemporary accounts of the appropriate terms of mutual accommodation often adopt this second, more ambitious approach. Traditional demands for tolerance are today being radicalized by those who argue that a genuinely just society requires more than that citizens with opposed views put up with each other; it also requires that they cultivate mutual respect for their different beliefs and ways of life.

There are therefore two sets of arguments for us to look at: arguments for toleration and arguments for respect. But before looking at each in turn, I first discuss two rather weak arguments that are sometimes used to defend both.

Stability and skepticism

Some argue for both forms of accommodation by suggesting that intolerance and disrespect are politically destabilizing; peace and order are more likely to be maintained to the extent that differing groups tolerate or cultivate respect for each other.

But arguments along these lines are problematic in two main ways. First, it is not obvious that pragmatic considerations of this sort will always tell in favor of toleration and mutual respect. It is at least possible to imagine political circumstances in which imposing uniformity will be a more effective strategy. In this context it is worth noting that John Locke, whose (first) *Letter on Toleration* is a classic defense of religious tolerance, argued in earlier works that pragmatic considerations support the state imposition of an intolerant form of uniformity. Against proponents of toleration, he suggested that religious liberty may "turn us loose to the tyranny of a religious rage."[4] The shifting sands of political strategy thus seem to be an unstable foundation for a policy of tolerant or respectful accommodation.

Second, and more importantly, the effort to reduce the discussion of the proper terms of accommodation to purely pragmatic considerations simplifies the issues at stake. To assume that what is mainly at issue is the preservation of political stability is already to make a controversial — and question-begging — judgment. Remember that the primary addressees of these arguments about tolerance and respect are those who take themselves to have *principled* reasons to object to the practices and beliefs of others. It is not clear that those with principled objections to something should always be swayed by the argument that intolerance of or disrespect for it would lead to conflict or disorder. Surely there are at least some cases in which our objections to a belief-system or way of life are powerful and serious enough for us to be prepared to risk some conflict and disorder in order to suppress it (think of slavery, dangerous cults, gross discrimination against women or racial minorities).

Of course, this does not mean that pragmatic considerations of this sort are wholly irrelevant; clearly, anyone contemplating political action has to weigh carefully any possibly destabilizing effects it may have. The point rather is that considerations of stability and order do not exhaust the range of issues that need to be addressed when we inquire into the proper terms of accommodation. This would simply miss the characteristic complexity of the relevant questions. These occur precisely along the interface where concerns about political stability encounter principled and often uncompromising commitment. In at least some cases, and from some reasonable points of view, principled commitment plausibly outweighs

---

[4] Locke (1993), p. 149.

the value of avoiding confrontation. The challenge, of course, is to delimit the range of such cases, and that is a complicated matter. But arguments that are from the outset insensitive to anything other than the imperative to maintain stability and order are certainly not up to this challenge. The search for adequate terms of accommodation among those who disagree is about more than securing a pragmatic *modus vivendi*.

Similarly unsatisfactory are arguments for either tolerance or respect that appeal to skepticism about ethics or value judgments. Skepticism of this sort, as we noted in chapter 1, essentially involves the denial that value judgments or ethical conclusions can ever be rationally shown to be sound or valid. Some suggest that accepting skepticism of this sort gives us some sort of reason to be tolerant or respectful of those who disagree with us. Because none of us can ever vindicate the truth or validity of our ethical beliefs and practices, the only humane option is to cultivate tolerance and respect for those of different persuasions.

But this is a bad argument. Far from supporting principles of toleration or respect, moral skepticism only undermines them, for these are them-selves principles with moral content. However they are interpreted, claims about the need to tolerate or respect those with different views express judgments about what we ought to be doing. But if, as moral skeptics maintain, we can never know for sure that such judgments are sound or correct, then pleas for tolerant or respectful accommodation turn out to be just as ungrounded as any other ethical position we might adopt. Faced with two views, one tolerant and another intolerant, moral skeptics must deny that one can be shown to be more sound than the other. Clearly, such a stance is cold comfort to proponents of toleration.

Furthermore, as with the arguments about political stability we have already rejected, arguments from moral skepticism cannot hope to do justice to the issues raised by ethical and religious disagreement. Again, the addressees of arguments for tolerance and respect are those who take themselves to have principled objections to the beliefs and practices of others. They are not going to be reassured that their concerns are being taken seriously if we proceed from the assumption that their objections reflect ethical beliefs that neither they, nor anyone else, could ever verify as sound. Still less will they think that such attitudes express any sort of genuine respect for them or their point of view.

Is intolerance futile?

One is not, as we have seen, intolerant of something just because one has principled objections to it. For one can have principled objections to something and nonetheless put up with it, that is, tolerate it. Intolerance, then, is a matter of *acting* on one's objections, and acting in such a way as to suppress or eliminate the beliefs or conduct in question. But presumably the underlying point of intolerance of this sort is not merely to stop certain forms of behavior or conduct, but also to eradicate the putatively confused, irrational, mistaken, or "sinful" beliefs that lead people to engage in it. Situations characteristically calling for toleration or intolerance are those in which differences over conduct are rooted in deeper conflicts over the truth or falsity of *beliefs*.

Perhaps the most common argument for toleration asserts that intolerance is futile because one cannot change people's minds and beliefs just by using force against them to suppress certain conduct. As Locke put it, "Such is the nature of the understanding that it cannot be compelled to the belief of anything by outward force. Confiscation of estate, imprisonment, torments, nothing of that nature can have any such efficacy as to make men change the inward judgment that they have framed of things."[5] This basic point had in fact been acknowledged by the more circumspect of the Christian theologians long before Locke. For example, although they were far from consistent in their commitment to toleration in all of their writings and doings, both St Augustine and St Thomas Aquinas at various points endorsed the claim that it is not so much inappropriate as *pointless* to use force to change peoples' beliefs. I can put a gun to your head and threaten to kill you if you do not accept Jesus, but clearly this is no way to induce sincere faith. "It is only light and evidence that can work a change in men's opinions; and that light can in no manner proceed from corporal sufferings, or other outward penalties."[6] The right way to proceed, then, is to tolerate the beliefs (and at least some of the practices) of those we believe to be wrong and seek to persuade them with arguments. But it is futile to

[5] Locke (1993), p. 395.
[6] Locke (1993), p. 395.

attempt to change their minds by force. Intolerance is thus fundamentally irrational.

But this standard argument invites a standard objection.[7] Certainly, I may not be able to convince you to accept a belief through naked, direct, and immediate threats of force. But such crude measures are not the only alternatives to purely discursive, argumentative, modes of suasion. Nor have intolerant governments, churches, and other institutions usually tried to foster doctrinal uniformity and suppress dissent in this direct way. Indeed, where they have succeeded, they have adopted a more sophisticated strategy, intended to undermine sources of dissent over the very long term. Censorship, adaptations in educational curricula, the use of propaganda, skillful exploitation of the widespread desire to conform and of the subtle sanctions of "peer-pressure," expulsion and suppression of dissenting groups, and efforts to render certain points of view invisible or rarely heard in public discussion may not be sufficient to change anyone's mind in the short term. But when applied consistently over long periods these forms of political power may decisively shape the contours of received orthodoxy within particular areas subject to them. This is why we do not find religious and ethical beliefs randomly distributed over the Earth's surface. Instead, distinctive ethical beliefs, religious traditions and folkways are typically concentrated in particular regions, a fact that invariably reflects distinctive features of their political history.

For example, there are today comparatively few Protestants in South America. This is certainly *not* because the Spanish and Portuguese colonists who brought Christianity to that region, or the local authorities that succeeded them, persuaded everyone with good arguments that Catholicism is true and Protestantism false. If the arguments were *that* good, one would expect them to have worked everywhere, and surely it cannot be that people in South America are brighter than everyone else. Nor does it seem right to say that the Catholic beliefs of the South American populations must be insincerely held because their prevalence in that area reflects the sustained application of political power in support of Catholic institutions and practices. Brazilian or Argentinian Catholics would doubtless be very insulted at any such suggestion. So would German Protestants, British Anglicans, Scottish Presbyterians, and Saudi Arabian Muslims.

---

[7] Waldron (1988).

It seems, then, that political power, when used wisely and over the long haul, *can* induce sincere belief.

Many have thought that this objection is fatal to defenses of toleration that appeal, like Locke's, to the irrationality of intolerance. But the argument can be made more sophisticated. And, as David Wootton has recently argued,[8] this more complex version of the argument is closer to the case that Locke developed than many of his critics have supposed. It is also a pioneering argument, in that it opened a line of thought that has been a mainstay of modern liberalism right down to the present.

A better argument

Two assumptions lie at the core of this more complex version of the argument. First, if intolerance is manifested in the use of force to alter the terms on which agents acquire ethical and religious beliefs, the question of the justifiability of intolerance cannot be separated from that of the justifiability of the use of force more generally. Would-be persecutors or intolerants are rarely isolated individuals; they are usually representatives of larger institutions who hope to recruit the power of the state and other social agencies to suppress dissent, control the terms of social discourse, encourage conformity, and promote particular beliefs and practices. So the matter of whether these forms of intolerance can be justified boils down to the question of whether using force for these purposes can be justified.

The second assumption concerns the interests of rational believers. As a believer, I seek truth and understanding. In cultivating and adopting certain beliefs, it matters, or *should* matter, to me that these beliefs are sound rather than unsound, coherent rather than incoherent, defensible rather than erroneous. Even in the case of purely descriptive beliefs about how the world *is* (e.g. empirical beliefs that the Earth is round, not flat, and rotates around the sun, not vice versa; or about how speciation occurs), most people prefer to be free of error, delusion, and confusion. That is presumably one reason why we are embarrassed when others expose our mistakes or ignorance.

But the stakes are higher still in the context of the prescriptive, action-guiding, beliefs over which people of differing ethical and religious

---

[8] See David Wootton's introductory remarks in Locke (1993), pp. 97–110.

persuasions disagree. For those who embrace beliefs of this kind do not merely give inward assent to propositions about the world. They also take themselves, in virtue of their ethical commitments, to have reasons to devote their lives to certain long-term activities and projects (e.g. a life of prayer, of evangelism, or of service to the needy, fighting for social justice, defending "traditional values," cultivating certain sorts of love or concern for others, promoting certain ways of living, and discouraging others). Given the large and often intense investments of personal energy to which these beliefs call us, it becomes particularly important that we verify that we are operating on the basis of something sound, well-grounded, and defensible rather than empty, confused, or delusory. Most of us would be profoundly disturbed to discover that we have devoted a lifetime of labor and endeavor to delusions, false idols, or confused fantasies. Everyone has an interest in living in the light of the truth rather than error, and one of our most important responsibilities to ourselves is to determine as best we can that this is the case.

As Locke saw, these two considerations combine to form a compelling case against intolerance. As autonomous agents and rational believers, we share an interest in identifying beliefs that are sound rather than unsound. What conditions should we choose for ourselves as a propitious basis on which to do so? This of course raises a large question, but the particular aspect of it that is relevant here is whether we could possibly regard the forcible imposition of uniformity by the state or by other powerful social organizations as desirable from this point of view. This seems unlikely. To authorize the powers that be to determine my beliefs for me, and then to inculcate them in me by force or long-term indoctrination, seems an irresponsible alienation of my own capacity to weigh and sift for myself the evidence before my own eyes. As Locke pointed out, this is tantamount to allowing our beliefs to be determined by such accidents as our place of birth.[9] But surely this is no more rational than deciding on our beliefs by tossing a coin. Given the importance we properly attach to getting our beliefs right, it seems reckless to trust to blind chance in this way. Rational believers would never barter away their epistemic responsibilities so cheaply and frivolously.

---

[9] Locke (1993), p. 396.

Living with objections

Mill's arguments in *On Liberty* take these Lockean considerations several steps further. On the one hand, whereas Locke advocated toleration among Christian denominations, but not between Christians and nonbelievers, Mill thought that the general argument applied across the board, to all forms of principled ethical disagreement, religious and otherwise. On the other, while Locke was mainly concerned with intolerance meted out directly at the hands of the *state*, Mill was additionally concerned about the more subtle ways in which the tides of fashion, informal social sanctions, and the entrenchment of a "conventional wisdom" threaten agents' ability to think responsibly about their own ethical commitments. In all these cases, various forms of force — some direct, some indirect — are mobilized to influence individuals' beliefs. But, like Locke before him, Mill insisted that this power, whatever form it takes, is inherently illegitimate.[10]

At the heart of Mill's case is the assumption that, setting aside the propositions of mathematics, geometry, and logic, accepting beliefs as true is almost never a matter of purely self-referential deductive inference. In most other areas, one must acknowledge that there are possible objections to what one thinks and does. One cannot therefore claim to have good reasons for holding some religious or ethical belief in the absence of any understanding of possible objections to one's own views:

> Three-fourths of the arguments for every disputed opinion consist in dispelling the appearances which favour some opinion different from it ...
> He who knows only his side of the case, knows little of that. His reasons may be good, and no one may have been able to refute them. But if he is equally unable to refute the reasons on the opposite side; if he does not so much as know what they are, he has no ground for preferring either opinion.[11]

On Mill's (surely correct) account, ethical beliefs and worldviews are ranged across a field of contestation, mutual incompatibility, tension, and reasonable doubt. To occupy a rational position in this field one cannot barricade oneself in behind unquestioned assumptions and blind oneself to the reasonable objections to which one's views are inevitably vulnerable. Sheltering one's beliefs from critical scrutiny in this way is a form of denial,

[10] Mill (1972), pp. 84ff.
[11] Mill (1972), p. 104.

a symptom of intellectual immaturity and indolence. It is also, for Mill, ultimately irrational. On his account, one cannot rationally apprehend one's own views apart from an understanding of their relation to those others that contest them. Beliefs have to be defended, whether to others or *oneself*, out in the open field.

These last considerations are particularly important because they allow us to rebut one of the most tempting and frequently cited objections to the general Mill/Locke line. This objection concedes that the argument makes sense from the standpoint of one whose views are not yet settled but who faces persecution or intolerance at the hands of those with firmer views. But it denies that it works so well when addressed to those who are justifiably confident of their beliefs and who contemplate intolerance to bring those still hesitant into the light.

But Mill's point is that intolerance is ultimately self-defeating even from this second point of view. For, on his view, justified confidence in one's own convictions can be acquired only under conditions in which one has an adequate opportunity to consider the objections they invite. This in turn requires the open expression of dissent, and a disposition to take it seriously and reckon with it. The suppression of dissent only erodes the foundations on which any legitimate confidence in one's own convictions can alone be based. Those who deny this confuse rational belief with the parroting of a dogma.

From toleration to neutrality

These are powerful arguments, and, if sound, they already move us some way toward those more demanding views of mutual accommodation that regard ethical and religious diversity as something to be respected and cultivated in its own right rather than merely tolerated. Still, while those who today advocate this more demanding model of accommodation have often drawn their inspiration from Mill, they also often regard Mill's arguments as importantly incomplete.

To see why, consider a democratic society dominated by a particular religious majority, the Caspians. This group is sufficiently numerous to guarantee enough votes to enact laws and constitutional principles inspired by distinctively Caspian religious beliefs. However, substantial minorities (Arcticans, Mediterraneans, etc.) in the same society conscientiously reject the majority's religious beliefs. Despite this, the Caspians play according to impeccably Millian rules. They do not attempt to persecute or suppress the dissenting minorities, they uphold their rights to freedom of speech, association, and worship, and they even grant Mill's point that the vitality and reflectiveness of the Caspian community can only be enhanced by living in a diverse, pluralist society in which not everyone believes the same thing. But despite having long abandoned, for good Millian reasons, efforts to use the power of the state to impose doctrinal uniformity, the Caspians see no reason to refrain from passing legislation and amending the constitution in ways to which minority groups object vehemently. Thanks to their efforts, for example, their constitution now explicitly dedicates Sunday to the glory of God; and, as part of this commitment, the Caspians successfully prohibit the sale and consumption of alcohol on Sundays even though many Mediterraneans and Arcticans would prefer to buy, sell, and enjoy alcohol throughout the weekend.

In response to complaints from the minorities, Caspian leaders say, "We are happy to acknowledge your freedom to worship and believe as you please; we uphold your freedom to criticize what we do; we gladly extend to you the freedom to participate in the democratic process on equal terms; and we are open to engaging you in dialogue about our respective differences. Still, this is a democracy and, under majority rule, we Caspians are perfectly entitled to commit the state to promoting our conception of the good life. It is, after all, our country. Until you can persuade enough Caspians to change their minds and come over to your point of view, there is nothing unfair in our expecting you to submit to our rules, even if they are inspired by beliefs you cannot personally accept."

This position is broadly consistent with the Millean or Lockean case for toleration; after all, the Caspians are not *intolerant* of dissent and diversity.[12]

---

[12] One might object that the Caspians violate Mill's Harm Principle (see chapter 8) in restricting the liberty to buy, sell, and consume alcohol on Sunday. Perhaps, but it is not clear that the Caspians' justification for this restriction must turn on a paternalist appeal to the welfare of those who wish to drink on Sunday (which would fall foul of the Harm Principle). The Caspians might argue, for example, that in this case the limitation of their liberty is necessary to prevent harm to others – e.g. damage to Caspians' legitimate interest in the preservation of a social practice that they see as valuable. I doubt whether Mill would have had much sympathy for an argument along these lines, but I am not sure he would have rejected it as contravening the Harm Principle. It is more likely that he would have viewed it simply as a bad argument.

Still, many contemporary liberals would insist nonetheless that the minorities in this society have a legitimate complaint, based on justice, against the way the Caspians treat them. These liberals, including Rawls, argue for a more demanding model of mutual accommodation organized around a requirement of *state neutrality*. On this view, genuinely fair terms of mutual accommodation require that as well as promoting toleration within civil society, the state also cultivate a stance of *neutrality* toward the ethical controversies that arise among their citizens.[13] The Caspians' behavior cannot be reconciled with state neutrality in the relevant sense. While the Caspians do not persecute dissenters, and do not seek to impose uniformity, they nevertheless expect nonCaspians to accept a constitutional order whose justification originates in religious beliefs that they conscientiously reject. As a result, state and law appear to take sides on ethical beliefs that are in dispute among citizens. The requirement of state neutrality, however, forbids the state from becoming partisan in this way.

The requirement of state neutrality is, as I have said, based on a claim about fairness and justice. This underlying claim is often cashed out in terms of unhelpfully vague notions of political equality, but can be captured more sharply in the following formulation, which I will call the 'inclusion principle':

> Citizens should not have to choose between their own reasonable ethical convictions and the ability to affirm the point of view from which public enactments are decided upon. That point of view must, rather, be structured so that it can be affirmed by holders of any reasonable ethical conception to which we can imagine individuals might become committed under conditions of freedom.

The inclusion principle is descended from, and closely related to, the contractualist accounts of political justification that we have encountered several times throughout this book, and so it is not surprising that philosophers like Rawls should be so strongly drawn to it. Contractualists propose to assess political arrangements by asking whether individuals under fair and reasonable conditions would freely accept them; as we noted in chapters 4 and 8, this test normally requires that we reconcile the exercise

---

[13] Defences of state neutrality can be found in Nozick (1974), p. 33; Dworkin (1985); Larmore (1987), ch. 3; (1996), ch. 6; (1999); Rawls (1993); (1999b), pp. 129–81.

of political power with (some conception of) citizens' autonomy. In a similar way, the inclusion principle requires that state power be exercised from a point of view that individuals can affirm from within their own freely determined system of convictions. It seems clear enough that the Caspians in our example violate this requirement.

Is neutrality possible?

The requirement of state neutrality has been widely criticized. Some charge that it is an incoherent, impossible ideal; others complain that it is undesirable in any case. Those tempted by the first sort of objection sometimes imply that proponents of state neutrality expect the state to avoid *any* ethical stance at all. Clearly, if the doctrine of liberal neutrality really is committed to this sweeping expectation, it describes a vain fantasy; states subject to this constraint could never do anything.

But objections along these lines caricature the neutralist view. The inclusion principle does not prohibit states from taking any ethical positions *whatsoever*. It requires, more weakly, that when states *do* adopt such positions, as they inevitably must (by enforcing legal requirements, pursuing public policies, and the like), they do so from a point of view that citizens can all affirm from within their diverging reasonable religious and ethical commitments.

Clarifying this point reveals much about the characteristic structure of doctrines of state neutrality. In particular, it explains why those doctrines require a distinction between two categories of ethical views: those that individuals may personally embrace but which cannot be expected to command general assent, and those ethical principles on which people with otherwise opposed views can nonetheless reasonably agree. The doctrine of neutrality does not forbid states from taking any recognizable ethical position at all, but rather restricts them to acting on principles of the second kind only. Thus, in Rawls's version of this neutralist view, the basic principles determining the permissible trajectory of law and public policy must be shown to be part of a possible "overlapping consensus."[14] By this Rawls meant a common fund of basic political commitments to which citizens with sharply divided ethical outlooks can repair for the purposes of

[14] Rawls (1993).

resolving their differences over public policy on fair and mutually agreeable terms.

According to Rawls in his later writings, the ingredients for such a consensus among members of the Western democracies are already latent in the public culture and institutions they share. He thus came to treat the political principles characteristic of this public culture as an implicit overlapping consensus to which liberal citizens can appeal when they engage each other in discussion about public policy. This led him, in his later work, to recast his theory of justice simply as an elaboration of these liberal democratic ideals, not (as he had originally conceived it) as a canonical theory for all societies under all historical conditions. Under this revision, its major principles purport to form an overlapping consensus about the terms of social justice in which reasonable citizens of liberal societies can (and allegedly in some ways already do) share, despite their many other religious and ethical disagreements. Rawls hoped that on this basis liberal democratic citizens need never choose between affirming his proposed principles of justice and any personal allegiance to deeply felt ethical and religious convictions. States can cultivate neutrality with respect to those disputed convictions, on this view, by acting only within the terms of those liberal democratic principles around which an overlapping consensus can coalesce.

As we have mentioned in previous chapters, this move carries a significant cost. Although Rawls maintained that the content of his proposed principles is largely unaffected by this adjustment, he readily acknowledged that it dramatically trims back their scope of application. So revised, his theory can get no traction in societies not already committed to the operative principles of liberal democracy, for (he maintained) only under these conditions is the relevant kind of overlapping consensus possible. Rawls's later theory thus became merely an elaboration of *one* historically contingent conception of justice that happens to be entrenched in a group of Western liberal societies at the turn of the twenty-first century, not a basis for making judgments about justice that transcends the boundaries of particular political cultures.

This also explains Rawls's caution about cosmopolitan redistributive justice. As we saw in chapter 6, he believed that the understandings of justice entrenched in the public cultures of different regions around the world are too diverse and fragmented to yield an international overlapping consensus around, say, a global difference principle. Instead, Rawls's "Law of Peoples" describes a model of international accommodation that negotiates reasonable terms of peaceful coexistence among societies committed to opposed conceptions of social justice.

But these features of Rawls's later position also raise doubts about the possibility of state neutrality even *within* those liberal societies to which he thought the requirement primarily applies. *Can* all reasonable citizens of liberal democracies unite around an identifiable and potentially coherent package of liberal democratic principles and regard it as "neutral" in the required sense? One could doubt this, on at least two grounds.

First, will not some citizens of liberal democracies reasonably reject the relevant principles? Clearly, the bare fact that principles are familiar and widely accepted within a particular political culture does not show that it is unreasonable for members of that culture to reject them. For example, must Marxists and anarchists who happen to live in liberal democracies be classed as "unreasonable" on Rawls's view? Second, even if all reasonable people who live under liberal democracy do feel able to endorse its core political principles, will they agree about what those principles *are*? This is not clear; we saw in chapter 9, for example, that the questions of what counts as democratic, and what basic democratic principles are, are themselves subject to considerable dispute.

Perhaps sensing these difficulties, some proponents of state neutrality ground the doctrine, not on a contingent convergence in political culture to be found in certain sorts of societies, but rather on an independently valid principle of equal respect for all.[15] But this only raises new questions about the basis and content of such a principle of respect, questions to which, it is fair to say, advocates of neutrality have yet to respond adequately.

Public reason

Another way in which critics often challenge the bare possibility of state neutrality is by objecting that there is no way for legislation and public policy to be entirely neutral in its effects on individuals and communities committed to different conceptions of the good life.

---

[15] Bird (1996); Larmore (1999).

Advocates of neutrality usually respond by conceding the point but denying its relevance. What matters, they say, is not "neutrality of effect" but "neutrality in justification." While laws and public policies cannot be wholly neutral in their effects, the terms on which they are justified can be neutral in the required sense. We can satisfy the inclusion principle by insuring that, whatever *effects* legislation may have, it is justified on the basis of principles and arguments that any reasonable person could accept without impugning their commitment to their personal ethical beliefs, or so neutralists argue.

This formulation of neutrality in terms of justification generates a notion of "public reason," an account of the legitimate terms on which arguments may be made in political contexts.[16] Thus Rawls insisted that, especially when they debate their most fundamental ("constitutionally essential") principles, citizens must identify arguments that their fellows cannot reasonably reject. Otherwise they are failing to act in accord with public reason, and falling short of an ideal of democratic civility. Consider those Christians in the United States who argue for a constitutional ban on same-sex marriage on the grounds that the Bible says homosexuality is sinful. Even supposing it to be sound, such an argument could not, on Rawls's account, be accepted by all reasonable people in society; citizens committed to public reason ought therefore to set it aside and make a case for their preferred political proposals on a less controversial basis.

Proponents of "public reason" thus contend that certain sorts of ethical claims — those that are in dispute among reasonable members of pluralist liberal societies — may not be used to justify political action. In public contexts, they must be "bracketed" and set to one side. For example, as we noted in chapter 3, the claims associated with various forms of perfectionism are often controversial; because some citizens reasonably reject particular perfectionist ideals of flourishing, arguments that appeal to such ideals must fall outside the scope of "public reason" as Rawls and others interpret it. Thus doctrines of neutrality and of "public reason" have acquired a reputation as "antiperfectionist." As we shall shortly see, perfectionists criticize this feature of appeals to "public reason" and argue that it objectionably discriminates against sound perfectionist arguments. But before considering objections along these lines, I briefly persist with

---

[16] Rawls (1993), lec. VI; (1999b), pp. 129–81.

the prior question of whether a genuinely neutral "public reason" is even possible.

In order for it to be so, it must be true that, once we have screened out the unacceptably "controversial" arguments that citizens might canvass, the remaining "public" reasons are sufficient to provide adequate justifications for political action. But this may not always, or even ever, be the case: the reasons we are left with may not be sufficient to decide the issue. In that case, we may be able adequately to justify policies and political principles only by drawing on precisely those reasons to which "neutrality in justification" forbids us to appeal. This concern is related to the objection to Rawlsian contractualism briefly canvassed at the very end of chapter 4. We saw there that contractualist approaches also attempt to bracket disagreements over perfectionist ideals and conceptions of well-being and seek political justifications that operate on a narrower, less contentious, basis. But we also worried that, by excluding judgments about human well-being, the contractualist framework may be *too* narrow to address all the relevant considerations. Given the close affinities between contractualism and the inclusion principle, it seems reasonable to conclude that these outstanding questions about the possibility of a neutral public reason turn ultimately on the cogency of the contractualist account of political justification itself.

Is neutrality desirable?

Even if state neutrality is possible, many critics complain that it is undesirable nonetheless. Some worry, for example, that it objectionably restricts political discussion. Neutrality in justification requires that we set aside our deeply held religious and ethical convictions when we address each other as citizens engaged in discussion of public principles and policies. But why should citizens be expected to restrict their political advocacy in this way? Why not follow Mill's recommendation and encourage the fullest possible discussion of the widest range of arguments for and against alternative political proposals?

Such objections, however, miss the point. Rawls and other advocates of public reason have always been careful to say that it does not restrict the expression of political views and opinions in civil society, and they happily endorse Mill's views about the need for freedom of speech and a rich marketplace of ideas. The constraints of public reason determine, not what citizens can permissibly *say* in political discussion, but rather which arguments, once articulated, they should together recognize as constituting valid or invalid grounds for political action. The question of which political opinions and arguments may permissibly be expressed is one thing. But that of which should be allowed to count as a valid basis for reaching acceptable political decisions is another, and the restrictions of public reason reach only this second question.

Restrictions of this sort are familiar in legal proceedings. For example, in reaching certain sorts of legal decisions, judges and juries are often expected to set aside certain sorts of considerations that might otherwise (rightly or wrongly) influence their judgments. While jurors (say) are always free to *air* these considerations, as when Ed Begley's character in *Twelve Angry Men* declares in the jury room that in his opinion the defendant is a born liar, they are supposed to set such judgments aside and reach decisions on other grounds. Public reason purports to operate in the same way: it excludes certain categories of arguments from counting for or against decisions about how to use state power. But that is not the same as limiting the permissible expression of these arguments.

A more troubling criticism has been pressed by perfectionists who contend that the ideal of a neutral public reason arbitrarily excludes arguments for political action that derive from sound, albeit controversial, conceptions of human flourishing. As Sher has it:

> Like most neutralists, I believe the fundamental issue is one of justification; but, unlike them, I do not believe that any kinds of reasons are in principle inadmissible in politics ... it is no less legitimate for governments than for private individuals to try to promote the good ... in our prior deliberation about which laws and policies to adopt, questions about how it is best to live [i.e. perfectionist conceptions of the good] may never simply be "taken off the agenda". In public as well as private life, the operative distinction is not between illegitimate and illegitimate reasons, but rather between good and bad ones.[17]

Suppose that we are justifiably confident that some policy will benefit society and its members, but that our reasons for believing this derive

---

[17] Sher (1997), pp. 4–5.

from a conception of human well-being that, while sound and defensible, many citizens reasonably reject. In such a case, the canons of public reason will block the proposed justification, and perhaps also the policy, even though it is sound and likely to improve citizens' lives. Why should (even reasonable) objections to otherwise perfectly sound political proposals be allowed to stand in the way of measures from which citizens only stand to gain? Is it desirable for rational policy-making to be held hostage to citizens' objections in this way? Perfectionist critics contend not. They argue that, under a regime of public reason, many potentially beneficial social policies will be ruled out on principle even before states have had an adequate opportunity to try them out and assess their actual benefits. This imposes an irrational limit on efforts to promote the human good by political means, or so perfectionists have charged.[18]

Giving neutrality its due

This argument, which is (not accidentally) reminiscent of Plato's perfectionist critique of democratic justice (see chapter 2), is certainly the most penetrating of the main criticisms of liberal neutrality. But there are several important replies to consider.

First, excluding perfectionist justifications is not equivalent to excluding all perfectionist policy. A policy's *effects* are one thing, and its *justification* another – public reason does not attempt to regulate the former. Thus it need not prohibit the adoption of legislation that perfectionists support because it is likely to promote the human good. It merely requires that, whether or not the policy furthers controversial perfectionist goals, its advocates offer their fellow citizens a justification couched in suitably uncontroversial terms.

Second, advocates of state neutrality often distinguish between ordinary legislation and what Rawls called "constitutional essentials," and argue that the strictures of public reason apply mainly to the latter, but more weakly, if at all, to the former. "Constitutional essentials" refers here to the bedrock of principle on which the legal and institutional architecture of any state is erected. They encompass constitutional law, the enumerated powers

[18] Sher (1997), p. 3; similar objections can be found in Raz (1986); Wall (1998); Chan (2000).

of the various branches of government, the terms of public decision-making, and the allocation of fundamental civil rights and liberties. It is these fundamental components of a legal order that, according to proponents of public reason, must be seen to remain neutral with respect to the diverse religious and ethical beliefs of citizens. But as long as it remains consistent with these bedrock rules, ordinary legislation need not always be neutral in this way; so at least some legislation justified on perfectionist grounds might be permissible on this basis.

Third, the perfectionist objection is open to the charge that it problematically idealizes the state. As Sher's comments illustrate, perfectionists deny that distinctions between justifications that are appropriately "public," "legitimate," or "neutral," independent of their soundness, serve any useful political purpose. This implies that when public officials are offered reasons for political action of various sorts, they need only consider whether they are sound or unsound and whether the proposed policies are likely to be effective. In other words, the capacities of the state are in principle limited only by considerations of effectiveness and by the requirement of sensitivity to sound reasons. The fact that a political argument is reasonably rejected by some citizens provides on this view no principled reason for officials to refrain from acting on it.

Perfectionists therefore assume that the state is in principle free to mobilize whatever social resources are effectively at its disposal in accordance with the dictates of right reason and citizens' common good. This is of course the old Platonic vision of the state as the site at which the full measure of human wisdom and rational foresight are concentrated and deployed to the advantage of all. In many ways, this is an inspiring ideal, but the objection is that it has little application to the realities of modern state authority and of the sharp ethical disagreements over which it characteristically presides. Making allowances for those realities weakens the perfectionist critique of neutrality.

The point here is not simply that modern nation-states fall far short of the Platonic ideal; it is rather that the ideals of political rule around which modern nation-states are organized are themselves fundamentally different. The self-image of the modern state is not that of a wise and benevolent guardian, whose primary responsibility is to attend and respond properly only to good arguments. Instead, we think of the state as an abstract and bureaucratic framework of institutions that claims, in some obscure sense, to speak and act in the name of the whole community of citizens it "represents."

This ideal of impartial representation defines a distinctive role for the state, and lends the inclusion principle special significance in the context of institutions that aspire to it. For, when citizens are fundamentally divided in their ethical and religious commitments, it is not clear how a state claiming to speak and act from a point of view representing them *all* can fairly commit itself, at the constitutional level, to norms that only some of them are in a reasonable position to embrace. This would, I think, continue to strike us as unfair even if the argument for the relevant norms were based on the soundest imaginable philosophical grounds. Those citizens who conscientiously reject them could quite reasonably complain that they are not being represented on the same terms as their fellows.

This circumstance creates a need for independent principles of mutual accommodation. Under modern conditions, citizens do not think of the vast legal apparatus of the state as either equipped or, more relevantly, *authorized* to act on the basis of whatever sound reasons come its way. That is simply not the kind of agency it purports to be. Rather, citizens think of public officials as having an overriding responsibility to represent them collectively on fair terms. The state and its cadre of officials are thus supposed to be accountable to *the citizenry* in whose name they speak and act, not to the truth about the good life. Encouraging the state to adopt a stance of neutrality toward the ethical controversies that arise among its citizens makes a certain sense as a model of mutual accommodation appropriate to this situation.

This neutralist proposal may raise all sorts of difficulties, but at least it engages a relevant problem. In contrast, the perfectionist assumption that, barring considerations of effectiveness, citizens' reasonable objections to sound political arguments cannot provide any principled reasons for official restraint seems not even to recognize it. It tacitly adopts an account of the relation between the state and its citizens that wishes the problem away rather than confronting it squarely. This does not show that the perfectionist critique is wrong, but it does suggest that it is misdirected. Perfectionists' objections may primarily apply, not directly to the requirement of state neutrality, but rather to the underlying (and currently dominant) conception of the state and its public role that gives that requirement its rationale.

Conclusions

I conclude by simply mentioning a somewhat different way in which questions about the accommodation of difference often arise and by describing their relation to the concerns of this chapter. Here, we have focused on issues surrounding the accommodation of ethical and political disagreements. These are distinctive in that they mainly concern the reconciliation of groups committed to opposed *beliefs*. But of course people often come into conflict, not only over what they believe, but also because of who they are. Hence the struggles against social exclusion and discrimination that women, the handicapped, members of ethnic, racial, and cultural minorities, those of nonheterosexual orientation and so many other marginalized groups have often faced. The need to address these forms of social exclusion based on identity lies behind currently popular ideals of "multiculturalism" and pleas for the recognition of difference.[19] The question here is how to adapt mainstream social norms and practices so as to more generously accommodate those bearing hitherto stigmatized or marginalized identities.

This project, which deserves consideration in its own right, stands at an angle to the questions explored in this chapter. Nonetheless, there is an important area of overlap, for racist, misogynist, homophobic, and similarly stigmatizing behavior characteristically reflects spurious *beliefs* about its victims. In the end, then, the effort to eradicate these forms of social exclusion cannot be divorced from the question of which beliefs we ought to tolerate, and those we ought not.

[19] See esp. Taylor (1994); Kymlicka (1989); (1995).

12   Radical criticism

A guiding aim of political philosophy is (or should be) to submit existing public institutions, along with any imaginable and realistically available alternatives, to what Karl Marx called "ruthless criticism." Such criticism, Marx wrote, should be "ruthless in two senses: the criticism must not be afraid of its own conclusions, nor of conflict with the powers that be."[1] A "ruthless social critic" must therefore stand back from prevailing social and political forms and achieve an appropriate critical distance from dominant practices and institutions.

But how should political philosophers cultivate this "standing back" from prevailing orthodoxies and forms of social organization? How can they attain the requisite critical distance? One answer to this question is presupposed in much of the discussion contained in this book. By carefully analyzing and applying various pertinent ethical ideals – notions of freedom, democracy, equality, justice, and the common good, for example – we can determine whether political institutions of one sort or another are *justified* from an appropriately detached, impartial point of view. Critical inquiry into political practices is on this view inquiry into their *justification conditions*, where "justification" is understood in terms of the satisfaction of various ethical expectations derived from such ordinary language concepts as justice, freedom, or the common good.

Many modern writers – including Marx himself – have, however, found this traditional approach to social criticism naïve and insufficiently "ruthless." They have argued that, to view our political situation in an appropriately detached and undeluded light, we must adopt a more radically critical posture, suspicious of the conventional ethical expectations around which the traditional discourse of political justification

---

[1] Marx (1978), p. 13.

is usually organized. This suggestion has been very influential, and many political philosophers writing today have been strongly drawn to it. For example, it lies behind several standard objections, often canvassed, to the approaches to political philosophy taken by Rawls and many of the other writers we have discussed in this book.[2] This final chapter attempts to retrieve and explain this line of argument for a more radically critical stance in political philosophy. It then goes on to assess the implications of this argument for the mode of analysis pursued in this book.

Rousseau's second *Discourse*

In general form, the line of argument I explore here can be traced back to Rousseau's remarkable *Discourse on the Origin of Inequality*, written in 1755.[3] Virtually single-handedly, this pioneering essay invented and defined the outlook of what we might today identify as the "radical left." The *Discourse* is a systematic and entirely subversive attack on the self-image of rational, enlightened, civilized society. In it, Rousseau contended that, quite contrary to their official pretensions, the institutions of modern civil society are oppressive, hierarchical, and profoundly dehumanizing. His discussion thus suggests a hypothesis about our vulnerability to falsifying forms of social consciousness. On this hypothesis, dominant forms of consciousness are "falsifying" in that they allegedly misrepresent existing configurations of social organization, moreover in a way that obscures their tendency to repress agents' real interests.

Critical philosophical reflection of the kind pioneered by Rousseau's *Discourse* represents an effort to identify and subvert these hypothesized forms of consciousness. As Marx would later put it, such reflection consists in "enabling the world to clarify its consciousness, in waking it from its dream about itself, in *explaining* to it the meaning of its own actions."[4] Marx's metaphor of waking someone from a dream is particularly apt. It captures the sense, shared by both Rousseau and Marx along with many other radical critics, that overcoming oppression requires agents actively to resist

---

[2] See McBride (1972); Young (1997), chs. 1, 4; Geuss (2005), pp. 29–39.

[3] Rousseau (1987), pp. 25–111; for more on Rousseau's role in this tradition, see Rosen (1996), ch. 3.

[4] Marx (1978), p. 15.

powerfully vivid forms of consciousness that may otherwise overwhelm their ability to appreciate their true political situation. Roughly two centuries after Rousseau, Max Horkheimer had essentially the same basic conception of social criticism in mind when he wrote: "The real social function of philosophy lies in its criticism of what is prevalent ... the chief aim of such criticism is to prevent mankind from losing itself in those ideas and activities which the existing organization of society instills into its members."[5]

Understood this way, then, "ruthless social criticism" does not make a preemptive strike against the status quo just for the sake of (what Horkheimer called) "superficial fault-finding with individual ideas or conditions." Rather, it is conceived as a reaction to systematic and preexisting forms of aggression perpetrated by dominant social forms against individuals and their interests, assaults that would otherwise pass unnoticed.

Like the writings of those critics he influenced, Rousseau's *Discourse* is as much concerned with the ideas and forms of "consciousness" that grow up around particular sets of social institutions as with those institutions themselves. This is the case because Rousseau accepted an assumption we have made throughout this book: that agents' willingness to cooperate in reproducing particular social arrangements, and to recognize and comply with the various conventional and institutional expectations, reflects beliefs about their supposed worthiness and value. So, for Rousseau, our domestication into civilized life is rarely effected through direct coercion, or through mindless training of the kind to which circus animals and rats in psychology laboratories are subjected. Rather, it is mediated by quite sincerely held assumptions about rights, entitlements, justice, the common good, the "public interest," and associated beliefs about appropriate ethical behavior. On Rousseau's account, then, to achieve a critical understanding of the workings of social institutions it is necessary to analyze not only the institutions themselves but also the dominant beliefs and ideas used to comprehend and defend them.

States of nature

That is why so much of Rousseau's discussion in the *Discourse* is developed in explicit opposition to, and in some ways as a caricature of, the

---

[5] Horkheimer (1972), pp. 264–5.

seventeenth-century theories of the social contract, particularly those of Hobbes and Locke. As we saw in chapter 3, Hobbes and Locke used the metaphor of a social contract by which agents escape a "state of nature" to highlight what they believed was at stake in the decision to reject or embrace the authority of the state. Once we view the stakes in the correct light, they thought, we are bound to conclude that we should reconcile ourselves with the state and accept its authority.

Rousseau granted, at least for the sake of argument, their general point that postulating a "state of nature" is a useful heuristic device for assessing the value of modern civic institutions. But he denied that Hobbes and Locke deployed it in a sufficiently critical way. He argued, rather, that their depictions of a "state of nature" were contaminated by assumptions drawn from the very forms of life they purported to be impartially evaluating.

For example, Rousseau objected to their assumption that individuals in a state of nature would already recognize certain "natural rights." As we noted in chapter 3, he held that our ability to recognize "rights" and forms of property ownership presupposes the development of civic and legal relations. He therefore dismissed as confused the Hobbesian and Lockean claim that such concepts could be available to individuals in a genuinely "natural," pre-civilized, situation. To think otherwise, he argued, illicitly imports artificial conventions into our conception of what is "naturally" human.

Similarly, Rousseau argued that Hobbes and Locke misidentified as "natural" forms of motivation that become predominant only under particular social conditions. For example, Hobbes cited ambition for personal "glory" and honor as a major cause of likely conflict among individuals in a state of nature. Rousseau was prepared to concede that this trait reflects certain psychological dispositions latent in our natural constitution. Nevertheless, he insisted that its emergence and tendency to spark damaging conflicts reflect, not a natural predilection toward competitive glory-seeking, but rather the ways in which artificial features of human social organization encourage particular forms of behavior and associated dispositions. For Rousseau, then, natural selfishness is not the cause of the personal ambition so prevalent in human societies. Rather, the reverse is true: the competitive character of modern social organization induces individuals to attach particular importance to honor, glory, and reputation.

As an antidote to such — as he saw it misleading and partial — conceptions of man's "natural" state, Rousseau offered a more radical interpretation of a "state of nature," purged of *any* influences that might plausibly be attributed to the artificial interventions of social organization in the formation of agents' character. Rousseau's natural man is moved only by the most primitive physiological impulses, lacks any self-awareness, has no moral beliefs, and indeed does not even possess a language. Despite these limitations, Rousseau nonetheless argued that in important respects the predicament of his "natural man" is preferable to that of civilized man. Unlike the latter, for example, Rousseau viewed him as wholly independent and self-sufficient: his actions are not dictated by the needs and demands of others, and his own needs and desires do not outrun his capacity to meet them by himself. As a result, he lives in harmony with his environment and largely at peace with others. He is wholly unaffected by the vain ambitions, resentful frustrations, and invidious obsessions about social standing and reputation that stalk the lives of people living under "civilized" conditions.

According to Rousseau, no truly impartial assessment of the costs and benefits of modern civic life can afford to ignore these (to him pathological) phenomena. However, Rousseau argued that, in building them into their accounts of state of nature, Hobbes and Locke insulated them from critical scrutiny and were thus unable to offer a truly balanced evaluation of the institutions they seek to recommend. By failing to notice these deficiencies while urging their readers to reconcile themselves with the institutions that perpetuate them, these theorists became unwitting agents of an oppressive and irrational form of life, or so Rousseau alleged.

Tainted origins

In articulating this critique of social-contract theory, Rousseau expressed an anxiety about the vulnerability of certain standard forms of philosophical reflection — in this case the techniques of contractualism as used by Hobbes and Locke — to becoming unwittingly complicit in oppressive schemes of power. Why might one find this suggestion plausible?

One answer, already suggested by Rousseau's analysis in the *Discourse*, involves a claim about the tainted origin of the abstract ethical concepts and ideals typically used in standard philosophical arguments for and against political institutions. "Abstract ethical ideals" here refers to the

fund of concepts that figure in ordinary discourse about the possible justifications for different possible social and political arrangements (i.e. conceptions of justice, fairness, the common good, human flourishing, etc.).

The effort to assess the legitimacy of particular social institutions in
terms of such abstract norms makes sense only if the relevant norms are
genuinely independent of the social forms that they are mobilized to assess.
But this (the argument runs) is typically not the case. The actual relation of
dependence between social forms and abstract ethical ideals is exactly the
reverse. It is not that existing social practices are legitimated by certain
independently "valid" principles or ethical standards. Rather, the stock of
justificatory concepts available to agents in particular societies is (on this
account) a function of the kind of social structures in which they live. These
concepts are therefore not appropriately independent of the social
environment that shapes them.

Rousseau's allegation that the social-contract theorists' account of the
state of nature was a misleading philosophical reflection of existing social
practices provided a prototype for this line of argument. But it was
developed far more systematically by Marx, who famously held that the
content of conventional beliefs about justice, along with ethical and
religious conceptions more generally, are determined by the conditions of
economic production ("modes of production") that prevail in the societies
and historical periods in which those beliefs arise.[6] For example, under
capitalism, economic life is based on relations of free exchange and so it
should not surprise us, Marx thought, that what are paradigmatically
recognized as "unjust" in capitalist societies are those actions that threaten
or undermine free exchange, or that do not treat people as autonomous
agents, free to dispose of their own assets and persons as they choose – that
is, forms of assault, theft, and fraud. Complicated doctrines about rights,
personal autonomy, property-ownership, privacy, impartiality, the "rule of
law," freedom, and equality have grown up around this core idea. According
to Marxians, these constitute a distinctively capitalist conception of justice.

Like the patterns of ethical beliefs that develop in other historical
periods, this conception marks as unjust or as otherwise questionable
conduct that might disrupt the prevailing mode of production. Agents
socialized into capitalist societies will therefore tend to perceive the routine

---

[6] See Marx (1978), pp. 146–202.

operation of capitalism as just and worthy of their rational support. This system of beliefs mobilizes social disapproval of actions that threaten capitalist exchange (especially theft, fraud, and assault) but does not mark as ethically problematic the ways in which the overall system works to the advantage of one class — the owners of capital — and against the interests of another — the largely dispossessed and poor working class. Such beliefs therefore protect capitalism from critical scrutiny and help to sustain it. In a comparable way, the religious and ethical beliefs prevalent in medieval Europe (oriented around hierarchical notions of bondage and service to sovereign lordship) reflected and helped to preserve feudal economic relations, or so Marx maintained.

This argument asserts a hypothesis about the "sociology of knowledge," that is about the social conditions under which certain beliefs become prevalent and compelling;[7] it adds to it a claim about the characteristic function of some of these beliefs in inducing compliance with existing forms of social organization. These claims are controversial, and clearly require complex empirical validation. But, if sound, they naturally imply that philosophical reflection conducted within the framework of conventional ethical beliefs will be biased in favor of the status quo, or at least fated to miss objectionable features of existing forms of organization. Perhaps that is why the institution of slavery, forms of racial injustice, and glaring social inequalities between men and women have so often escaped the attention of historically influential philosophers ostensibly committed to promoting ideals of justice and the human good.

The agonistic character of social life

These claims are obviously controversial, but suppose for the sake of argument that we reject traditional inquiry into the ethical justification of political institutions for something like these reasons. What role is then left for the political philosopher to perform? To put the same question somewhat differently: Apart from rejecting standard approaches to the subject, does the "ruthless social critic" have any positive proposal to offer about how philosophers might more fruitfully contribute to an understanding of political life?

[7] See Mannheim (1985).

It is difficult to give a wholly representative general answer to this question, for the various philosophers and schools of thought that have shared something like Rousseau's critical orientation form a quite diverse group. For example, Rousseau, Marx, members of the Frankfurt School,[8] Foucault, and those they have influenced disagree profoundly with each other about exactly how to understand the social institutions they seek to criticize. Despite these differences, however, several themes consistently recur in their writings. These allow us to outline certain characteristic topographical features of the philosophical territory on which these otherwise disparate figures stand.

Perhaps the most obvious and important recurring trope in the writings of radical critics from Rousseau to Foucault has been a stress on the agonistic character of social and political life. That Rousseau himself shared this assumption that human politics is fundamentally a struggle for power and control over others can be obscured by his depiction of the state of nature as a situation of peace and self-sufficiency. But of course his point was precisely that this halcyon tranquility is immediately disrupted once his hypothesized state of nature is replaced by organized civil society. The clear implication of the Rousseauan analysis is that the appearance and proliferation of needs and desires that agents cannot satisfy by themselves are both cause and symptom of social, economic, and political development. To satisfy such needs, concerted collective action is required; this cannot occur without the power and control needed to recruit other agents to the increasingly complex tasks required to meet them. Inevitably, this will to control, whatever shape it assumes, encounters opposition. For Rousseau the resulting social conflicts form the substance of human civilization and its history.

Marx's famous "historical materialism" — the view that human history is *nothing but* a succession of different ways of organizing economic production — tells a very similar story. On his account, our collective efforts to gain mastery of our natural environment, to exploit the resources of the world to satisfy our desires, necessarily become a struggle to assert control over each other. If great cities are to be built, lavish palaces to be constructed, or cheap consumer goods to be made available to a mass market, the actions of large

---

[8] For a useful overview of the Frankfurt School, see Held (1980); the best and most accessible analytical study of Frankfurt School "critical theory" remains Geuss (1981).

numbers of people must be coordinated in complex ways. This cannot be expected to happen automatically. Resistance to the required routines must somehow be overcome, whether by direct force, or the more subtle inculcation of ethical beliefs likely to foster cooperation. On this view, such phenomena as the division of labor, slavery, and the emergence of social classes, as well as the complex conventional beliefs that sustain these practices, are all to be analyzed as manifestations of human powers struggling to gain control over the world and each other.

Like Rousseau, then, Marx placed great stress on economic development as the motor driving the various distinctive patterns of social power that have succeeded each other across human history. For Marx, the key to decoding these configurations of power is to lay bare the relations of economic dependence that underlie them. The effect of this exercise is to expose a gap between the official pretensions of social organizations and their actual operation. It is not merely that their day-to-day functioning fails to live up to the ethical ideals they profess. Rather, it is that viewing them through the lens of conventionally accepted ethical ideas completely misrepresents their true character. The task for the "ruthless social critic" is to highlight the tensions between that underlying character and the distorting gloss of conventional orthodoxy.[9]

Unmasking power

This book opened with a contrast between two faces of political life, one cloudlessly routine, the other stormily violent. The agonistic conception of social existence just described blurs that contrast. For it naturally encourages a suspicion of the surface appearance of peaceful, harmonious, mutual reconciliation that stable social and political routines tend to refract. Rather than assuming that social and political stability is a symptom of genuine harmony among individuals and groups, this view expects there to be deep conflict and dissonance simmering beneath the surface. From this point of view, a primary intellectual task is to cultivate an honest

---

[9] It is important to stress that one can share that general goal while rejecting Marx's particular view that social and political power is always reducible to underlying economic relations. It is perfectly compatible, for example, with the more flexible understanding of power to be found in the writings of Nietzsche and Foucault.

and unsentimental appreciation of these inner tensions, and accurately to map the ways in which conflict is, under different regimes of organization, suppressed or managed. Thus Foucault:

> One of the tasks that seems immediate and urgent to me, over and above anything else, is this: that we should indicate and show up, even where they are hidden, all the relationships of political power which actually control the social body and oppress or repress it ... It seems to me that the real task in a society such as ours is to criticize the workings of institutions, which appear to be neutral and independent; to criticize and attack them in such a manner that the political violence which has always exercised itself obscurely through them will be unmasked, so that one can fight against them.[10]

This understanding of the point of intellectual inquiry into social and political life is another enduring mainstay in the broad tradition of thought that we are exploring here.

Foucault himself pursued this project in a series of pioneering (albeit very controversial) historical studies of the social management of sexuality, deviance, and criminality, and of the various conceptions of knowledge and expertise implicated in it.[11] But contemporary political philosophy provides many other cases of theorists who have applied a similar mode of analysis to other areas of social life.[12] Consider, for example, the way in which (self-described) "critical legal scholars" have sought to expose the ways in which what may appear to be the "impartial" operation of the rule of law in fact disguises various unacknowledged political agendas. These theorists have hoped to explode the conventional image of the law as an impartial, "gapless," and coherent body of rules, insulated from the domain of political struggles. They have tried to do so by documenting the ways in which legal practices are merely another venue in which underlying political conflicts are carried on.[13]

The same effort to expose hidden conflict also animates the partly overlapping effort on the part of contemporary theorists of race and gender to show how seemingly neutral institutions and modes of thought in

---

[10] In Davidson (1997), p. 130.

[11] See Foucault (1984).

[12] For an interesting effort to look at democratic theory from this standpoint, see Flyvberg (1998).

[13] See, for example, Unger (1986) and the essays in Kairys (1990).

fact conceal various "gendered" practices or tacit forms of racism.[14] The feminist attack on conventional distinctions between "public" and "private" is a case in point. As feminist critics have vigorously argued, such distinctions tend to define (for instance) the domestic sphere as "private" and beyond the reach of public control. This protects the privileges that men have traditionally enjoyed over women in these settings. From this point of view, the division between "public" and "private" is not an innocent intellectual distinction with no political implications. Rather, it plays an active role in skewing relations of power between men and women, heightening women's vulnerability to abuse and exploitation and perpetuating their longstanding subordination.[15] This argument therefore carries the important implication that the subversion of settled belief is often necessary for emancipation and liberation.

Dissonance, history, and Utopia

It is helpful at this point to recall some aspects of Rawls's later writings. In the previous chapter, we noted that the later Rawls recast his theory of justice as a possible "overlapping consensus" on which citizens of liberal democratic societies could agree despite widely conflicting personal convictions. The contrast with the ambitions announced in Foucault's manifesto just quoted could not be starker. While Rawls seems determined to overcome conflict and dissensus by specifying a basis for common agreement in public life, Foucault aims explicitly to subvert apparent consensus, stability, and order by excavating and indeed sometimes inciting latent tensions that (by hypothesis) hold them in place. The point is precisely to disturb settled beliefs by actively introducing a dissonant voice.

Those drawn to this more Foucaultian approach frequently criticize the Rawlsian quest for political consensus as a form of "depoliticization." Underlying this charge once again is the assumption that the "political" is unavoidably an arena of struggle and contest. The allegation is then that, in seeking to dissolve conflicts in "remainderless justification

---

[14] E.g. Delgado and Stefancic (2001); Young (1997).
[15] See Elshtain (1981); Okin (1989); Pateman (1993).

and reconciliation,"[16] Rawls and others are engaged in a misguided and ultimately dishonest effort to "displace politics." Thus

> they confine politics (conceptually and territorially) to the juridical, administrative, or regulative tasks of stabilizing moral and political subjects, building consensus, maintaining agreements . . . They assume that the task of political theory is to resolve institutional questions, to get politics right, over, and done with, to free modern subjects and their sets of arrangements of political conflict and instability.[17]

This line of argument helps explain an otherwise unexpected antipathy to utopianism found among writers who share a critical orientation. One might think that those who wish to offer a genuinely *radical* critique of existing arrangements would seek to criticize them from the point of view of some utopian ideal. But in fact they have more usually rejected this approach to social criticism and indeed often used the word "utopian" as a term of abuse. Their standard complaint about utopian ideals parallels the objection to Rawls just discussed: utopianism, they argue, exemplifies a vain hankering after reconciliation, harmony, consensus, and closure – a world, as they would put it, beyond politics. Indulging utopian idealism, on this view, betrays a withdrawal from politics, disengagement from the struggles of the day, and is perhaps symptomatic (as Nietzsche suggested in the context of Christian asceticism) of a certain sort of weariness and debility.

A consequence of this position is that achieving an appropriate critical distance from prevailing orthodoxies will not be a matter of retreating to some ideal standpoint beyond the particularities of history. Rather, it will have to be introduced by exploring the alternative possibilities latent within the particular historical situation within which critics find themselves. That is why radical critics from Rousseau to Foucault have characteristically regarded historical awareness as an essential attribute of sound critical reflection on politics. As Paul Veyne has put it in a helpful essay describing Foucault's own position:

> The present is never indifferent. To be a philosopher is [for Foucault] to make a diagnosis of present possibilities and to draw up a strategic map – with the secret hope of influencing the choice of combats. Enclosed in his own

---

[16] Honig (1993), pp. 160–1.

[17] Honig (1993), p. 2; see also p. 198.

finitude, in his own time, man cannot think just anything at any time. Try asking the Romans to abolish slavery or to think about an international equilibrium.[18]

Historical awareness is, on this view, an important resource for social criticism because it can disclose the fissures that exist, often hidden, within currently dominant social arrangements. If the agonistic hypothesis is true, dominant configurations of social power typically suppress, marginalize, and forget historically available alternative modes of thought and life. Historical understanding can bring these antagonisms out into the open, and perhaps explain how alternatives to the present order remain latently suppressed *within* currently hegemonic structures. This allows the social theorist to achieve critical distance without recourse to utopian ideals that stand outside the ebb and flow of history.[19]

Assessment

What I have been describing is less a determinate philosophical position than a particular kind of intellectual attitude that many have thought it important to cultivate in the context of social and political life. Rather than attempting a comprehensive survey of the various, often very different, views defended by those who have shared that attitude, my aim has simply been to offer a broad explanation of its characteristic concerns and philosophical rationale.

As we have seen, those who adopt it have often seen a sharp antagonism between their own concerns and the more traditional approaches in political philosophy that have dominated this book. In assessing this suggestion, it is essential to distinguish between the following two possible objections that it might imply:

Strong claim: the philosophical discourse of political justification – that is, the effort to assess social and political institutions in terms of conventional conceptions of justice and ethics – leads either to a facile utopianism or to a premature reconciliation with existing social forms. It must therefore be discarded entirely as a basis for social criticism.

---

[18] Quoted in Davidson (1997), p. 230.
[19] See on this Geuss (2001); (2005).

Weak claim: there is a standing danger that an uncritical acceptance of conventional ethical beliefs and expectations will lead political philosophers to overlook problematic features of prevailing political arrangements.

The strong claim, which poses the more serious threat to the line of thought pursued in this book, is too strong and should be rejected.

One reason for this is that – as we have seen – it rests on highly speculative claims about the tainted origin and protective function of conventional ethical beliefs. It would be surprising if there were no relation at all between patterns of social organization and the various ethical expectations and self-understandings that characteristically develop among those immersed within them. But it does not follow that such self-understandings are powerless to motivate serious criticism of existing social practices. At the very least there remains the possibility that we can expose hypocrisy when institutions and agents act in ways that are demonstrably contrary to their own professed commitments. In various works Michael Walzer has pressed this point with great vigor:

> The substructure of the ethical world is a matter of deep and apparently unending controversy. Meanwhile, however, we are living in the superstructure. The building is large, its construction elaborate and confusing. But here I can offer some guidance: a tour of the rooms, so to speak, a discussion of architectural principles ... But that's not to suggest that we can do nothing more than describe the judgments and justifications that people commonly put forward. We can analyze these moral claims, seek out their coherence, lay bare the principles that they exemplify ... And then we can expose the hypocrisy of ... [those]... who publicly acknowledge these commitments while seeking in fact their own advantage. The exposure of hypocrisy is certainly the most ordinary, and it may also be the most important form of moral criticism. We are rarely called upon to invent new ethical principles; if we did that, our criticism would not be comprehensible to the people whose behavior we wanted to condemn. Rather, we hold such people to their own principles.[20]

As we remarked in chapter 1, criticism of this kind plausibly helped to abolish slavery, secured women the vote, gave us universal public education and can fairly claim at least some responsibility for the establishment of the welfare state. In the context of what came before, these are hardly

---

[20] Walzer (1977), p. xv; see also Walzer (1987).

reactionary achievements, and they do not deserve our contempt. These considerations suggest that the relation between dominant practices and prevailing ethical norms is more complex than proponents of the strong claim sometimes suggest.

A second problem with the strong claim is that it is simply unclear how meaningful social criticism can avoid appealing (at least tacitly) to standard ethical concepts and allied notions of justification. The point here is not simply that abandoning the traditional categories of ethics would deprive us of an important rhetorical weapon, although that is surely true (what would political criticism *sound like* stripped of allegations of injustice, unfairness, discrimination, violation, corruption, vice, hypocrisy, or inequity?). The deeper issue rather is that it is difficult to see the point of the sort of radical criticism we have been exploring unless we view it as guided by implicit ethical principles of a familiar kind.

The point is nicely illustrated by a particular exchange between Noam Chomsky and Foucault in a televised public debate that took place in the early 1970s. This was not a debate between a conservative and a radical, but one between two men ostensibly committed to a struggle against oppression. Chomsky, however, describes the battle he is waging as inspired by a "vision of a just and free society" and therefore as itself a "just" struggle. Foucault, however, rejects this view:

> So it is in the name of a purer justice that you [Chomsky] criticize the functioning of justice [referring to the operation of conventional legal systems in capitalist societies]? There is an important question for us here. It is true that in all social struggles there is a question of "justice." To put it more precisely, the fight against class justice, against its injustice, is always part of the social struggle ... but if justice is at stake in a struggle, then it is as an instrument of power; it is not in the hope that finally one day, in this or another society, people will be rewarded according to their merits, or punished according to the faults. Rather than thinking of the social struggle in terms of "justice," one has to emphasize justice in terms of the social struggle.[21]

To this Chomsky responds, "Yeah, but surely you believe that your role in the war is a just role, that you are fighting a just war, to bring in a concept

---

[21] Davidson (1997), pp. 135–6.

from another domain."[22] But Foucault seems unhappy with this formulation: "If you like, I will be a little bit Nietzschean about this; in other words, it seems to me that the idea of justice in itself is an idea which in effect has been invented and put to work in different types of societies as an instrument of a certain political and economic power or as a weapon against that power."[23]

The problem with this answer is that it is unclear why, and for whom, the struggle against oppressive forms of social power *matters* from a Foucaultian standpoint. The natural answer is that it matters because those who are oppressed are the victims of injustices that ought to be resisted and removed. An answer along these lines presupposes that justice and injustice can be recognized independently of contingent struggles over power. But Foucault rejects this kind of answer because he refuses to define the "social struggle in terms of justice." But if the plight of oppressed groups does not require our attention because their cause is in an independent sense just, what other grounds might there be for caring about it?

Perhaps the answer is that we are ourselves members of the oppressed groups, or have some personal sympathy with them and want therefore to conduct the battle of ideas on their behalf. This answer may be behind a prevalent tendency in contemporary political philosophy to write from the point of view of specific identity groups, a tendency exemplified in the development of critical theories of race, of gender, and of sexual orientation.

But citing identity or sympathy in this way seems a rather feeble and *ad hoc* basis on which to justify the strong priority given in these theories to the interests of relevant groups in overcoming oppression, discrimination and other burdens. What if one is not, personally, a member of the relevant group, or lacks any particular sympathy with their plight? More pointedly still, what if one's own sympathies lie with the forces of reaction and not with those they oppress? Would one then not have reasons to pursue some counter-critical form of theoretical reflection, trying to reinforce the various ideological delusions that help sustain one's position of power?

Some will reply that such objections betray, yet again, a suspect drive to displace politics in the sense described earlier. If, as agonists like Foucault

---

[22] Davidson (1997), p. 136.

[23] Davidson (1997), p. 138.

insist, politics *just is* a contention of irreconcilable partialities, in the end the only honest way of proceeding in political life is to fight one's corner whether or not others have any sympathy for one's own point of view. From this angle, the suggestion that one must first vindicate the justice of one's cause to everyone's satisfaction before entering the fray is simply a way of postponing active engagement, another example of the depoliticization effected by utopian idealism in politics. As Foucault bluntly says: "One makes war to win, not because it is just."[24]

There is something to this reply, but it misses the main point. The issue is not whether to join the fray at all, but rather how we determine which side we ought to be on and which struggles deserve our attention and investments of energy. The search for ideal conceptions of justice of the sort developed by (at least the early) Rawls and others needs to be understood in this light. Their purpose is not to delay or avoid political conflict, nor to construct aesthetically sublime ideals to contemplate when we are weary of the messy, imperfect, political struggles going on around us. It is instead to provide intelligent guidance about the relative significance and priority of the different political fights we might pick.

Everyone knows that conflict is unavoidable in politics. We cannot advance the interests of all agents and groups simultaneously: "Freedom for the pike is death for the minnows."[25] A major purpose of ideals of justice is to explain whose conflicting interests, whose conflicting freedoms, and whose conflicting claims merit our attention, and in what order. Different explanations will be more or less plausible, reasonable, convincing, and cogent; there is no obvious reason to think that we cannot tell the difference. Foucault's refusal even to enter this discussion deprives him of the ability to assess the relative urgency of the claims for which he urged us to struggle; as a result his critical stance seems incomplete and unsatisfactory. It is so because it lacks the very component the strong claim urges us to discard.

Envoi

It remains therefore to consider the second, weaker, allegation laid out above. This claim strikes me as largely uncontroversial, and perfectly

---

[24] Davidson (1997), p. 136.
[25] Tawney (1964), p. 164.

compatible with the tenor of the arguments we have considered in this text. No doubt the dogmas of conventional wisdom are a perennial temptation. But there is no reason to suppose that philosophical inquiry into the possible justifications for different political arrangements must automatically yield to that temptation.

At various points in this book, we have considered political positions or practices that invite certain objections, and have decided that the objections overwhelm familiar efforts to defend them. For example, in chapters 5 and 6 we rejected the increasingly popular view that the free market is a sufficient agent of distributive justice. We also questioned the commonly accepted assumption that requirements of distributive justice should apply primarily within states, but far more weakly, if at all, beyond their borders. Our discussion of political obligation in chapter 7 exposed the puzzling quality of our practices of authority, and in chapter 8 we had unexpected difficulty vindicating the claims often made today on behalf of democratic procedures. In all these cases, our arguments pointed firmly away from the conventional wisdom. If they have any merit, then, there is little reason to doubt the critical credentials of traditional justificatory analysis, or their ability to call complacent orthodoxies into question. There need be no conflict between the weak claim and the arguments explored in this book.

This does not mean, however, that the weak claim is so banal as to have no critical significance in the context of contemporary political theory. For it seems to me that this entirely valid stricture has been neglected in at least one tendency prevalent in the writings of political philosophers today; I am referring to their frequent readiness to identify themselves and their intellectual activities by reference to "liberalism" or (sometimes) "liberal democracy," and to organize discussion in the field around oppositions between "liberals" and their "opponents."

It is important to stress that in criticizing this tendency I am not necessarily opposing any of the political practices or ideals for which liberals have historically struggled. For example, freedom of speech, equality before the law, and checks on the arbitrary abuse of state power are all vital historical achievements that I would not want to reverse. But our appreciation of these accomplishments should depend neither on their credentials as "liberal" nor on our desire to remain loyal to a tradition that defines our supposedly "shared" values. Rather, it should reflect our considered view that in upholding these principles our societies are better, more just, more humane, more likely to promote human good, more rational, and so on. That these also happen to be "liberal" principles is, or should be, quite incidental to this judgment.

But in recent years there has been a strong tendency to fixate on "liberalism" and to allow specifically liberal questions and assumptions to dominate and guide discussion in political philosophy. This tendency is pervasive but is exemplified very clearly by the revisions (noted several times in earlier chapters) that Rawls made to his theory of justice in the latter part of his career. Under these revisions, Rawls's theory became quite explicitly a "liberal" theory, setting out from, and defining itself in terms of, the commitments and aspirations of liberal democratic public culture.

But why should "liberalism" assume this central importance in political philosophy? One answer, suggested by Rawls and many others, goes like this: "Liberal values are *our* values. The radical critics are right to reject utopian forms of political philosophy.[26] We cannot and should not seek to step outside our own historical situation. We must make the best of what we have. In our case, that involves drawing out the implications of our commitment to liberal values of freedom, equality, impartial justice, free and fair elections, and the rest."

Thus Rawls argued quite explicitly that among the central roles of political philosophy presupposed in his later theory is the effort "to calm our frustration and rage against our society and its history by showing us the way in which its institutions, when properly understood from a philosophical point of view, are rational." Thus he hoped that his theory might "reconcile us in part to our condition," where "our condition" refers to our involuntary enrollment in institutions committed to the ideals of liberal democratic freedom.[27] In these passages, Rawls comes very close to endorsing Hegel's view that the point of philosophical reflection in politics is to explain the inner rationality of existing forms of life, with a view to helping us feel at home within them.

As a human goal, there is nothing wrong with seeking a "home in the world." However, as Marx rightly complained, under some circumstances it can become an excuse for reconciling oneself prematurely with the present

---

[26] For Rawls's own anti-utopianism (which he calls "reasonable utopianism") see Rawls (1999b), pp. 11–23.

[27] Rawls (2001), pp. 3–4.

and its ruling ideals. Rawls and others may be right that liberalism is susceptible of coherent philosophical systematization and that it represents our core values; it certainly enjoys unrivalled historical salience. But from none of this does it follow that we are entitled to feel at home in its world, or that liberalism provides a propitious framework for thinking clearly and pertinently about the most serious problems we face, particularly those at the global level.

With this in mind, I end with closing words of Rousseau's *Discourse*: "It is obviously contrary to the law of nature, however it may be defined . . . for an imbecile to lead a wise man, and for a handful of people to gorge themselves on superfluities while the starving multitude lacks necessities." As our discussions of global justice and war in chapters 5, 6, and 10 underlined, the phenomena that Rousseau mentions here – foolish and dangerous political leadership on the one hand and an amazing affluence largely indifferent to widespread deprivation on the other – remain all too familiar features of the present global order. While we cannot blame liberal democracy for creating them, liberal democratic societies have proven remarkably tolerant of these problems and very half-hearted in their efforts to solve them. As we noted at the end of chapter 6, these global challenges define an important and exciting agenda for the future of political philosophy. But as long as they remain locked within the framework of liberalism and fail to look beyond its horizons, political philosophers are fated to underestimate these challenges. They will pursue them from a cramped and parochial point of view, ill-adapted to the pertinent issues and unlikely to yield much insight into them. In struggling to overcome these prejudices, we still have something important to learn from our radical critics.

Bibliography

Anderson, E. (1999), "What is the Point of Equality?", *Ethics* **109/2**, pp. 287–337

Aristotle (1981), *The Politics* (London: Penguin)

Arrow, Kenneth (1963), *Social Choice and Individual Values* (New Haven: Yale University Press)

Atiyah, P. S. (1995), *Law and Modern Society* (Oxford: Oxford University Press)

Auden, W. H. (1991), *Collected Poems*, ed. Edward Mendelson (London: Faber)

Beitz, Charles (1989), *Political Equality: An Essay in Democratic Theory* (Princeton: Princeton University Press)

(1999), *Political Theory and International Relations* (Princeton: Princeton University Press)

Bentham, Jeremy (2002), *Rights, Representation, and Reform: Nonsense upon Stilts and Other Writings on the French Revolution*, eds. Philip Schofield, Catherine Pease-Watkin, and Cyprian Blamires (Oxford: Oxford University Press)

Beran, H. (1987), *The Consent Theory of Political Obligation* (London: Croom Helm)

Berlin, Isaiah (1969), *Four Essays on Liberty* (Oxford: Oxford University Press)

Bird, Colin (1996), "Mutual Respect and Neutral Justification," *Ethics* 7/1, pp. 62–96

(1999), *The Myth of Liberal Individualism* (Cambridge: Cambridge University Press)

(2000), "The Possibility of Self-Government," *American Political Science Review* **94/2**, pp. 563–77

Blake, Michael (2001), "Distributive Justice, State Coercion, and Autonomy," *Philosophy and Public Affairs* 30/3, pp. 257–96

Carter, Ian (1999), *A Measure of Freedom* (Oxford: Oxford University Press)

Chan, Joseph (2000), "Legitimacy, Unanimity and Perfectionism," *Philosophy and Public Affairs* **29/1**, pp. 5–43

Christiano, Thomas (1996), *The Rule of the Many* (Boulder, CO: Westview)

Cohen, Gerald (2000), *If You're an Egalitarian, How Come You're So Rich?* (Cambridge, MA: Harvard University Press)

Cohen, Joshua (1989), "Deliberation and Democratic Legitimacy," in Robert Goodin and Alan Hamlin (eds.), *The Good Polity* (Oxford: Blackwell)

Davidson, Arnold (1997) (ed.), *Foucault and his Interlocutors* (Chicago: University of Chicago Press)

Delgado, Richard, and Stefancic, Jean (2001) (eds.), *Critical Race Theory: An Introduction* (New York: New York University Press)

Dewey, John (1939), *Intelligence in the Modern World: John Dewey's Philisophy*, ed. Joseph Ratner (New York: Modern Library)

Downs, Anthony (1957), *An Economic Theory of Democracy* (New York: Harper)

Dworkin, R. (1985), "Liberalism," in *A Matter of Principle* (Cambridge, MA: Harvard University Press), pp. 181–205

　(1986), *Law's Empire* (Cambridge, MA: Harvard University Press)

Edgeworth, F.Y. (1967), *Mathematical Psychics: An Essay on the Application of Mathematics to the Moral Sciences* (New York: A. M. Kelley)

Elshtain, Jean Bethke (1981), *Public Man, Private Woman* (Princeton: Princeton University Press)

　(2004), "But Was It Just? Reflections on the Iraq War," in *Nexus: A Journal of Opinion* 9, pp. 1–9. Available online at <http://www.nexusjournal.org/ separate%20pdf/Volume9/ElshtainArticle.pdf>

Engels, Frederick (1958), *The Condition of the Working Class in England*, ed. W.O. Henderson, and W.H. Chaloner (Oxford: Oxford University Press)

Finnis, John (1980), *Natural Law and Natural Rights* (Oxford: Oxford University Press)

Flyvberg, Bent (1998), *Rationality and Power: Democracy in Practice* (Chicago: University of Chicago Press)

Foucault, Michel (1984), *The Foucault Reader*, ed. Paul Rabinow (New York: Pantheon)

Frank, Robert (1985), *Choosing the Right Pond* (Oxford: Oxford University Press)

Frankfurt, Harry (1988), "Equality as a Moral Ideal," in Harry Frankfurt, *The Importance of What We Care About* (Cambridge: Cambridge University Press), pp. 134–59

Freeman, Samuel (2001), "Illiberal Libertarianism: Why Libertarianism is Not a Liberal View," *Philosophy and Public Affairs* **30/2**, pp. 105–51

Gallie, W.B. (1956), "Essentially Contested Concepts," *Proceedings of the Aristotelian Society* 56, pp. 167–220

Galston, William (2002), *Liberal Pluralism* (Cambridge: Cambridge University Press)

Gans, C. (1992), *Philosophical Anarchism and Political Disobedience* (Cambridge: Cambridge University Press)

Gauthier, David (1986), *Morals by Agreement* (Oxford: Oxford University Press)

Geuss, Raymond (1981), *The Idea of a Critical Theory: Habermas and the Frankfurt School* (Cambridge: Cambridge University Press)

(2001), *History and Illusion in Politics* (Cambridge: Cambridge University Press)

(2005), *Outside Ethics* (Princeton: Princeton University Press)

Green, L. (1990), *The Authority of the State* (Oxford: Oxford University Press)

Grotius, Hugo (1901), *The Rights of War and Peace*, trans. A. C. Campbell (Westport: Hyperion)

Gutmann, Amy, and Thompson, Dennis (1996), *Democracy and Disagreement* (Cambridge, MA: Harvard University Press)

Haksar, Vinit (1979), *Equality, Liberty and Perfectionism* (Oxford: Oxford University Press)

Hardin, Russell (1993), "Public Choice versus Democracy," in David Copp, Jean Hampton, and John Roemer (eds.), *The Idea of Democracy* (Cambridge: Cambridge University Press)

Hare, R. M. (1981), *Moral Thinking: its Levels, Methods and Point* (Oxford: Oxford University Press)

Harrison, Edward (1987), *Darkness at Night: A Riddle of the Universe* (Cambridge, MA: Harvard University Press)

Hart, H. L. A. (1975), "Rawls on Liberty and Its Priority," in Norman Daniels (ed.), *Reading Rawls* (New York: Basic), pp. 249–52

(1997), *The Concept of Law*, 2nd edn (Oxford: Oxford University Press)

Hayek, Friedrich (1937), "Economics and Knowledge," *Economica* 4, pp. 33–54

(1976), *Law, Legislation and Liberty, II: The Mirage of Social Justice* (Chicago: University of Chicago Press)

Held, David (1980), *Introduction to Critical Theory: Horkheimer to Habermas* (Berkeley: University of California Press)

Hobbes, Thomas (1994), *Leviathan*, ed. E. Curley (Indianapolis: Hackett)

(1998), *De Cive*, ed. and trans. Richard Tuck and Michael Silverthorne (Cambridge: Cambridge University Press)

Holmes, Robert (1989), *On War and Morality* (Princeton: Princeton University Press)

Holmes, Stephen, and Sunstein, Cass (1999), *The Cost of Rights* (New York: Norton)

Honig, Bonnie (1993), *Political Theory and the Displacement of Politics* (Ithaca: Cornell University Press)

Horkheimer, Max (1972), *Critical Theory*, trans. Matthew O'Connell et al. (New York: Herder and Herder)

Horton, J. (1992), *Political Obligation* (Atlantic Highlands: Humanities Press)

Hume, David (1969), *A Treatise of Human Nature* (London: Penguin)

(1985), "On the Original Contract," in Eugene Miller (ed.), *Essays Moral, Political and Literary* (Indianapolis: Liberty Fund)

Hurka, Thomas (1993), *Perfectionism* (Oxford: Oxford University Press)

Jevons, W. S. (1988), *The Theory of Political Economy* (London: Macmillan)

Joad, C. E. M. (1939), *Why War?* (London: Penguin)

Johnston, David (1994), *The Idea of a Liberal Theory* (Princeton: Princeton University Press)

Kant, Immanuel (1991), *Political Writings*, ed. Hans Reiss, trans. H. B. Nisbett (Cambridge: Cambridge University Press)

(1993), *Grounding for the Metaphysics of Morals*, trans. James Ellington (Indianapolis: Hackett)

Kairys, David (1990) (ed.), *The Politics of Law: A Progressive Critique* (New York: Pantheon)

Kekes, John (1997), *Against Liberalism* (Ithaca: Cornell University Press)

King, Martin Luther (1989), "Letter from Birmingham Jail," in Paul Harris, *Civil Disobedience* (Lanham: University Press of America)

Klosko, George (1992), *The Principle of Fairness and Political Obligation* (Lanham: Rowman and Littlefield)

(2005), *Political Obligations* (Oxford: Oxford University Press)

Kymlicka, Will (1989), *Liberalism, Community and Culture* (Oxford: Oxford University Press)

(1995), *Multicultural Citizenship* (Oxford: Oxford University Press)

(2002), *Contemporary Political Philosophy: An Introduction* (Oxford: Oxford University Press)

Lane, Robert E. (2000), *The Loss of Happiness in the Market Democracies* (New Haven: Yale University Press)

Larmore, Charles (1987), *Patterns of Moral Complexity* (Cambridge: Cambridge University Press)

(1996), *The Morals of Modernity* (Cambridge: Cambridge University Press)

(1999), "The Moral Basis of Political Liberalism," *Journal of Philosophy* 96/12, pp. 599–612

Lively, Jack (1975), *Democracy* (Oxford: Blackwell)

Locke, John (1993), *The Political Writings of John Locke*, ed. David Wootton (New York: Mentor)

McBride, William (1972), "Social Theory *sub specie aeternitatis*," review of J. Rawls's *A Theory of Justice*, *Yale Law Journal* 81/5 (April 1972), pp. 980–1003

MacIntyre, Alasdair (1984), *After Virtue* (Notre Dame: University of Notre Dame Press)

McMahan, Jeff (2004), "The Ethics of Killing in War," *Ethics* **114**, pp. 693–733

MacNamara, Robert (2005), "Apocalypse Soon," in *Foreign Policy* (May/June 2005), pp. 28–36

Manin, Bernard (1997), *The Principles of Representative Government* (Cambridge: Cambridge University Press)

Mannheim, Karl (1985), *Ideology and Utopia: An Introduction to the Sociology of Knowledge*, trans. Louis Wirth and Edward Shils (San Diego: Harcourt Brace)

Marx, Karl (1978), *The Marx—Engels Reader*, ed. Robert Tucker (New York: Norton)

Mearsheimer, John (2001), *The Tragedy of Great Power Politics* (New York: Norton)

Mill, John Stuart (1972), *Utilitarianism, On Liberty, and Considerations on Representative Government* (London: Everyman)

Miller, David (1995), *On Nationality* (Oxford: Oxford University Press)

Miller, Richard (1998), "Cosmopolitan Respect and Patriotic Concern," *Philosophy and Public Affairs* 27/3, pp. 202—24

Milner, Murray (2004), *Freaks, Geeks, and Cool Kids: American Teenagers and the Culture of Consumption* (London: Routledge)

Moellendorf, Darrell (2002), *Cosmopolitan Justice* (Boulder, CO: Westview)

Murphy Liam, and Nagel, Thomas (2002), *The Myth of Ownership* (Oxford: Oxford University Press)

Nagel, Thomas (2004), "The Problem of Global Justice," *Philosophy and Public Affairs* 33/2, pp. 113—47

Nozick, Robert (1974), *Anarchy, State and Utopia* (New York: Basic Books)

Nussbaum, Martha (2006), *The Frontiers of Justice* (Cambridge, MA: Harvard University Press)

Okin, Susan (1989), *Justice, Gender and the Family* (New York: Basic Books)

Oldfield, A. (1990), *Citizenship and Community: Civic Republicanism and the Modern World* (London: Routledge)

Paley, William (1828), *The Principles of Moral and Political Philosophy* (Boston: Whitaker)

Pateman, Carole (1970), *Participation and Democratic Theory* (Cambridge: Cambridge University Press)

  (1983), "Feminist Criticisms of the Public/Private Dichotomy," in Stanley Benn and Gerald Gaus (eds.), *Public and Private in Social Life* (London: Croom Helm)

Penn, William (1682), *A Frame of Government of Pennsylvania*, excerpts online at <http://www.constitution.org/bcp/frampenn.htm>

Pettit, Philip (1999), *Republicanism: A Theory of Freedom and Government* (Oxford: Oxford University Press)

Plato (1992), *The Republic*, ed. G.M.A. Grube and C.D.C. Reeve (Indianapolis: Hackett)

Pogge, Thomas (1994), "An Egalitarian Law of Peoples," *Philosophy and Public Affairs* 23/3, pp. 195—225

  (2002), *World Poverty and Human Rights* (Cambridge: Polity)

Popper, Karl (1966), *The Open Society and its Enemies* (Princeton: Princeton University Press)

Przworski, Adam (1991), *Democracy and the Market* (Cambridge: Cambridge University Press)

Rawls, John (1993), *Political Liberalism* (New York: Columbia University Press)

(1999a), *A Theory of Justice: Revised Edition* (Cambridge, MA: Harvard University Press)

(1999b), *The Law of Peoples* (Cambridge, MA: Harvard University Press)

(2001), *Justice as Fairness: A Restatement* (Cambridge, MA: Harvard University Press)

Raz, Joseph (1986), *The Morality of Freedom* (Oxford: Oxford University Press)

Riker, William (1988), *Liberalism against Populism* (Prospect Heights: Waveland)

Rosen, Michael (1996), *On Voluntary Servitude* (Cambridge, MA: Harvard University Press)

Rousseau, Jean-Jacques (1987), *The Basic Political Writings*, ed. and trans. Donald Cress (Indianapolis: Hackett)

(1990), "The State of War," in Grace Roosevelt (ed.), *Reading Rousseau in the Nuclear Age* (Philadelphia: Temple University Press), pp. 185–98

Sandel, Michael (1982), *Liberalism and the Limits of Justice* (Cambridge: Cambridge University Press)

(1996), *Democracy's Discontent: America in Search of a Public Philosophy* (Cambridge, MA: Harvard University Press)

Scanlon, Thomas (1998), *What We Owe Each Other* (Cambridge, MA: Harvard University Press)

Schumpeter, Joseph (1956), *Capitalism, Socialism and Democracy* (New York: Harper)

Schwartz, Barry (2004), *The Paradox of Choice: Why More is Less* (New York: ECCO)

Sen, Amartya (2000), *Development as Freedom* (New York: Anchor)

Sher, George (1997), *Beyond Neutrality* (Cambridge: Cambridge University Press)

Sidwick, Henry (1981), *The Methods of Ethics* (Indianapolis: Hackett)

Simmons, A. John (1979), *Moral Principles and Political Obligation* (Princeton: Princeton University Press)

(2001), *Justification and Legitimacy* (Cambridge: Cambridge University Press)

Singer, Peter (1972), "Famine, Affluence and Morality," *Philosophy and Public Affairs* 1/3, pp. 229–43

(1993), *Practical Ethics* (Cambridge: Cambridge University Press)

(2002), *One World* (New Haven: Yale University Press)

Skinner, Quentin (1998), *Liberty before Liberalism* (Cambridge: Cambridge University Press)

(2001), "A Third Concept of Liberty," in *Proceedings of the British Academy* 117, pp. 237–69

Stone, Julius (1984), *Visions of World Order: Between State Power and Human Justice* (Baltimore: Johns Hopkins University Press)

Taurek, John (1977), "Should the Numbers Count?" *Philosophy and Public Affairs* 6/4, pp. 293–316

Tawney, Richard (1964), *Equality* (London: George Allen and Unwin)

Taylor, Charles (1985), "Atomism," in Charles Taylor, *Philosophical Papers*, II (Cambridge: Cambridge University Press), pp. 197–210

(1994), *Multiculturalism: Examining the Politics of Recognition*, ed. Amy Gutmann (Princeton: Princeton University Press)

(1995), "Cross-Purposes: The Liberal-Communitarian Debate," in *Philosophical Arguments* (Cambridge, MA: Harvard University Press), ch. 10

Unger, Roberto (1986), *The Critical Legal Studies Movement* (Cambridge, MA: Harvard University Press)

Vattel, E. (1844), *Law of Nations* (Philadelphia: T. and J.V. Johnson)

Waldron, Jeremy (1988), "Locke: Toleration and the Rationality of Persecution," in Susan Mendus (ed.), *Justifying Toleration: Philosophical and Historical Perspectives* (Cambridge: Cambridge University Press), pp. 61–86

Wall, Steven (1998), *Liberalism, Perfectionism and Restraint* (Cambridge: Cambridge University Press)

Walzer, Michael (1973), "Political Action: The Problem of Dirty Hands," *Philosophy and Public Affairs* 2/2, pp. 160–80

(1977), *Just and Unjust Wars* (New York: Basic)

(1983), *Spheres of Justice* (New York: Basic)

(1987), *Interpretation and Social Criticism* (Cambridge, MA: Harvard University Press)

Weldon, T.D. (1947), *States and Morals* (New York: Whittlesley House)

Williams, B.A.O. (1985), *Ethics and the Limits of Philosophy* (Cambridge, MA: Harvard University Press)

Wolff, Robert (1970), *In Defense of Anarchism* (New York: Harper)

Yates, Michael (2003), *Naming the System: Inequality and Work in the Global Economy* (New York: Monthly Review Press)

Young, Iris (1990), *Justice and the Politics of Difference* (Princeton: Princeton University Press)

(1997), *Intersecting Voices* (Princeton: Princeton University Press)

Index